MR. T
The Man with the Gold

MR. T

The Man with the Gold

An Autobiography by Mr. T

ST. MARTIN'S PRESS
NEW YORK

Library of Congress Cataloging in Publication Data
Mr. T
    Mr. T
    1. Mr. T.   2. Entertainers—United
States—Biography.   I. Title.
PN2287.M78A35   1984   791.43′028′0924 [B]   84-11783
ISBN 0-312-55089-8

First Edition

10 9 8 7 6 5 4 3 2 1

Dedication

I dedicate this book to my mother and my daughter, Lisa. For without their love, sacrifices, understanding, caring, patience and loyalty, neither life nor work would bring fulfillment.

I also dedicate this book to the men who have had the greatest influence on my life:

1. Jesus—for being my Saviour
2. My father—for loving my mother and doing the best he could
3. The Reverend Dr. M. L. King, Jr.—for giving me hope and inspiration
4. The Reverend Henry Hardy—for bringing me closer to God and being my pastor at Cosmopolitan Community Church.

I am indebted and sincerely grateful to all of them.

Contents

*I live by the Golden Rule—
the man with the gold rules.*

1 WHO IS MR. T?

SO YOU WANT TO MEET MR. T, PERSONAL AND UP close. The man with the gold, not just around his neck but deep down in his heart. Well, this is my story about my life, and I wrote it myself— without a ghostwriter, because if I had a ghost-writer my book would have become his story instead of my story. I am sure there will be other books about me, but they won't tell it like it is. So if you want to read the honest-to-goodness truth about Mr. T, this is it. But, on the other hand, if you want to read lies, scandals and half truths, then read someone else's point of view about Mr. T. Lies sell more books and make more money than the truth because that's what a lot of you want to read and hear. Even though we know the truth yet we still lie. I am glad I follow the teachings of Jesus, and he said, "Speak the truth and the truth shall set you free." So here is the unadulterated truth, told, written and spoken in such terms that even a fool can understand what I am talking about.

I have something to say, and I said it in this book the way I talk. It's unconventional and not like everybody else's style, but this is me. This is the me that makes me me. Now, you all know I'm not a Harvard graduate. I'm not a Fancy Dan, I'm not a proper-speaking guy. I just say it like it is, and put it out there. It might not be as smooth and flowing as other folks' books, but this is my book and I wrote it my way. It reads like me. I might have made it pretty, but then that don't sound like Mr. T. I talk about this and that, and jump and move around, but by the time it's over I'm sure you'll understand what happened, what's going on. It might not grab you straight off, but when you read it through, you'll know something about this character, this Mr. T.

You'll learn how I went from rags to riches, from welfare to faring well and from the ghetto to the get more. You'll learn about Mr. T: the father, the son and the born-again Christian. Some things will shock and amaze you, while others will make you cry and laugh. You will feel my heart, my pain, my joy and my sorrow. You will become a part of me, and thus when you finish reading my autobiography you will know Mr. T. You'll know that I was a follower, now a leader, a doer and always an individual. You may find some contradictions, but what the heck, I am a very controversial guy. Some may see me as a bit outspoken and may criticize some of my actions. But this doesn't bother me because I am not here for a popularity contest. Unlike an elected official, I am not trying to win popularity, but I am just trying to proclaim the truth and the teachings of Jesus Christ. Unlike most Hollywood celebrities, I try to devote most of my attention to representing the church for the good of mankind. Locally, nationally and internationally, I think this involvement is the greatest thing I have done. I feel it is my duty to make certain that the rights of all people are protected, especially people who are voiceless and powerless. That's why I feel the church must be present to raise a voice and cry out. Because the Blessed of us must try to save the less of us.

Just think for a moment how hard I had it growing up in poverty and being a poor, nappy-headed, snotty-nosed, raggedy, hungry, black child. Now, I am not bitter nor do I hate anybody, I just want you to know where I came from. I should make it clear right now that my sole purpose and reason for writing this book is not to make a million dollars, but to let you, the public, know who Mr. T really is and what Mr. T is trying to do. That's what this book is about, not just some gossip about my private life. This is no "celebrity" story here.

Now let's be honest with each other: You don't know Mr. T, do you? I mean really know Mr. T? I know you think you know him, because you have read a couple of articles about him in several different papers and magazines. But you can't really understand Mr. T or truly know him just by reading some short and inaccurate article or listening to some tall tale about him. Now if you want the truth and nothing but the truth, you keep reading this book. Don't listen to someone who claims to have gone to school with him. Don't listen to some disgruntled chick who claims to have been his lover once. But listen to Mr. T when he speaks because it's time he tells it like it is, with no holds barred and no punches pulled. I'm going to tell you the hard cold facts about me and I am not ashamed of anything that I've done, because if a push becomes a shove I'll do it all again. Everything that I did was done in the name of survival, so don't try to question my judgment on any certain occasion but put yourself in my position at the time of that decision.

I will guarantee that when you finish this book you will owe me an apology. Because so many of you see me as a big, black, strong, musclebound nigger, who is mean, mad, angry, hateful, vengeful, cocky and arrogant. Which is all untrue. Very few of you see the Godly qualities in me because even though we know the truth we still lie. That's why it's so important that I come at a time like this. I come maybe not exactly like John the Baptist or Moses, but I come. I come to you with a message of love. It's nothing new. It's as old as the Scriptures but modern as tomorrow's sunrise. Now please don't get sidetracked and start looking in the other direction just because I have been chosen by God Almighty to be one of his messengers and news carriers. Look beyond the color of my skin, my combat boots, my hairstyle, and my gold.

Now if I can get you past all this makeup maybe you can see the man for what he really is—a man of God who would rather spend his weekends at hospitals visiting and praying with the sick or fulfilling a dying child's last wish than go to a party with rich folks. In fact, let's get this whole business out of the way right now.

My hairstyle is from Africa, it's from the Mandinka tribe, the Mandinka warriors, a proud people. My beat-up, run-over, taped-up, raggedy and old combat boots used to belong to my father before they were handed down to me. I wear my father's boots with pride because they help me not to forget where I come from and they tell me that I have to finish his journey.

Now the reason I wear mismatched socks is because there are a lot of poor children who don't have a pair of matched socks, and people laugh at them. So I wear mismatched socks so people can laugh at me, instead of the poor kids. Plus I am making a fashion statement: Just wear what you got and be thankful.

The gold chains are a symbol that reminds me of my great African ancestors, who were brought over here as slaves with iron chains on their ankles, their wrists, their necks and sometimes around their waists. I turned my chains into gold, so my statement is this: The fact that I wear gold chains instead of iron chains is because I am still a slave, only my price tag is higher now. I am still bought and sold by the powers that be in this society, white people, but this time they pay me on demand, millions and millions of dollars for my services. I demand it and they pay it. Yes, I am still a slave in this society, but I am free by God. "How are you still a slave, Mr. T?" You see, the only thing that interests this society is money. And the only thing that it fears and respects is more money.

It took me eight years to complete this book (and it was eight years ago that I bought my first gold chain—1976) and eight years ago society had no money interest in this book, because I was just a small-time slave with no money value. The white man took the chains off my legs, wrists and body but he placed them around my brain. He shackled my mind by refusing me entrance into schools of higher education and jobs with higher pay and position. Yes, I am still a slave. Even with all of my fame, fortune, money and power, I am still a nigger to the white man. That's why I serve God, because He don't make junk. You see the white folks made a "nigger" but God made a man!

But you see I got to get away from what the white man is thinking of what I am. He might say I'm nothing. But I got to know I'm a child of God, I'm something special. When people say, "Mr. T, you ain't nothing!" I smile at them because I know I'm a product of God. God don't make mistakes. God knows exactly what He's doing.

Now I notice when I talk about prejudice and racism, white folk think I'm attacking them. They say, "Mr. T hates whites." No, man! I don't hate white folk, there is no hatred in my heart. But I have to tell it like it is. Now let's be serious for a moment: We all know there is a lot of ugliness in this world. I'm just trying to put it out there so we can see it and do something about it.

Some white folks see me as defiant because I don't bow and scrape to them. You see, I answer only to God and they don't like that. I am loved and hated by the same people for the same reason. Some people love me because they see strength in me. Others say, "I'd like to be like him but since I'm not, I don't like him." So they are jealous and envious. You see, what I got attracts people, they want to see this man with all this gold, this funny haircut, bulging muscles, beat-up combat boots and rapid-fire speech. So while they are marveling at my appearance, I slip my message in on them. And I am blessed with the gift to know what I'm talking about. Because I can't lead where I don't go and I can't teach what I don't know.

I believe my message is very important but I also realize that a lot of people do not agree with what I have to say and they think I am not sincere. I say to them, I am more than a mindless, muscular, money machine or a walking jewelry store. People don't understand me, so they tear me down and spread lies about me.

That's why I love children so much. They are so young, innocent, pure and honest, with virgin minds. They are a very important part of my life, especially since I have a daughter myself (Lisa). I know it is very important to talk to children while they are still young. You see, children don't know racial hatred, prejudice, or jealousy. All of that is taught by the parents. Children are not born to hate another race. Why do children love me so much? Well, they see what you adults don't want to see—they see my heart and my love for them. I am a real true hero to them, so kids listen to me, not because they fear me but because they look up to me.

I want to save them while they are still young and have a chance. I want them to know the dangers of drugs, alcohol, smoking and dropping out of school. I try to set a good example for all children of all races to follow. I am trying to give them someone who is strong in spiritual beliefs and educational values, as well as physical powers. I am trying to be a positive image for them.

Now as their hero my advice to them is: Stay away from drugs, listen to your parents and stay in school. I don't want a kid to try to be tough like me, but to have a tender heart. Be a scientist, a doctor, an astronaut, because everyone can't be Mr. T. For a person to really truly be like me that person would have to be a Child of God who ain't afraid to take a stand. Because if you don't stand up for something, then you will sit down for anything.

Read on, open your heart, enjoy the book and, most important, go in peace, my brothers and sisters.

MEET MY FATHER AND MOTHER

S I WRITE THESE PAGES ABOUT MY FAMILY, I want you to know that it didn't sit too well with them, because they didn't want you people to know certain things about us. But you see, the story must be told. I am not ashamed of my family, or where we come from, or anything I have done.

The main reason I am writing about my family is to let the world know how tough it was, and by my doing this, maybe other poor families with broken homes can come back together, because they will at least know that they are not alone.

I know a lot of things in this chapter will hit home with some of you, especially if you are black, Mexican, or Puerto Rican—and some white people too. But, as you read, don't feel sorry for me because I grew up with such circumstances. I just want you to know that these conditions made me what I am today.

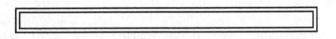

Let me introduce you to my father first, the man behind the man. You can call him the Reverend Nathaniel Buddy Tureaud, Sr., because my father is a minister. When I was little I used to love to look and listen as my father would walk around the house praying. I would be so moved behind that. Now if you wanted to hear some real serious preaching, you should have been at his church on Sunday morning. Sometimes he would just be in the pulpit talking, then all of a sudden he would get warmed up and feel the spirit and start preaching. He would have the whole church shouting and hollering. My father had a powerful voice and a knowledge of the Bible that was truly outstanding, and when he would preach you could almost feel yourself standing there next to Moses as he parted the Red Sea or watching Jesus carrying the cross up Mt. Calvary, the crown of thorns on his head. The way he delivered his message was like nothing I ever heard, and when I was small listening to my father preach it seemed that when he spoke, he spoke to me and only to me. I was so captured by what he was saying and the way he was saying it.

□ ■ □

Being the son of a minister was not easy. They say the preacher's children are the worst in the neighborhood, but we were not *that* bad. My father would definitely keep us in line. He didn't like to be embarrassed; he was a proud man and he wanted to be proud of his children, so he raised us with discipline. My father did not believe in sparing the rod.

My younger years are still fresh on my mind: I used to be in church all the time, because my father said, "Be there or else" . . . and we all knew what that "else" meant. In the church he would have some of us singing in the choir and the rest being ushers collecting the money. I would be sitting in church on a Sunday morning at 11:00 A.M., the temperature about ninety, and I would be wearing some wool, I mean some heavy wool snow pants in church in the summertime. They were the only pants I had, and they were raggedy with holes in them because I had just gotten them from my next older brother (hand-me-downs).

My father was stern, but he could also be nice and gentle. I remember when we would take some of my brothers and myself for a ride in his beat-up, smoky, run-down, four-door cream-colored 1956 Plymouth. My father would ask, "Who wants to go with me?" and I would shout, "I do!" I didn't care where he was going, I just wanted to go with him and be with him. Sometimes he would call me his "little man," and I would stick my chest out and act like my father. I always looked up to my father and respected him for what he was, a very strong and courageous man who didn't fear the living, the dead or the unborn.

I have watched my father stand up to three men at a time and not back down. I think, because he was a minister, the only thing my father feared was God. My father was not a bully. He was just a brave and tough man who demanded respect from everyone, and didn't take no mess.

□ ■ □

My father was a junkman also; he would go into the white folks' neighborhood and get their throwaways. Sometimes he would bring home good things, like toys, bicycles, food and old clothes . . . they were old clothes to the white folks, but new clothes to us. He started taking some of my brothers with him to let the white folks know how poor he was. Back then, when white folks knew that you were very poor, they would give you a lot, and my father capitalized on that. I guess you could say my father had a genius for knowing what the white folks liked to see—they liked to see blacks begging and needing something from them.

My father would take about five of my brothers with him, and he would go into the white neighborhood and take anything the whites didn't want. When those white folks saw my father and my brothers, dressed real bummy, looking through their backyards for anything that they (the whites) didn't want, that made them feel real big. It sent them on an ego trip to see a black man with his sons loading up things they had just thrown away. My father came around so much, with that smile and big "Thank you" on his lips, that those rich whites really started liking him. I mean they would buy extra food and give it to him. They would invite my brothers to play with their sons. Sometimes they would even invite my father and brothers to stay for dinner—yes, dinner over at the rich white folks' house! From that, my father got a chance to meet other rich people; then he would run down the story of his life and I mean that was incredible . . . it would bring tears to your eyes.

My father was a real smooth talker. He could talk for days as long as he had an audience, and he never had a problem finding an audience when he was invited to an all-white gathering. You know, white folks are always curious about blacks. They want to know what makes us tick, how we live, what it's like to live in poverty, why blacks have so many children. My father would tell them everything they thought they wanted to know about him or other blacks. The more my father would talk, the larger the crowd became around him—it seemed like my father got some type of energy from the crowd—and those white folks would be putting things in the bags for us to take when we left.

I must admit, they were very generous to us. I guess they considered us to be "good niggers," and therefore we were all right. They would even take us on trips with them and to their family reunions to meet more of their relatives. You should have seen my father, how cool he was. He played his hand like a riverboat gambler, and I think he should have received an Academy Award for best actor because he was simply outstanding . . . he was truly at his best. My father used to tell me, "Son, sometimes it takes a lie to get by," and I believe him.

My father told me a lot of things that really stuck with me, like "From small acorns large oak trees grow." He was trying to tell me to have patience. I remember he told me that I would have everything I wanted, it was just a matter of time. It was strange, though, that my father would tell me that, because he was very short on patience. He did not believe in waiting on anything. I guess that's the reason I am so impatient; I learned it from my father.

☐ ■ ☐

He was an amazing man. He was a fighter for his rights. He would not let anybody push him around, he didn't believe in cowardice.

My father was poor, but he was proud, and he knew how to get his money's worth on everything he bought. I remember when I was small, my father took the whole family to the shoe store; we were all trying on shoes and when the salesman told my father how much the shoes would cost, my father told the salesman how much he would pay for them, and the salesman said, "No deal." You should have seen my father coming to each of us, snatching the shoes off our feet and saying, "Come on, let's get out of here." I never saw my father pay the amount on a price tag; he would always talk the man down to a lower price.

I have seen my father get two and three months behind in rent and tell the landlord that the building should be condemned because it had so many faults and violations. I have watched my father argue with the light man, the gas man, the coal man, bill collectors, the police and the store clerks. My father's most famous words were, "They didn't know who I was and I demand respect." He definitely demanded respect, from everyone he met. Soon, the whole community knew about my father.

I remember one day in 1958, when we lived at 4848 South Wentworth, which is the Dan Ryan Expressway now, a man came to our house trying to collect a bill. The man said, "Reverend Tureaud, we really need payment on this past-due bill." My father said, "I ain't got it, I ain't gonna get it, and if I had it, I wouldn't give it to you! Now get out of my house!"

As we began to grow older, my father got a lot more

respect, or perhaps I should say a lot more people feared him. People used to call him "the man with the sons." You see, by then my seven brothers had gotten bigger, with nice size, too. People knew that if they messed with my father, they would have to tangle with his eight sons.

□ ■ □

But times got hard for my father. When I was small he used to work driving a bakery truck; I remember he'd bring the truck home with him at night. Then he got laid off and he couldn't find another job, couldn't even get in the door. Now with all those kids things got tough. One winter, my father and brothers had to chop down the wooden fence in our front yard, to burn it in the stove and give us heat.

My father tried to get other jobs, he wasn't afraid to work, he wasn't afraid to get himself dirty—he even worked as a junkman, and he'd have us all going into abandoned buildings collecting scrap we could sell.

Now pretty soon my father figured out how it was and that he had to beat the Man at his own game, because if you don't play the game, you starve to death. My father wanted the best for his family, but something went wrong and he had to use another plan. He realized it was easier for a black family to get on welfare than for a black man to get a job even though he's qualified. They want to keep you down, suppress you— that's the name of the game. But you couldn't get on welfare if there was a man in the house, so when I was five my father left us.

I was real hurt and angry—and so were my brothers—but we didn't know what was going on, what my father's game plan really was. You see, he didn't really desert us, he didn't disown us and say, "I ain't going to give you no money." No, my father would find work wherever he could and send money back to my mother.

But we didn't know that. There are things you can't outright explain step by step to children because kids are going to talk. He couldn't tell me what he was doing, I wouldn't have understood, I would have just said, "Wow, you're leaving. What is this here?" When the social worker comes knocking at the door, you can't tell children, "Tell her I'm not home." The kid goes to the door and says, "My mama say she ain't home."

No, you got to do the whole thing, you got to actually stay away. You can't keep any of your clothes in the house, you got to let the kids think you are really gone. So I was hurt but I didn't know.

Now after my father left, we had to make it on our own. The boys in the family became men and the girls became women. We were downright angry and hostile to my father, but my mother never stopped telling us to always love our father. I used to get so mad at him, and say, "I don't have a father. God is my father." Then my mother would interrupt me and say, "Son, God is your heavenly father, and although your earthly father might not have done all he should and could do as a father, he will always be your father." You know, if my mother hadn't told us that we would have killed my father, or seriously injured him for deserting the family. We were angry, hurt, poor, and had no way out and nobody to turn to.

But we were too young, we didn't understand how it was, and that my father was trying to do the best he could for us, and helping us whenever he could. I didn't understand till I got older and observed other families and how it was. You know, everybody's out to beat the system, because the system's out to beat you. In the ghetto you just hang on. They give you just enough, so you got to scrape and scratch on your own. So I started to understand, he hadn't just left us, he hadn't washed his hands of us and forgotten us. He was just playing the white man's game and trying to provide the best he could for us.

One time when I was in high school I went to talk to my

father and I told him, "Daddy, you don't have to say you are sorry, because your eyes and face say it. Besides, I understand the way it is now, and we all still love you." I shook my father's hand and gave him a big hug, then we both started crying. I have no hard feelings now. Who am I—or who are you—to judge my father? I am at peace with myself; God forgives, so can I.

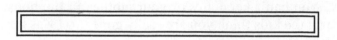

I want to talk about my mother—I mean the heart, body and soul of my mother—because I believe my mother is one of God's greatest creations. I want to talk about the anatomy of my mother—her hands, her feet, and her knees, because those parts are all so very special to me. It was her feet that carried her across town to do domestic work for the white folks; and once at those white folks' houses, my mother had to get down on her hands and knees to scrub floors, scrub toilets and wash dirty, stinky diapers.

I remember how early in the morning she had to rise and then stand outside in the cold Chicago snow, waiting for a bus. I say every time I think about my mother, it sends a certain feeling up and down my body. I say whatever it is about your mother that causes a little emotional wheel to turn when you think of her, I want you to know I feel the same way about my mother's hands, feet and knees, because it was those hands, feet and knees that did so much for me and the rest of her children.

Now I say, not only did my mother's hands, feet and knees go to work for me or go to school for me when I was bad, but she used her feet to walk against my sickness when my body was ill and racked with pain. It was my mother who walked the floor with me, on her feet all night long, talking to God;

then she would get down on her knees to pray some more, still holding me in her hands. My mother walked until my fever came down or left my body completely. I am just trying to tell you how I feel about my mother.

I believe the genius of God's soul expresses itself through the body of a mother like no other. There are a lot of important parts of a mother's anatomy, but I want to speak on a couple of parts right now. My mother—she slept on her back, she lay on her side, she sat on her buttocks, she crawled on her hands and knees, but she stood up on her feet. Yes, my mother's feet are unique . . . even though she carried a very heavy burden on her shoulders. Every time I speak of my mother, I hold my head up high, stick out my chest and strut proudly down the street, like a peacock in full bloom.

The main reason why I truly love my mother is because she didn't abort me. For that alone I want to say, "Thank you, Mother, and God Bless You." I am glad my mother didn't abort any of my brothers and sisters either. My mother told me that she couldn't and wouldn't even if she had to, "because life is precious and a gift from God."

Nobody made as many sacrifices as my mother, and for every sacrifice that she made, God rewarded her with a credit. Every inch added on to my mother's once streamlined waist when she was pregnant was a sacrifice; the first month when I was in there and her waistline got out of shape one inch, the universe piled up one credit on her behalf; the more inches, the more credits. And you know, my mother remembers when she used to look like "the girl from Ipanema, tall and tan and young and lovely . . . walking like the girl from Ipanema." My mother didn't forget that eight or nine months later when she looked like "the girl on her way back from Ipanema, couldn't hardly make it; so tired and slow!" For every varicose vein, the universe piled up credits; for every morning of nausea, the universe piled up credits; for every discomfort and for every kick that I gave her, for every effort my mother's body had to make—her heart had to pump for two, her urinary tract had to work for two, her digestive tract had to work for two—for all of that God rewarded her with credits; for every hour of pain that she endured in labor to bring life from her womb, God said she is due credit. Those pains were sacrifices. For every time-consuming and energy-sapping effort that she put into raising a family, washing and cooking, and then for every time I cried and my mother didn't know why, God said, "She deserves credits."

□ ■ □

As I look back on my younger days, I am ashamed of myself, because I was a bad little boy then. My mother was so understanding and had so much love in her heart that she overlooked my shortcomings; and besides, after seven sons already, she was used to bad boys! I thank God for my mother, and every chance I get I call to let her know how much I appreciate her and love her. My mother means so much to me—she's been my inspiration, my light when times got dark, she's been my partner when I couldn't find a friend. I remember when I was small how I used to cuddle up to my mother and she would hold me and sing me a song so sweet and so soft. As I write this book, especially this part about my mother, and I look back on all she's been through and how tall she stood, I am crying because I love her so much. God knows that she suffered a lot, but she loved us still. Like they say, "There ain't no love like a mother's love."

My mother reminds me of that spiritual sermon entitled "The Eagle Stirred Her Nest." If you have ever seen a bird fight over her young, then you would know what I am talking about. Well, here my mother had eight sons, who could and would fight anybody, but she would protect us as if we couldn't protect ourselves. I remember one time a fight broke out and my mother ran downstairs with a golf club ready to do battle with anybody, even though her sons were on the case. She was strong and courageous—and she feared nothing but the Good Lord. My mother stands about five foot six and weighs about one hundred fifty pounds, but if she had to protect us, you would have sworn that she was taller and bigger than an oak tree.

As I said, my mother went through an awful lot. I remember when my mother would go hungry so that her children could eat. I know that when I was growing up I was kind of bad and I hung out with the wrong crowd, but no matter what I was doing, when my mother called me I would run toward her. I know of all her sons I was the worst. I got the most whippings and used to stay on punishment the longest. My mother would put me in the "dark room" when I was bad and I would start crying, but she would just ignore me. Then I thought that my mother was the meanest lady in the whole world. Sometimes I would get so mad I'd say to her, "You make me sick," but God and my mother knew that I didn't mean it. I remember the times when I got sick and my mother would feel my head and throat and then lay me down in her bed and sleep in a chair next to me. She didn't need a thermometer or have to rush me to the doctor at the slightest sickness for all that modern medicine; she would just tell me, "Son, you've been running too much, you've got to rest some." She would nurse me back to health, make special meals for me, and at night I could hear her praying to God for me to get well soon. Words can't say what my mother meant and means to me, and I can't do enough to repay her for all that she has done for me. I guess the only payment she ever wanted was for me to grow up and carry on her teachings . . . to share, to love, to be kind and always take God with me wherever I go.

My mother is never given the credit that she deserves and earned. My mother always seemed to be paying her dues for a club she isn't even a member of. One of these days, I am sure she will be rewarded for all the work that she has done here. She will find her resting place with the angels, because sleep is the only freedom she knows.

I have so much respect and praise for my mother—not

because she raised twelve children right, but because she taught us to *be* something in life. She told us to stay in school so we could get the kind of jobs that we wanted, and sometimes she would help me with my homework. She always said, "Don't be bitter, don't hate, don't hold grudges, and never forget to pray." I remember a lot of times when we didn't have enough to eat, and my mother would say, "Just be thankful for what we do have and more will come." Then she would tell us about the time Jesus fed the multitude (five thousand people) with two fish and five loaves of bread; and she told us that one man in the crowd was ungrateful because he got a small piece of food; and because he was so ungrateful for what he did have, Jesus took that from him and gave it to someone who was thankful. And then she told us, "A little bit of something is always better than a whole lot of nothing." I found that out at an early age, but it wasn't an easy lesson for me to learn. You see, of all my mother's children, I was the one with the hardest head . . . I wouldn't do right to save my life.

As I look back on those days, I feel ashamed and embarrassed, because my mother worked so hard to keep the family together. I would have rather died and burned in hell than disrespect my mother. Sure, I was bad, but I wasn't that bad. I never cursed my mother, nor raised a hand at her, but I know a lot of people who did and still do, and I'd like to add that they are not friends of mine. Your mother is your first cause and your first love, and if a man (or woman) disrespects his mother, he will disrespect anybody.

I really feel sorry for those families that fuss and fight all the time. To this day, I have never heard my mother or father curse, so I must have learned all of my bad words in the streets. My mother really practices what she preaches; she would never tell us to do something that she wouldn't do or didn't already do. My mother was a very positive image to me and the rest of the family. She was not the fussy and loud type, she was always soft-spoken and quiet. I wish you could have seen her going about the house singing those spirituals and doing the chores; everybody would be outside playing and my mother would be inside cooking and listening to religious programs on the radio. She didn't like gossiping with the neighbors and, as a matter of fact, the neighbors used to talk about her because she wouldn't go out with them. I mean these so-called mothers would have babies all around the house and leave the house and the kids all by themselves. Sometimes they would even have the audacity to ask my mother to babysit for them, as if she didn't have enough work to do already. They envied my mother and wondered how she could make it without a man in the house, and my mother used to tell them, "I've got eight men in this house." That shocked the hell out of them.

I didn't understand a lot of things my mother did because I was too small and as they say, "When I was a child I acted like a child." Now I am a man so I put away childish things. My mother knew I couldn't understand, but she also knew that what she was doing, I would benefit from later. Sure, we were on welfare, relief and Aid to Dependent Children and everything else we could get on to make it. I remember when my mother had to walk three miles in both directions to the welfare office, even in the winter, just to get a little bag of food for us to eat, and she did this on those cold wintery Chicago mornings and then when she got home, she would chop wood to put into that old potbelly stove to heat the house. Meanwhile, she took everything in stride; she held her head up high and kept right on stepping.

Even though many times my mother hardly had enough food and money for us, she would always find an extra quarter to give to someone less fortunate than we were. She would always quote the Bible and say, "Blessed be the cheerful giver" and "It is better to give than to receive." I learned my lesson from that, and to this day I will never pass a beggar and not help him, I will never pass a blind man and not put money in his cup. My mother taught me that. She used to say, "Be sensitive, put yourself in the other person's shoes." My mother, at times, seemed to be carrying the world on her shoulders. She was so concerned with humanity. I used to wonder where she got her strength and energy from, and to this day I still don't know how she did it—how she made it through.

It's so hard to try to describe my mother's endurance, her patience, her love, her feelings for her family, her spiritual convictions, her right to be, her loyalty and her pride in parenthood. I will just say that my mother was God-sent. Behind every great man, there is a mother. You've just met the mother behind Mr. T.

3 LIVING IN THE GHETTO

I WAS BORN IN THE CITY OF CHICAGO ON THE SOUTH Side in a section known as the ghetto. I was the eighth son and the baby boy, the tenth child out of twelve in all. I was born on May 21, 1952, at Cook County Hospital and weighed in at eight and one-half pounds. The name that appeared on my birth certificate was Lawrence Tureaud (my father later changed it to Lawrence Tero). I changed it to Mr. T in 1972—but that comes later.

Now let me take you back into my childhood, or my very young and restless years. Then again, maybe you can call them my scars, cuts and bruises years. 'Cause when I look back on my early years, it seems like what I most remember is getting hurt, bruised and kicked around. Life was all cuts and bruises, accidents and aggressions, new threats and constant dangers. Survival was an open question and security was an unknown word. But I guess I was blessed with a power of self-healing and I made it through.

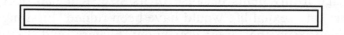

I remember when I was three years old and living in Robins, Illinois, a town on the south side of Chicago. I was running to an ice cream truck to get some free ice cream. I slipped and fell to the ground, my left arm landing on a broken bottle. I got up with a piece of glass still stuck in my arm and I was screaming. My mother took the glass out and bandaged the wound. Some days when it would get real hot and my bandage wasn't clean, the sore would be smelling. I mean it would be stinking. That sore took a very long time to heal and I'd like to add that I didn't get taken to the hospital for that cut. But the wound healed itself finally, when I was not ripping and running.

Sometimes my mother would tell me how bad I was because I had so many scars and cuts. She would say, "You can tell the bad kids anywhere because they are the ones with all the scars on their bodies and faces." That would scare me and I would try to avoid being scratched up or cut again. But I wasn't that lucky. Somehow, I would catch the bad end of everything. Once I was playing in the house (I was still three years old) and running from room to room. I would run around the potbelly stove that was real hot. Next to the stove was a pile of wood that had already been chopped into small chunks so it could fit neatly into the stove. Now, in the stove was a poke-iron (used to stir the fire), made of steel, which was sticking halfway out of the stove; it was red hot. As I ran around the house jumping, stomping and bouncing, I didn't know I was jarring the poke-iron from the stove. As I began to make another trip around the stove, all of a sudden the poke-iron fell out of the stove, the handle part hitting the floor first and the red-hot tip striking me. I was badly burned on my groin area right near my penis. I guess I escaped permanent damage to my penis because of its size; if it had been any bigger, my sexual life would have been ruined. First my skin bubbled up in that area; you know, blisters, and they were real tender. The slightest touch would make me cry. I couldn't wear diapers because the diapers would rub up against the burn and that would bring about too much pain—more than I could bear. I could not walk for two weeks. That wound took much longer to heal than all the others. But after a couple of months of doctoring by my mother, I was like new, and ready for the next accident.

Deep in my heart, I think and believe that I have been spared for some divine purpose. You see, I have suffered more cuts, bruises and near-fatal accidents than anyone can imagine. Once, when the church took us on their annual summer picnic, I went climbing in a tree with my brother Joe, who was higher up in the tree than me. I was trying to keep up with him when I spotted this real big apple, and not watching where my foot was going, I just started reaching for it. I made a couple of steps on a branch that could not hold my weight. The branch broke and I fell about twenty-five or thirty feet to the ground. I was unconscious the remainder of the day. And when I awoke I didn't know who or where I was. I was given an orange earlier that morning, but I didn't know who had given it to me. It actually took me until the next day to fully recover from my temporary state of amnesia.

I remember when I cut my right hand. I was five years old. I was pushing one of my brothers at the time and I cut it on the rim of a tricycle he was on. My hand slipped down on the wheel, which didn't have any rubber on it, and my hand got cut on the ragged edge of the rim, which was very sharp. I didn't even know I had been cut; it happened so fast and it was so painless that my brother had to tell me. I remember telling him that it was my turn to ride and his turn to push, but my brother, Gus, got up and said, "Oooohh, man, your hand is bleeding!" I didn't cry but looked at it and I could see my bone because it was such a deep cut, my flesh was parted like the Red Sea and blood was dripping all on the ground. I went upstairs to tell my mother, who started to panic but didn't. She calmly wrapped my hand with some rags to try to stop the bleeding. Then my father took me to the hospital and there I remember getting five shots; one in my left arm, two in my right arm and two in my butt. The next thing I knew I was at home with this big wrap on my arm and fifteen stitches in my hand. It took fifteen stitches to close the wound. I guess that's the reason why I'm left-handed today; when my right hand was cut and I was unable to use it, I had to use my left hand.

The stitches stayed in my hand for so long that I ended up pulling some of them out myself. Ordinarily, stitches are supposed to stay in for a couple of weeks, but these stayed in my hand for two months. That's right, two months. I will never forget when my mother took me to Cook County Hospital to get the remainder of the stitches out of my hand and the doctor told me that I was lucky to have my hand because the bandage was not changed regularly. My hand almost got infected, it was nearly frostbitten from the winter air, and I was using it before it had healed well enough. I was doing push-ups on my hand, crawling around on the floor and everything else with that hand. At the time, when the doctor told me that I was lucky to have my hand, I was too young to understand the full impact of what he was saying. But now I know, and I truly believe that I have been blessed.

One day my brother Joe and I were playing; he was running and, as usual, I was trying to keep up. I fell down on some rocks and glass and I was cut twice in the stomach by some glass. I got up to my feet and pulled my shirt up so that I could see my stomach and the wound. When I raised my shirt, my brother Joe saw the cut and hollered, "Oh, Lawrence, your guts are coming out!" Then I started to cry. The cut looked worse than it actually was, but my brother Joe thought for sure my guts were coming out. The wound healed, but left a bad scar. This cut on my stomach today looks like a fancy letter "T" . . . it really does.

And then I got on to bigger things when we moved to the Taylor Homes. I began to play with bullets. You see, I would always be experimenting with something; I was a curious kid. I just never feared danger. I would find bullets on the street or in empty lots. I separated the gunpowder from the lead, then I would pour the gunpowder on the ground in a straight line and light a fire to it and watch it burn. The dangerous part came when I was opening the bullet. I would chop the lead off from the shell with a small, sharp hatchet. One day when I was chopping the lead off, I struck a blow right in the middle of the shell. The bullet went off and grazed my right eyebrow—the scar is still there today. The sound was loud because it was a .38 bullet. My mother was in the front of the house at the time of the accident, so she did not hear the noise or, then again, she probably heard it and paid no attention to it. When you live in the ghetto, you hear gunshots all the time. Good thing she didn't hear the noise and find me holding my eye; she might have had a heart attack because she had already been through so much with me. I was really blessed the bullet didn't hit my eye, but there was a lot of blood from my eyebrow. I ran into the house to the mirror to see how bad the wound was, then I grabbed a shirt and held it to my eyebrow to stop the bleeding. I didn't want my mother to know what had happened to me so I stayed in my room the rest of the day. At one moment, I thought I would have to tell her because I was getting scared. The blood wouldn't stop flowing and the room looked a mess, with blood everywhere. I lay back with my head in a good position for a long time, the shirt pressed against the wound. The bleeding finally stopped and the wound started closing. It took a while for my mother to find out, but when she did, the wound had just about healed. She asked me what happened; I told her that I fell off a bicycle. She followed that with some good motherly advice: "Don't ride a bicycle until you learn how to stay on it."

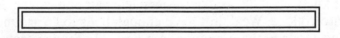

I started school in Kankakee, Illinois. It was a very good school, about 5 percent black and 95 percent white. They did not have a kindergarten, so I went straight to first grade. I was the poorest kid in the classroom (but not the poorest in the school because some of my brothers and sisters were enrolled in the school also). I remember my school days very well. I was picked up by a big yellow school bus and once on the bus all the kids would look at and compare their lunches. But not me; I would hide my lunch bag behind my back because I had egg sandwiches or peanut butter and jelly sandwiches on homemade biscuits. The biscuits would be nice 'n' hot in the morning while we were on the bus, but when I was ready for lunch at noon, these biscuits would be all crumbled up, hard and cold. My family was so poor I could not afford to buy a bottle of milk, which only cost one cent in 1957. I had a hard time falling asleep because I didn't have a rug to sleep on. We were supposed to bring a rug from home, but I didn't have one at home either. I was the only kid in the class who almost failed the first grade simply because I didn't have a rug to sleep on. I remember I used to sit and stare out of the window and say to myself, "When I grow up . . ." what all I would do and be.

Kankakee, Illinois, was then a small country suburb of Chicago. The house we stayed in was big—well, when I was very small I thought the house was real big. It was the type of house that sat on top of blocks and bricks and was made only of wood, with thousands of cracks in it. Every time the wind would blow the house sort of shifted and whistled. It was heated by one of those potbelly stoves. I never will forget living there during the winter months. It used to be so cold in our house that we had to sleep fully clothed to keep warm. I never knew what it was like to sleep in a pair of pajamas until I got into college. We didn't have enough beds to go around, so we had to sleep three or four to a bed. My four sisters slept together in one bed, my four oldest brothers slept in another bed, and my other three brothers plus myself slept in the last bed. I really had it bad because I was the youngest. I would find myself on the edge of the bed with no cover at all, and don't mention a pillow because you know who got that . . . the oldest brothers sleeping in the bed at the time. Sometimes I would urinate in the bed and wet my brothers. We would all jump up out of the bed, stinking, wet and cold. My brothers would get really mad then. After that, I would find myself sleeping on the floor for a long time. I can't really remember when I actually got to sleep in a bed all to myself, but I think I was about eleven or twelve years old, when enough of my brothers had moved out of the house.

□ ■ □

One thing I got tired of hearing was that I was "the baby boy" of the family. It was true, that I *was* the baby boy, but my older brothers didn't have to drive it into the ground. Everywhere I would go, if I was with one of my brothers or even with my father, I would be introduced as, "This is my baby brother," or "This is my baby son." That word "baby" stuck with me a long time. Then one day, one of my brothers started calling me "Truck" and that was to become my nickname. A couple of years later, I found out they gave me that name because I have a big and long head. My brothers would tease me about it and I would tell my father and he would whip all of them who were laughing.

Sometimes my brothers would call me "Football Front and Basketball Back," or "Balloon Head," "Water Head" and even "Pumpkin Head." They used to say, "Boy, you should be very smart and have lots of sense because you have a very big head."

In our family we pride ourselves on being the best of whatever, and that pride was instilled in us by our father, who was so proud of having eight sons. I remember sometimes my father would get our names confused and forget who was who, and he would call me by my brothers' names until he got tired of trying to figure out which son I was; then he would just say, "Boy, come over here." I guess it was very easy for him to get us confused because we all sort of favor one another. You see, most of my brothers have round-like heads and we all used to keep our hair cut very short, almost bald. Once in a while my mother would get us mixed up, all except me. I sort of stood out like a sore thumb in everything I did or said. When it came to talking, I would talk for hours without stopping. I could hold a conversation for a while, then it would turn into a monologue and I would be center stage all alone, at my best. I was never bashful or shy. The more people listened the better. I would astound the listening audience, which consisted mostly of my older brothers, uncles and aunts, and sometimes my sisters. My talking ability sometimes surprised even me, to know that I had all this speaking power.

Being the youngest brother really had its disadvantages, from hand-me-down clothing to leftover food. When we ate, I would get the smallest portion of food—that is, when we had food. When I went to school and the teacher would say everyone should eat three meals a day, I thought that was only for the rich white kids. I didn't get three meals a day until I was a senior in high school and that was because the family had gotten a whole lot smaller. It truly was by the grace of God that we made it through. Times were always tight and the money was never right. Everyone had to sacrifice something. We could not afford a TV, new or used. Toys at Christmas were a no-no. Clothes for Easter were impossible, it was taboo to even think of clothes for Easter. My parents would tell us we were not poor, we were just less fortunate than others. But we had good health, matter of fact, all the eight boys and four girls were in excellent health. We didn't have vitamins or four glasses of milk a day; we didn't know the meaning of protein, minerals, iron. The only iron we knew about was the iron we collected when we were junkmen—we would take pounds of iron and copper to the junkyard for money. Our favorite meal was beans, beans, beans, and sometimes we would have oatmeal; the problem was that there was never enough to go around. But what little we did have, my mother and father would bless it and thank God for another day.

In my family there was no favorite child, no special individual in my father's eyes. But being the youngest son, I sure felt like I was the forgotten person. I used to watch my oldest brothers wear clothes, then pass them down the line to the next brother, then the next, and the next, and lastly, they would get to me. If it was a sweater, by the time I got it, it was stretched out of shape, with many holes in it and the color faded out of it. If it was a coat or jacket, the lining would be torn up, the zipper torn loose from the coat or jacket and the sleeve coming apart from the rest of the garment. If it was a pair of shoes, the soles would be worn out with holes in the bottom, run over to the side, shoestrings broken and one longer than the other. My brothers' pants would be too big for me and would have patches in the knees, be busted in the seams, with the zipper broken and one leg with a cuff and one leg without, and stains all over them.

I also wore a lot of my big brothers' lumberjack shirts, those all-cotton plaid long-sleeve shirts. They were the only kind of shirt my father would buy. When I wore them to school the wind and cold air would go right up my sleeves. I tried rolling up the sleeves and putting the shirttail in my pants, but that didn't help at all. All the kids at school would laugh at me and say, "I seen your brother wearing that same shirt yesterday, haha." I would always be ready to fight them, because the truth hurts.

Speaking of fights, I had so many I can't count them, and every time I was caught fighting, I got suspended for three or more days, after which my mother or father had to bring me back to school. In a funny kind of way, I don't think my father got mad when I got suspended for fighting, as long as I won. My father would ask me, "What happened? Who started the fight? What did you do?" I would tell my father what happened and he would say, "Okay," then walk away. I was suspended so many times the principal threatened to send me to reform school.

Once I almost got suspended for not letting a teacher hit me. It all started when this teacher tried to keep me after school during lunch time. I was still a kid and in grammar school, but I could get mean and nasty when I wanted to. This teacher said, "Everybody can go home for lunch but you." I told her that I was not going to stay after school. She said, "You will," and I said, "I won't." All of a sudden she grabbed a yardstick and, waving the yardstick in the air, she said she'd beat my behind with it. I told her that nobody gives me a whipping but my father. She said, "Oh, yeah," and drew back the stick to hit me, but I grabbed the stick from her and broke it. She looked at me and was scared to death by the look that I gave her. She ran to the next room and got this male teacher. You know how men are—they try to put on a tough act in front of women but he didn't scare me. I told him that if he hit me I was going to get my big brother on him (everybody knew the reputation of my brothers). The male teacher, whose name was Mr. Young, thought for a minute, then told my teacher maybe it was best to send me home and have me bring my mother back with me.

I was sent home with a note stating that my mother should come to school and meet with my teacher and the principal to discuss my attitude and meanness. Good thing my mother did not work, because if she did, she would have gotten fired for missing so many days from work coming up to school and seeing about me. It was really funny—my mother did come to school with me and she met the principal and my teacher (who thought she was the finest female teacher at the school). My teacher told her a lie. She didn't tell my mother that she tried to hit me with a yardstick, but she did tell her that I was going to get my brothers on Mr. Young. My mother said with ease, "Which one of your brothers were you gonna get on Mr.

Young?" I said, "My brother Charles." When my father heard about this teacher trying to hit me and running out to get a male teacher to help her, he got real mad and said, "If any teacher hits you, I'll come up there and turn that school upside down, and when I get finished with Mr. Young, he will look like Mr. Old!" The whole family started laughing. One thing my father didn't like was someone else hitting his children. He also stressed the importance of fighting for respect.

I remember one day I was walking to 47th Street, and I was confronted by four boys much bigger than me who demanded my money. I only had about sixty cents, but they took that and one of them hit me in the chest. Then they asked me where I lived; I told them. They also asked me my name and I told them. Then one of them asked if Gus and Nathaniel Tero were my brothers. I said yes. The one who had taken my money gave it back to me and the other two said, "Please don't tell your brothers," and that they were sorry. The one who hit me told me to hit him back as many times as I liked, but not to tell my brothers that he had hit me. I didn't tell my brothers, but I did walk away with a smile on my face, knowing that my brothers were taking care of business.

My brothers made it a point to see that I was strong and muscular in the Tero tradition. When I was young, my brothers had me doing pushups and situps every day until I started developing some muscles. Once I learned all the exercises, I had to do them every day and all my brothers would sit around and watch, making comments about how tall I would be, what my arm and chest measurements should be when I grew up. They stayed on me night and day. I had to race with them, climb trees with them, take long walks with them, do jumping jacks until I fell out, and since I did not have a bicycle, they would make me run along with them while they rode their bicycles. My mother would sometimes worry that they might be a little too rough on me, but they would reply,

"We're making him tough. We don't want a sissy for a li'l brother; then who'll protect the family?"

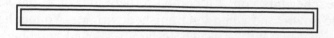

Now let me tell you all about the heart of the ghetto, where I lived in one building for twelve years. My family moved into the Robert Taylor housing projects for low-income families on March 2, 1962, when I was ten. We moved into the second project building, south of 39th Street, located at 4022 South State Street, and we occupied apartment 1010, which had four bedrooms. That's right. Fourteen people living in a four-bedroom apartment. The building was sixteen stories high with ten apartments on each floor. There were two elevators in each building, and two stairwells, one at each end of the building. Each floor had a laundry room and garbage chute leading to the incinerator. Also, there was what was called a gallery with a fence that stood about four feet high on all sixteen floors. Each building had its own parking lot, and a tunnel-like opening on the first floor which was called the "breezeway."

When we moved into the "projects" in 1962, things weren't that bad—at least, not as bad as they are now.

I remember when we first moved into the projects. It was almost like a prison. The security guards would "write you up" if they caught you playing in the stairwell. They would "write you up" for curfew if you were out after 10:30 P.M., and then they would send their reports to the main office, and if any family got over three violations in one year the office would send them a notice to move. Some people were put out by the sheriff's office. Yes. The Chicago Housing Authority was very strict then and—would you believe it?—back then they had screening processes and long waiting lists! That was back in 1962 through 1965, but it is not that way now. If you go into the projects every day for a week and see one security guard, one time, you have seen a miracle! In 1979, you wouldn't find a screening process or a waiting list; as a matter of fact, some teenagers sixteen and seventeen years old have apartments in the same building as their mothers.

There is a song that's entitled "Everything Must Change," and it goes on to say "nothing stays the same." That stands true for the projects—everything has changed, drastically. The buildings, the landscape, and most of all the people. The change was for the worse, of course. Crime is up so high in the projects that the criminals themselves are frightened to death. Drugs are affecting everyone, the young and the old. Education in the area isn't worth two pennies; the medical facilities are always overcrowded and poorly staffed. The playgrounds and playlots are all torn up. The swings are broken and the sliding boards have broken beer bottles on them. The basketball courts are ruined—bent rims, if not broken off—the softball diamond is filled with rocks and broken glass. The schools in the area look like bomb targets—the windows are boarded up with paint all over the doors and walls.

I saw so much while living in the projects—such as the lady next door being pushed out of her tenth-floor bodroom window by one of her boyfriends as her children watched. I've seen gangs sweep through the neighborhood and beat up everybody in sight twice a week. As my childhood progressed in the projects, conditions got a lot more messy and bloody. Young boys—guys I used to hang around with, twelve and thirteen years old—were strung out on drugs while their older brothers and sisters encouraged them by telling them how cool they were. Little girls ten and eleven years of age were engaging in sex in the stairwells with three and four boys at a time. And sometimes grown men were indulging in the activity at hand. I have seen thirteen to twenty guys beat up one man for nothing. Delivery trucks were broken into and the drivers were beaten and robbed. Brothers and sisters (siblings) would fight and beat their mother like she was some criminal in the night.

It isn't easy to get out of the projects alive and healthy. Some people get out, but they aren't healthy, and some get out only to be buried at a nearby cemetery. Robert Taylor projects has claimed a lot of lives . . . young and old, girls and boys, mamas and papas. A security guard shot and killed a partner of mine who lived on the same floor I did; the guard said he "shot in self-defense," because my friend "laughed at him." Men snatching ladies' purses and feeling all over their bodies was a common sight. I have seen grown men throw firecrackers into crowded elevators and young boys throw bottles off the gallery down on the heads of people passing by. It was rough in the ghetto, and even worse in the projects.

In the projects people are stacked on top of each other like pancakes. Living in the projects is like living on top of a time bomb. Sooner or later it's going to explode. The projects are a meeting place for thugs, much like a headquarters for crime. Living in the projects will either make you or break you. You will either fall into the clutches of the ghetto syndrome or you will barely escape the long, hard, lowlife living. Nobody lives in the projects without being affected by the sad surroundings. Living in the projects is worse than having a nightmare because the projects are real; you go to sleep and wake up the next morning and the projects are still there. The projects are a concrete jungle in the sky, where the animals are human beings. The projects are nothing but a large zoo where the main attraction is black people in a cage . . . a cage with a big steel fence stretching from floor to floor with holes just big enough to stick your fingers through.

However, there is a necessity for the cagelike structures. The fences on the galleries were extended from floor to ceiling to prevent people from throwing objects over the gallery onto people's heads. Once my brother was hit on the head with a bottle; the bottle was thrown from the fourteenth floor of another building, and it took twelve stitches to close the wound. Sometimes you could look out of your window and see men and boys urinating off the gallery, wetting people who were walking into the building. People would take their garbage and throw it over the gallery, instead of putting it in the incinerator.

I can't blame everything on the system, even though the system had a lot to do with the decline in conditions of ghetto living. The people who lived in the projects were also to blame though. I am talking about those adult women who have sexual relationships with men, and sometimes boys, in cars in the parking lot. How could children possibly respect their mothers when their mothers didn't respect themselves? I have seen plenty of fights start because a mother was screwing the whole neighborhood, and the men she had an affair with would brag about it to the mother's children, saying, "Your momma ain't shit; I screwed her in the back seat of my car last night." A couple of guys were shot in the back by a woman's sons for that type of talk. Now, if these things sound too gruesome for you, you might as well stop reading this book right now, because I lived in the projects for twelve years, and a lot happened in those twelve years.

Everybody who lived in the projects was poor. Ninety-five percent of the families were without a father, and 85 percent of the families were on welfare, A.D.C., General Assistance and the food stamp program. There is hatred, jealousy, ignorance, poverty and lack of proper health care in the projects. It is my sincere belief that the Robert Taylor Homes (ironically, they have the audacity to call them "Homes") were built and designed with black people in mind. The Housing Authority in downtown Chicago calls the projects "a housing development"; I call them the ghetto. Rich people call them the projects, I call them the rejects. The politicians call the projects homes, but I consider them to be a concrete reservation. You can call the projects what you want, but I see them as a monster society has created. I am not just talking about the Robert Taylor projects, I am talking about all the projects; they may have different names, but the plan and objective is still the same . . . to put all black people in a single area.

All big cities have housing projects—Los Angeles, Detroit, St. Louis, New York and Chicago. In Chicago, you will find Altgeld Gardens on 130th Street, Ida B. Wells on 39th and King Drive, Stateway Gardens on 35th and State Street, Henry Horner at Damen and Lake Streets, and don't forget, last but not least, Cabrini Green on the northwest side of town. If you've lived in one project, you have lived in them all, because they are all the same, just with different names. If you once lived in the projects I say to you, count your blessings. If you are living in the projects presently I say to you, don't give up and don't give in. Don't give up the struggle to better your situation, and don't give up your desire to get out of the projects. I got out, so can you. I know it's rough, but keep fighting and never quit.

Some of you might be thinking it's easy for me to say, "Don't give up," since I no longer live in the projects, but that's not true, because even though I live in a nice apartment and am successful in my endeavors, when I come back to try to inspire and motivate my less fortunate black brothers and sisters, it hurts me to see the things I see. What do I see? I see babies having babies. I see windows broken out of these so-called "homes." I see little children running about half naked and sick. I see elevators broken and the stairwell lights not working properly.

You must understand that I paid and am still paying my dues. I haven't forgotten where I came from. I know the problems that a typical project dweller faces from day to day—sometimes you wonder where the next meal will come from, you wonder if your welfare check will be on time, and if it is, will someone break into your mailbox and steal it. I know about the noise in the projects . . . the elevator emergency bell ringing all night long; people hollering and screaming so much that if someone was in trouble, you wouldn't recognize it; guns shooting every night, people racing cars in the small parking lot, teenagers shooting off firecrackers, kids five and six years old staying up until two and three in the morning, kids beating up on the sliding boards with sticks, people playing music loud enough to drown out the speakers at Soldier's Field.

In the projects there is no justice. One building's residents fight the other's. The stores in the areas don't stay open too late, because the people from the projects steal from the stores in the daytime and break in at night. I have seen a number of businesses move out of the area because of the projects. I have seen the Bowman Milk dairy truck get ripped off every day and I do mean every day! I mean it was just unbelievable how they used to steal from the Bowman dairy trucks—men would get so bold as to dress up like dairy workers and just haul big crates of milk into the projects in broad daylight.

The police didn't do much; they were afraid to come into the projects. When they did come, it was with a show of force. They would arrive with six to seven squad cars and two paddy wagons. As badly as the police were needed in the projects, the residents would resent them coming in. People would throw bottles at them from their windows; they would throw balloons filled with urine at the police and shout dirty names at them. Then, when somebody really needed the cops, they took a long time responding, and people wondered why. The only way that police responded quickly was if they received a call stating that a police officer was hemmed up in the projects and in trouble. No sooner was the phone hung up, than there were a dozen police cars, four or five wagons and three or four unmarked cars (detectives). Police would run everywhere with guns in hand, some with shotguns and automatic rifles. I know you probably think I am exaggerating, but it is the truth.

What do you think happened the day when that white policeman was shot in the all-black Cabrini Green project back in the summer of 1973? There were so many police out there that day you would have thought it was a police convention. There were police everywhere, and they had sealed off the entire area in a matter of seconds. They didn't allow anyone to enter or leave. The police meant business; they went into every apartment and searched it from top to bottom. They broke down doors, arrested people for just standing around talking, threw people against the wall, searched them and held them at gunpoint. They made residents leave their apartments while they ransacked the place looking for weapons and the killers. The police terrorized the entire neighborhood in their attempt to find who had committed the crime against a fellow officer. They finally found the weapon, which was a rifle, in an apartment, and soon the whole building and the other projects in the area were under a police state, or house arrest.

It didn't take the police long to find the two black men who were responsible for the shooting death of one of "Chicago's Finest." To be truthful, I really didn't think those two black men would make it to court. I thought they would be killed in jail (by accident, of course), but they made it to court and were found guilty and sentenced to life in prison. After that incident, Cabrini Green was placed on probation (curfew) and police were visible every two minutes, twenty-four hours a day. They even had policemen walking the beat as well as police riding four deep in a car—they were determined to bring Cabrini Green back to law and order.

You know, they never really brought law and order—nor safety—to Cabrini Green. Since the shooting of that police officer, crime has increased in and about Cabrini Green. There have been many robberies, stabbings, rapes and killings there. In the last couple of months alone (since this writing), there have been over seven sniper attacks, four resulting in death. The same thing goes on in every project; but why is Cabrini Green so highly publicized? Well, in and around Cabrini, the crime is no longer black-on-black crime, it's black on white . . . black on any and everybody. When blacks start robbing, raping and killing whites who come around the projects, then the powers that be say, "Something must be done to rectify this situation." But as long as it's black-on-black crime, who cares?

That's why the projects are built for blacks . . . so they can kill each other! A black woman coming from work falls victim to the local rapist, so what? Black women have been getting raped or beaten up ever since the projects have been inhabited. Now, if a white woman gets raped or beaten up in any project, watch what happens. In August 1979 a white woman, eighteen years old and from Tennessee, was dragged from her car and raped repeatedly by two black men. When the ordeal was over, she ran from the building and flagged down a police car. She told them what had happened and within seconds police were all over the place. On the seventh floor of that building the police found the men who raped her, and the bond for those men was set at $75,000. Then, on August 2, 1979, a Canadian doctor was robbed and shot to death near 21st and State Streets. The man accused in that killing is a black man, and his bond was set at $750,000.

But when you have black-on-black crime, you can kill your black father, mother, sister, brother or friends and all you might receive is a slap on the wrist. Your bond might be a mere $2,000 . . . and it's unusual to see it that high. But that's black-on-black crime and it's all right as long as it's among ourselves. But the minute a black steps out of line and messes with white folks, "NIGGER," you're in big trouble. Take another case, in another housing project, this time in Cleveland, Ohio. I am talking about the accused killer of an FBI agent, Melvin "Boy" Guyon. His bond was set at $1.3 million. I wonder if John Wayne Gacy's (the mass murderer of thirty-three young men and boys) bond was that high? I wonder if James Earl Ray's bond was that high? I know you remember James Earl Ray; he's the white man who killed Dr. Martin Luther King, Jr.

Don't get me wrong—I don't like to see or hear of anyone getting hurt in any way, but I did want to make a point and put something on your mind. Black-on-black crime is encouraged by the nature of the projects and allowed to run rampant by the powers that be. That's why it isn't easy growing up in the projects, and if you lived to see your fifteenth birthday, it was a miracle.

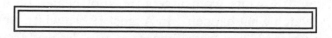

If you live in the projects and want to survive, you've got to deal with the lawlessness, the violence, the constant threat to life and limb. Now my family, we had our own justice system. We have our own laws and when they are broken or violated, someone must pay and pay they do. When someone does something to a family member, we don't call the police for a number of reasons: (1) it takes them too long to respond; (2) they are not really interested because it is black-on-black crime; and (3) justice is too slow and the punishment is a slap on the wrist, and the criminal is back on the street the very next day.

I remember in 1973 when I was still living in the Robert Taylor projects, a dope addict broke into the house of one of my brothers on 40th and Wabash. The guy took my brother's TV and thirty dollars from the apartment. Now he had to sell the TV to get a fix, so he came over to the projects to try to get rid of the TV real fast, and he started at the sixteenth floor, going from apartment to apartment, floor to floor. Now, all criminals make mistakes. Some make one, some make three or four, but they are all costly. This dope addict who broke into my brother's apartment made three mistakes: (1) he broke into my brother's apartment; (2) he tried to sell the TV to my mother; and (3) he came looking for me with a gun in his hand and a couple of companions. That was his worst mistake.

Yes, he tried to sell my brother's TV to my mother—ain't that something? About five minutes after he left her door, my brother called my mother and told her that someone had broken into his house and taken his money and TV. Then my mother said, "A man just tried to sell me the same TV." My mother then called the rest of my brothers and told them what happened. I was downtown, not knowing what was going on, but upon my arrival home, I was quickly informed. The first thing I did was change clothes. I changed out of my suit into a black turtleneck sweater, black pair of pants, black combat boots and black gloves. I went outside to question some of the local punks, thugs, winos and low-lifes. But as usual, nobody knew anything . . . well, not yet. You know, I was really mad behind that, so I told them: "If you really don't know anything, don't be around here when I come back, because if you are, someone is going to get hurt." I came back exactly ten minutes later and I walked right up to five of the local thugs who were sitting on a car. I grabbed two of them and asked them again, "Still don't know anything?" They replied, "No!" Then I said, "I'm going to kick your ass for the things you've done before. Like snatching that lady's purse three weeks ago." I started slapping them, then I threw both of them down to the ground and began to kick the hell out of them. That's when the other three jumped in and that was what I was waiting for. Now it was a fair fight (five against one). We started to fight. They jumped on me and then they jumped right off me, rather I threw them off. I gave two of them a flying drop kick, one a punch to the throat, and one I kept picking up and throwing back to the ground. The other, I held his head by the hair and kept punching to the face until his nose and mouth were bleeding. I went back to the two I had kicked and grabbed their heads and started to run them into each other until they were also bleeding. The one I had hit in the throat, I grabbed him and hit him in the stomach so hard he folded up like a suitcase and rolled over. I picked up the one I had thrown to the ground a couple of times, and he begged me to stop and said he had enough and he would tell me whatever I wanted to know. He told me the man I was after was tall, thin, about six feet four, a known drug addict, and they called him "TV Man," because all he steals is TVs and radios. One of the other guys told me that this addict's girlfriend stayed in the next building and sometimes he's there.

It is strange: The only way to get results sometimes is you have to go upside someone's head. After getting the information, I went upstairs to my house and changed back into my suit to pay this "TV Man" a visit. When I went to visit this dude, I went with the intention that we could work the problem out. Now, I always carry a weapon when I'm in my suits, a four-shot derringer in the waistline of my pants. I had it with me when I went calling on TV Man. I arrived at the apartment and knocked on the door and he answered. I asked him if he could step outside because I wanted to talk to him. He was shocked as hell when I said in a mean tone, "I want the TV you stole today!" He tried to play the nut role, saying, "What TV?" I said, "Look, man, I didn't come up here to play, I want the TV you took from that apartment on Wabash, it belongs to my brother." He said, "That wasn't me, I do take TVs but not that one—what kind was it?" I said, "You either give me the TV or you give me some ass, either one—don't make me no difference. I'll be back tomorrow at twelve noon."

But he was not there the next day. As a matter of fact, no

one was there. I sensed that there would be trouble so I changed weapons. I put the derringer up and started wearing my snubnose .38 pistol in an upside-down holster. Lo and behold, two days later, I was confronted by this addict and three or four other people. I couldn't see them all because it was dark and some of the sidewalk lights were out.

One thing for sure, they had definitely laid for me. I had just come back from the ice cream truck, and I had an ice cream bar in my left hand, my walking cane in the other, and I was wearing my white gloves, white shoes, a blue pinstriped suit, white and blue tie, and sunglasses. Underneath my suit, on the left-hand side, I had my pistol. There is a commercial about a deodorant that goes: "Are your underarms safe? If not use this spray . . . !" Well, I say your arms might be safe, but your body won't be, not out there in the streets. The only way your arm will be safe is if you have a pistol under it.

Anyway, I was walking back to the building, not paying any attention to the people standing up ahead because it was hot that night and people are always out. Besides, it was only 10:00 P.M. Right in front of my building I was approached by none other than TV Man, who had with him his girlfriend and two other guys as backup. He stopped and said, "I heard you were up to my house looking for me and scared my wife and kids." I said, "I was there but no one was home." He said, "You're a liar, motherfucker, and you kicked the screen door in. Motherfucker—I'll blow your head off!" All this was said angrily while he waved his gun around my head. I knew I had to think fast because he was a junkie and it is hard to reason with them; besides I thought the other two guys had guns also. So I said smoothly, "I see you have a gun, do I have a gun? Is this the way you want to come to me, with a gun? Did I have a gun when I talked to you a couple of days ago?" Then he said thoughtfully, "You are right." I knew he had the drop on me, he already had his gun out and I couldn't go for mine. So I told them, "If you shoot and kill me, you forget that I have seven brothers and you will have to shoot and kill them because they will find you." As I talked I started growing in confidence and getting ready to make my move. I told myself, "If I'm gonna die, I'm not gonna die standing still." I then told them, "One of my brothers is upstairs and he has a rifle pointed down and I'm not worried anymore. If you don't believe me, look up there."

If he had looked for one split second, I would have had my gun out and firing. But he didn't. Instead he began to apologize, saying he didn't know it was my brother's apartment. He said, "You got the TV back, what else do you want?" (Yes, we did get the TV back. It was sold to a lady on the sixth floor for $60—(it cost $319)—so my brother and I went into this lady's apartment and told her what happened, took the TV and told her never to buy stolen property again.) I told him I wanted the $30 that had been taken also. He said abruptly, "It was not thirty dollars, it was fifteen." I said, "All right, give me fifteen dollars."

At this time, one of his buddies told him, "You don't have to apologize for breaking into someone's house, we don't care whose house we break into." I said, "Shut up, fat boy. You don't have nothing to do with this." He said, "Don't point your finger at me, nigger." I threw my ice cream down and dropped my cane and glasses to the ground. At the time, the fat one started walking toward TV Man, saying, "Give me the gun, I'll shoot this motherfucker." Then I realized that TV Man was the only one with a gun. Suddenly fat boy and TV Man started wrestling for the *gun!* At first, I was stunned, then I told myself to move.

I began to walk away, at the same time unbuttoning my suit coat. Some of my friends came by and asked me what was wrong and I pushed them back, saying nothing. I turned around with my pistol in my hand and, because there were some kids around, fired one shot in the air. Then I told TV Man and his buddy, real loud, "You want to shoot, let's start shooting." They ran like hell in different directions, screaming at the same time. I stood there with my gun in my hand watching to see which one had the gun, and it turned out to be TV Man.

I chased him, and he was so scared that as he ran, he used up all his bullets. I heard his gun go click! click! And he said, "Uh! Uh! Shit!" I said, "You done ran out of bullets, man, you're dead now." I shot a couple of more times and continued chasing him. We ran through the playground, jumped over a fence, then ran around the building. I mean we were running. He was running for his life and I was going to take it. He ran around the building and hid behind a big pole. I was running so fast that I ran right past him. When I realized that he was behind the pole, he broke out and started running again. I quickly turned and shot. You should have heard that loud sound when that bullet hit the pole. After that shot, I ran out of bullets, but I always keep extra rounds in my pocket. So I began to chase him again, unloading and reloading my gun all at the same time. By the time I had my gun loaded up he was opening the door of the stairway and I quickly got in a crouched position, took aim, and fired three shots. Pow! Pow! Pow! Man, he was lucky, or I just couldn't shoot straight.

I wasn't no fool. I wasn't going to follow him in that stairway, so I turned and ran out front of the building to look up. By looking up, I could tell what floor he stopped at and what apartment he went into. I watched and waited for twenty minutes but didn't see anything. So I ran to my building and went to my house. First I changed clothes. I put on my streetfighting clothes, which were my black turtleneck sweater, black pants, black combat boots, black gloves with holes in them, and my black skull cap. Naturally, while all this was going on my mother was crying and pleading with me not to go back out there. My mother knew it was a game of death and it was being played for keeps.

As I changed my weapons for the kill, my heart was

beginning to feel a burden of sadness because I was disobeying my mother's wishes and, God knew, that was the last thing I ever wanted to do. My mother begged me not to go. I told her, "He pulled a gun on me and tried to kill me. I wasn't gonna let him get away with that." I left the house with an arsenal of weapons. I had a .357 Magnum strapped to my side, just like a gunslinger of the Old West, a belt of bullets and shotgun shells around my neck and under my arm, my 30-30 Winchester rifle with an infrared scope on it and my sawed-off twelve-gauge shotgun in my hands.

I went to his building and then walked up the stairs to the fourteenth floor. At every floor, I would carefully open the stairway door, sticking my pump shotgun in the crack then immediately jumping out on the floor with my finger on the trigger ready to shoot. I finally made it to the fourteenth floor where TV Man was supposedly staying. After opening the stairway door of the fourteenth floor, I got down on my stomach and began to crawl. It was really rough crawling with all that stuff on me. I mean, some bullets were coming out of my pockets and the butt of the gun was dragging on the floor, making a lot of noise. I crawled to his apartment door, where I sat for about two or three minutes thinking. I thought: Suppose TV Man is not inside and his girlfriend is in there with the children? Well, I didn't have a quarrel with them, only with him. So I decided not to. Then another thought passed me. I thought he would be hiding behind his lady and kids. I said to myself, TV Man, you got away this time but I will catch you later.

I caught the elevator down and went home. When I arrived, my mother was so glad to see me back all in one piece that she said, "No more fighting, son, two wrongs don't make a right." I said, "I know, I know," and went straight to my room and fell asleep with my gun on my side and all my clothes on so I could be ready when the morning came.

When morning came, I was ready. I got up at 7:00 A.M. and was on the go. I had neighborhood spies looking for him too, but I couldn't trust my spies—sure, they would tell me if TV Man was in the area but they would also tell him if I was in the area too. So I couldn't trust anyone. Some days passed by and I was still on my search. One day I saw TV Man in the area and ran over fast. When I got to the building he was gone and the guy he was with was still there, like he didn't know what was going on. I told him, "If I ever catch you with TV Man again, I will kill you, and the next time he comes in the area you better tell him you can't be caught with him or else you will get killed."

That same afternoon I went to the police station to swear out a warrant for his arrest. I told the police that he had pulled a gun on me and had three people with him. That way, if he should come up dead somewhere, they would know that I had killed him in self-defense and it was not premeditated murder.

I went to the police station clean as usual, three-piece suit, bowtie, and briefcase in hand. I told the officer who was taking the report that "My life is being threatened and I'm afraid to come and go in my own neighborhood. I'm a law-abiding citizen, respectable, and an upstanding young man in the community." Then I think I blew the officer's mind. I said, "Officer, what should I do if I see him again? I'm so terrified." The officer said protectively, "Don't waste no time in calling us and make sure you state there's a warrant out for this person's arrest." I then replied, "Thank you, officer, you've been most kind, and have a good day."

Now, you know very well that was all an act. I was no more afraid of him than of the man in the moon. I would have fought all three of them had he not pulled his gun. I would rather have a good knock-down, drag-out fistfight than make love. You see I loved to fight. I would fight at the drop of a hat. Anyway, I made my point with the police. I gave them a good impression. The police saw me as a very clean cat who was trying to make an honest living while this hoodlum was trying to rip me off (which was true).

About three weeks later, I got a call at work from the police department via the courts that they had my man. Now I was happy and sad because I really didn't want them to catch him. I just wanted them to know so I could have my alibi together when I killed this guy. It was kill or be killed. That's the law of the jungle (or ghetto). I could visualize the judge saying, "Case closed, Mr. T killed him in self-defense." Meanwhile, we were in court for TV Man's bond hearing. His court-appointed lawyer was trying to have him released on a recognizance bond, but TV Man didn't want to be set free because I told him, "The minute you walk outside, that will be the second you die. I don't threaten, I promise and it shall come to pass."

The judge denied bail because he had three other previous warrants out when the police caught him—coming out of an apartment with a TV in his hands. I showed no emotion while the judge read his record out loud. I mean, this guy had a criminal record stretching all the way back to early childhood. He had jumped bond three times, broken parole twice, committed purse snatching, robbery, robbery with a deadly weapon, home invasion, grand theft, possession of stolen property, possession of drugs, assault and battery and disorderly conduct. The judge said, "This man has done everything on paper except rape and kill, and who knows, he may have done that too. It would be against my good conscience to let this man walk the street again . . . you've heard the type of life he leads. This man can't be helped . . . he was born to be bad."

And with that, I left the courthouse and a month later TV Man was found guilty of all charges and sentenced to prison for no less than five years and no more than fifteen years. I personally doubt he did even two years, but that's the way life is in the ghetto.

□ ■ □

In 1974 my mother was robbed on an elevator in the Robert Taylor housing projects and threatened with death. It wasn't enough that the punks took the money (over two hundred dollars), but one of the punks wanted to kill her, saying, "I oughta cut this bitch's throat." Needless to say, my mother hasn't been quite the same after that; would you be? Since that day, I have declared a personal war on criminals. When that happened to my mother I said to myself: All criminals beware and don't cross my path, because you will only find death and destruction. The day my mother was robbed I was so mad, more angry and hurt than I'd ever been in my entire life. I said, "Why my mother?" She never hurt anyone. The one I love so dearly, the one who taught me to share and pray. My mother would have given the money to them had they really needed it and asked her for it. But they chose to rob her instead. So, I grabbed my sawed-off twelve-gauge pump shotgun (which I kept loaded), my 30-30 Winchester rifle and my .357 Magnum with the nine-inch barrel and put on my hunting jacket, with extra bullets in the pocket. I was going hunting, looking for big game—two black punks. One had a mustache, plaid shirt, uncombed natural, black shoes, and was tall and thin, about six feet three inches. The other was unshaven, wore a brown hat and a leather jacket, and was about six feet one inch, wearing a short natural and blue pants. The Lord have mercy on their souls because their asses belong to me.

When I arrived on the scene at my mother's house with a sawed-off shotgun in one hand, my 30-30 Winchester rifle in the other hand and my .357 Magnum strapped to my hip, I saw my mother shaking. She was scared and crying—a nervous wreck. I laid my weapons down and held my mother in my arms, telling her not to worry, I would protect her and I would get the guys who robbed her whatever it took to do it. I waited for the rest of my brothers to come and map out our plan of attack. Shortly, the whole family was on the scene. I told my sisters and father to "Stay with Mother because we have a lot of work to do."

My brothers and I left with fire burning in our eyes, revenge on our minds and pain in our hearts. We used three cars. We didn't split up; we stayed together. We covered an area that consisted of 35th Street to 55th Street, from King Drive to Halsted Street. We went into dope dens, pool halls, bars, restaurants, taverns, stores, laundromats, boys' clubs, gas stations, alley garages, parking lots, playgrounds, and kicked down some doors. We went everywhere that "niggers" hung out. We also warned people not to be caught with these two guys.

We didn't find them that night, but we brought down so much heat in the area that crime stopped for weeks. "Niggers" that usually hung out on corners and in hallways weren't there anymore. We questioned some of the other local thugs in the area and no one knew anything or had seen anything. Now you know somebody was lying to me and that made me even madder. I knew somebody who lived in the building had set my mother up, but the biggest mistake was not telling the two robbers that the lady they were going to rob had eight sons who didn't take no shit! We talked, we walked, we looked, we searched, we stayed around the area; we didn't eat; we didn't sleep. "Niggers" started getting nervous— beginning to panic because everywhere they went, one of my brothers was on the scene purposely, to make them sweat.

Soon we got our first break in the case—after we announced the $1,000 reward for information. The break came when a local thug tried to con us. It turned out that he did not have any information at all, but he tried to run the game on us. You see we had given him the $1,000 up front (eight hundreds and four fifties) to let him know we were for real. Then he began to talk in circles, but we checked out his story anyway. We made sure he was lying, and then we came back looking for him, but by that time, he was gone.

It didn't take us long to find him. He was standing in line getting ready to buy some liquor. My brothers and I ran in this crowded store and grabbed him and the two guys he had with him. We dragged them outside and commenced to beat them. We kicked and beat on them like they were bass drums. Within minutes the news of the beating spread around the neighborhood and everybody really knew we meant business. At that point, I said, "Damn the reward, let's just beat the hell out of everybody until we find them," and my brothers replied, "Good idea!"

My mother was robbed on Tuesday, and I found the guys who did it a week later on a Thursday. I would like to add that up until that point I had never killed anyone before. I will not say what I did to those two niggers who robbed and threatened to kill my mother, but I will say this: "No one will ever see them again and I don't have no hurt in my heart anymore." I am at peace once again because I did what had to be done. And I pity the fool who don't protect his mother. In the process of finding those two guys, fourteen people got beaten up pretty badly, three women got slapped around for interfering with us, and a lot of property was damaged. Other people's stolen goods were recovered and we made three citizen's arrests and brought the crime-ridden area to peace for a week.

□　■　□

One year later two black punks tried to rob my father. It was on a hot summer evening about 5:15 P.M. My father was sitting in front of the building, which he often does. I had just come in and said a few words to my father and then told him I was just going to change clothes and I would be right down. I lived on the second floor. It was a two-story apartment building with four apartments. Now this building was like a fortress because the whole building was owned by our family and occupied by the family. After we moved from the projects I shared an apartment with one of my brothers and one of my sisters stayed across the hall. Two more of my brothers lived directly under my apartment, on the first floor. My oldest brother lived down the street and around the corner. So you see, we had the area pretty much sewn up.

The two punks saw my father sitting out there by himself, an old man in his late sixties; they thought he must be easy prey. Those punks were really stupid. I was upstairs with the windows in my apartment open for some air to flow through. I had the record player on and the music was sort of high. As those two punks approached my father, they asked, "Where is your money, old man?" So my father began to yell out to me. At first, I didn't hear him because the music was too loud (later I begged my father to forgive me for not hearing him the first time). My father yelled out my name again and this time I ran to the window and looked out. I saw my father standing by two guys, then he said, "These two men tried to rob me," at the same time the two men said, "No, we didn't, brother."

Ain't that some shit? Here's two punks trying to rob my father who brought me into this world and they have the nerve to call me brother! Damn! I ran back and grabbed my .357 Magnum and returned to the window and saw the two guys running. I fired three shots from the window. Then I jumped from my window on the second floor to the ground with nothing on but my underwear (a pair of white shorts) and my .357 Magnum in my left hand. I jumped out of the window instead of running down the stairs because it was faster. It was a miracle that the gun did not discharge when I hit the ground, because I don't know if I had my finger on the trigger or not. When I did hit the ground, I landed on my feet and immediately started to run. I was running in my underwear with a big gun in my hand chasing two black guys down the street.

Every three or four steps, I would take a shot at them. This was the time of day when everyone would be returning home from work. The streets were crowded with cars, buses and people. I chased these two guys five blocks, shooting and running. We ran across 55th and Garfield. I jumped over one car, stepped on the hood of another, and ran around a bus full of people. Three cars ran into each other because the drivers were watching me run in my underwear with this big gun in my hand. I chased and shot at these guys until they got out of sight and I ran out of bullets. On my fourth or fifth shot I could have sworn that I shot one of them in the back near his shoulder. When I got to the area where one of them had fallen from the shot, there was some blood but not enough for me to be satisfied with, so I can't take credit for something that I am not sure of. In chasing them, I had two goals: (1) to capture them or kill them, and (2) not to shoot an innocent bystander, which I didn't.

I returned to my house, walking slowly and feeling dejected because I didn't get them. I was walking back home with my gun in my hand wearing only underwear. I received a lot of stares but one thing's for sure, people got out of my way in a hurry.

My brothers and I didn't catch them, although we combed the area for days and weeks. We had some clues but no answers. I don't think people in the neighborhood knew these guys because after we turned the area upside down and inside out like we did, if anyone knew something they would have told us. So to this day, I'm still looking for those two punks. They might be in jail or they might be dead, but I am sure I will continue my search until I die or they die.

□　■　□

I remember the last time the family was "called to arms." One day one of my sisters and her baby were home all alone. It was getting late in the evening when three men kicked in the door. My sister grabbed the baby and said, "What do you want?" The men, all carrying guns, said, "Where is your man?" My sister said, "I don't know." Then, one asked, "Where is the stuff?" (meaning drugs) and started tearing up the apartment. One guy put his gun to the baby's head, saying, "You better tell me or I will kill this baby." My sister cried and said, "I don't know," which she didn't. Finally, they left, saying, "You tell your man we are looking for him." My sister came home to my mother and told her what happened. Mother then called all her sons. The family gathered up and my sister told us what they looked like, what they were wearing and everything. We then caught up with my sister's boyfriend and questioned him. My brothers wanted to beat him up for bringing my sister and the baby into that mess. He told us where the three punks hung out and where we could probably find them.

So, the next day, after careful planning, we decided to pay them a visit. My brothers who had to work took the day off and we rehearsed what we were going to do until we had it down like clockwork. We went in five cars. In the first car were Clarence and William; in car number two Jesse and Charles; in car number three Gus and Nate; in car number four Joe and Angie (another sister); and I rode by myself in the last car because I was carrying the heavy stuff. I had two shotguns, one a sawed-off pump and the other a sawed-off double barrel, both twelve-gauges. I also had a carbine with a banana clip. I had two ropes in case we had to climb on the roof, plus two sledgehammers for breaking down doors. We arrived at our destination and did everything just as we had planned.

We parked the cars around the corner and each one of us got to our designated spot. Charles and William had a corner apiece; Clarence was positioned across the street with a .38 revolver on his hip, holding onto a parking meter like a drunk; Gus waited outside, almost directly in front of the door; Jesse had the alley covered; Nate climbed on top of the roof with the carbine, and I stood in the back door with my pump shotgun ready. Now it was Joe and Angie's time to do their thing—go into this pool hall and ask for our man by name or ask where they could buy some drugs. I've forgotten his name, but he was there.

He told Joe and Angie, "Be cool, baby, let me finish this game," but Angie said, "C'mon, brother, we don't have all day." So he put down the pool cue and motioned to his two buddies, "Let's go." Joe asked, "Who are they?" playing dumb. The guy said, "The stuff is at the house." Joe said, "Okay," then signaled to Gus, who shouted the signal to everyone else. With that, I entered the pool hall from the back door and yelled out, "The first one that moves will be the first that dies!" Everybody in the place froze; nobody even blinked. Angie, who had her hand in her jacket pocket, holding her finger on the trigger of a two-shot derringer, told the three men to step outside. As each one came out the door, Joe searched them for weapons, but they were clean. As everybody was stepping away from the pool hall, two of their buddies approached; one had a bottle behind his back and the other had a gun inside his pants under his shirt. The guy with the bottle stopped and started backing up, saying, "Let my friends go." Gus said, "What's that behind your back?" At that moment, William, who was positioned on the corner, snuck up behind the guy and cracked him upside the head with his gun. The one with the gun tried to go for it but Gus yelled to Joe, "He's got a gun," and Joe started kicking until he got close enough to grab him. Clarence crossed over to our side of the street to help William and Joe beat them up. Nate, who was on the roof, pointed down with the carbine and told the first three guys, "Don't move." I was at the door along with Angie and Gus, and I suggested we go into the alley. As we were taking them to the alley their main man said, "You can't do this to me, I have a reputation. I am the king on this block." And Nate said, jumping down from the roof, "Okay, king, we gonna crown you." At that point Nate hit him with the butt of the carbine rifle again and again until blood started gushing down from his lips and nose. Then, Nate started knocking his head against the concrete wall. Jesse and Gus started yelling, "That was our sister and niece you pulled the gun on"—beating them at the same time.

You might call that a senseless beating, vicious and cruel punishment. You might even say we shouldn't have taken the law into our own hands. But we call it justice; we call it revenge; we call it protecting our family; we call it, "Don't mess with the Teroes." Now, I don't know what happened to those five guys we beat unmercifully in that alley that night, but who cares? I know I don't, my sister don't, my niece don't, my brothers don't and all those poor helpless souls in the area don't either. All I am saying is this: If you hit one of us, we gonna hit you back. . . . An eye for an eye and a tooth for a tooth.

That was the last time the family was "called to arms," because, I guess, we were all grown up and had escaped the projects. But it was only by sticking together as a family that we'd been able to survive the violence and the damage that threatens everybody in the projects. In the projects the deck is stacked against any child surviving his childhood. The projects are a disease that destroys those who live there.

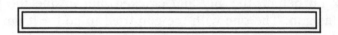

Who is to blame for this, you might ask. The black man on the corner will answer, "The white man—he got all the jobs, and he don't want to hire me because I am black." Ask the black mother of eight children who is to blame and she will say her man, the guy who fathered her children and left her holding the bag. Ask the black preacher with the church next door to a tavern who is to blame and he will say the liquor stores—there are two or three in each city block. Ask the black school teacher who is to blame and he will say, "The parents, because it is their duty to punish the children when they disobey." Ask the white doctor who is the only medical physician in the large black area who is to blame and he will say, "Improper medicine and treatment, ignorance, and not enough neighborhood clinics." Then ask the neighborhood merchant who is to blame and he will tell you this: "It's those young punks who hang on the corners day in and day out. The police who don't do anything about their hanging around, the politician who only comes around when he needs you to vote for him. Then last but not least, it's those pimps and drug dealers who bring the areas down." There you have it—a whole list of suspects to blame for the black man being in this position.

Well, I am going to tell you what I think. Who is to blame? . . . I am to blame and you are to blame. I know what's going on in your mind, you are probably saying, "How can I be to blame, I haven't done anything." Well, see there, that's just it—you haven't done *anything!* Maybe if you start doing something, things will change—if you do something right, do something legal, something productive. Now let me tell you why I am to blame. I am to blame because I haven't done all that I could and should in the black community. I haven't given enough of myself wholeheartedly to the cause of human dignity. Sometimes we can't find time because we are too busy doing nothing.

Well, I don't know how to fix the sad situation in the projects, but I will say this, if you live in the projects long enough, no matter how strong your willpower is, you will be caught up in what I call "Project Paralysis."

Most of the people who lived in the projects just didn't care because of what Project Paralysis is, a contagious disease which affects your mind and your attitude. What are the early signs or symptoms showing that you have contracted the disease? One, you don't want to work; two, you just want to sit around the house all the time; three, you become part of the criminal element and start hanging out with the wrong crowd; four, you start disrespecting your parents and everybody else; and five, you get involved with the drug and alcohol scene.

Now, the dictionary defines *paralysis* as (1) "loss or impairment of the ability to move or have sensation in a bodily part as a result of injury to or disease of its nerve supply," or (2) "partial or complete inability to move, function, or stoppage of activity," and (3) "to make helpless or unable to move; to impair the progress or function of, make inoperative or powerless." Project Paralysis starts in the mind, and before long, it will spread throughout your entire life. It makes the body lazy and the brain forget. This disease affects everyone who enters the projects, and no one is immune. When you see stealing, robbing, killing, raping, poverty, ignorance, stupidity, drug addiction and apathy—you witness Project Paralysis. It is no accident that you find more liquor stores than medical facilities in the ghetto, more taverns than schools, more pool halls than boys' clubs, more hangouts than libraries. Project Paralysis is a terrible disease because it clogs the conscience. It blocks the blood flow to the brain and wrecks the respiratory system. It smears the senses, it harms the heart, and it fractures the families. I wonder, do you really understand what I mean about this disease?

Project Paralysis makes you think small, think negative, feel sorry for yourself. It makes parents pitiful. If you have Project Paralysis you won't register to vote.

The big question is, can Project Paralysis be cured?

Well, to this date, we are still researching. We have not yet found a 100 percent cure for the disease but we are still trying. A couple of years ago, some concerned leaders and specialists thought they had found the cure. They thought that if we tightened down on all the welfare recipients, that would make the people cooperate. They found out that cutting the welfare down and investigating welfare cases in the projects only made the project dwellers angry. The caseworkers would come out to visit the families in the projects to write their reports but all they found was heartache and pain . . . their own! When caseworkers visited the projects, the females were raped and harassed; the male caseworkers were beaten, robbed and threatened with death. The so-called investigation was ended, and the disease of Project Paralysis remained and kept spreading.

You might ask how many people are affected by this disease. I say nine out of every ten project-dwellers have the disease and they are carriers, too. That's right . . . if you have it, you are going to spread it. Some victims found their own cure for Project Paralysis, and it was a drug overdose—the easy way out. They ended their long, agonizing hours, days and years of poverty, frustration and pain, sorrow and nothingness. Drugs are one way out, but that way is the back way, the coward's way. Some victims believed that jail was a better place to be than the projects. I can understand what the residents are saying, what they feel, because I lived in the projects for twelve long, painful, hungry and depressing years.

How did I get out of the projects alive and healthy? Well, it was through faith and believing—the faith that I have in my God and the belief that I have in myself. I would like to give you a secret for life . . . believe in yourself and never ever let anyone discourage you from the goodness that you feel about you. For example, once I mentioned to a friend of mine that I was going to purchase this particular building. He laughed at me and said, "If you buy this building, I will buy this entire block." The other people who happened to be around at the time laughed at me as if I were a clown. Now, if they were my true friends, they would have been glad for me to get my wish. Yet, they laughed. Now, if you have made up your mind that you are going to make it, you had better be prepared to take quite a few insults, people laughing in your face, because that's the name of the game in the ghetto. The people in the ghetto are in a valley of despair and these people refuse to let you climb out. It takes a lot to be a winner, and nothing to be a loser. You don't have to go to school, sacrifice or keep your mind healthy to be a loser. Reverend Jesse Jackson said it best when he stated, "It's all right to live in the ghetto, as long as the ghetto doesn't live in you." That message stuck in my mind when I was living in the projects. I said to myself, I live here in the projects but I refuse to let the projects live within me. I am not going to be filthy, nasty, ignorant, low-lifed, and most importantly, I will give due respect to all. With that affirmation, I became a winner, I became proud of myself, proud of being black. I knew there was nothing I could do overnight to change my situation, so I started getting my head together.

Now after your head is together, you will have no problem being a winner. Whatever the body does, it is a result of the head. You cut off the head when you stop going to school and start hanging out on the corners. You cut off the head when you get involved with drugs and crime. You cut off the head by thinking that you are too cool to work, and if you would work, you think that you are too big and important to take a small job with small pay. You see, that is one of the biggest problems that the people in the projects have . . . they want big-time pay but only have small-time skills. They want the biggest and the best, but will only give the smallest and worst in return. In the ghetto, it's every man's dream to live high on the hog, to drive big Cadillacs, wear diamond rings and custom "threads," to have a big bankroll in his pocket and to live downtown in one of those lush, plush condos. So all day long, the black man and the black teenager sit around the house and stand along the streets wishing, hoping and fantasizing. That is a daily ritual in the ghetto—to wake up and go stand on the corner and watch the world go by.

As I look back on my project-dwelling years, I recall how hard it was for me to stay on the right track. It was hard for me to stay in high school; sure I was the football and wrestling star in high school, but I was nothing at home. At home we didn't have food to eat or money to spend for necessities; welfare checks were always late. I needed some clothes and shoes. I was ashamed of wearing the same old clothes. I liked school but it was hard for me to go every day. I was hungry every day, but I used to try to fake it around my buddies and the girls. Some guys would come to school wearing nice clothes every day, with money in their pockets. I was in such bad shape that I had to beg and borrow money to rent a tuxedo for my prom. There is an old saying that goes, "Into each one's life some rain must fall." Well, let me tell you, the rain surely fell in my life—not only did it rain, it poured and it stormed, but fate was kind. My mother used to tell me that "Sorrow and sickness may endure for a night but morning follows." She said, "Son, you must pay your dues." I remember when she would tell me how bad and rough times were when she was a little girl; she told me how far she had to walk to school and back—half the time without any shoes on her feet. She told me that when she got older, she had to scrub the white women's floors on her hands and knees and when she was finished, she was not allowed to look the white women in the face when she talked to them. My mother told me that she was never allowed to enter a white woman's house through the front door, only from the back. After she would tell me about her days in the South, she would then say, "Son, learn all you can while you can." My mother was so encouraging to me. If other children had the opportunity to have a loving mother like mine, maybe there would be less crime and more success.

I really feel sorry for all the people who didn't/don't have a mother like mine. I know a lot of kids who were raised with both parents in the house and they had all the necessities of life . . . but what about now? Some are addicted to drugs, some are thugs, pimps and dropouts. Every once in a while, I look back at my own high school years. What do I find? The most attractive girl in my school isn't so pretty to look at anymore, she's a prostitute, and the best student I knew, well, he started off on a good foot by going to college, but he got hooked on drugs and dropped out. Now you can find him on either 39th Street or 43rd Street barely holding on.

So you see, it's not where you come from, but where you are going that counts. It's not where you start, but where you finish. The best way to avoid Project Paralysis is never to move into the projects . . . but where else can you go when you are "lo' and po' "? If you have to live there, then please honor that place with your presence, make a negative into a positive. Hold your head up high and, most of all, never ever forget, "God helps those who help themselves." I am living proof!

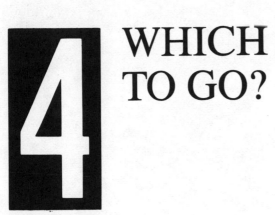

4 WHICH WAY TO GO?

**HERE ARE ONLY TWO WAYS OUT OF THE** ghetto for most black kids—school and sports. School opens the mind, nourishes the spirit and gives you the tools to compete in the world. Sports give you the chance to be the best, the chance to *win* and be somebody, gain honors, be proud. Sports give a ghetto kid the chance to win because there are rules; the competition can be tough but it's fair. In the ghetto life isn't fair, there are no rules, so you *can't* win.

Now I always did so like the rougher things in life, the rougher sports, 'cause sports were a way of me working off anxieties and tension. If I hadn't had wrestling or football, I'd have gone berserk or turned to drugs. It was an outlet for me from being suppressed in the ghetto and not having the things I wanted.

Also the trophies were something to look forward to, to work for, to get some pride and self-respect. It's like some little glue that holds you together, you can see your progress. And it was something to keep me occupied. My mother always said, "Idle hands are the Devil's workshop." If I'm not doing something constructive, I'm doing something destructive. You see, this is important in the ghetto. If I wasn't playing football, there was too big a gap there—you get out of school at 1:15 P.M., what are you going to do? Hang out, sitting on the fender of some car? That's why kids get into trouble. "I had nothing to do." The problem with the average kid in the ghetto is that he doesn't have anything to do, so he turns to crime or to violence. 'Cause it's something *to do*.

Sports was the key to unlock the door to the ghetto. I wanted to be a football player or a boxer, something that would give me big money, fast and legally—unlike some guy who might say, "I can buy these drugs and turn them over fast and make more money than Pa ever could and have this and have that." But, you see, the trouble with that is, it just don't work, you find yourself in another trap. Now if I could make it in sports, I could get out and write my own ticket. But I also knew I had to do well in school.

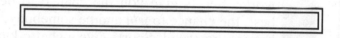

My eight years in grammar school were memorable because of the various teachers I had. It was also very important that I was enrolled in a mostly white school, which enabled me to interact with white boys and girls without problems. I learned a lot. Not just in the classroom, but in social acceptance and racial relationships. Children don't know about the ugliness of racial hatred, prejudice, jealousy or envy; all that is taught by the parents. I know through experience that black children and white children can play together, go to school together, and have fun all day long together without any problem. But as soon as a parent comes in, here comes the trouble. The parent will say, "What are you doing playing with that 'honkey'?" or "What are you doing playing with that 'nigger'?" And the children grow up with that hatred in their hearts and they don't even know why. Because their parents said so.

In grammar school my first four teachers were white and my last four teachers were black (three women and one man). I will never forget my third-grade teacher because she was so beautiful. Well, anyway, I passed her grade and went on to the fourth, then to the fifth grade. I was attending Edward Hartigan School and my teacher's name was Mrs. Style. She was rough and tough. If you were late coming to school and she knew you were playing around, she would grab you by the collar and lift you off the ground and sling you in your seat. She was a for-real black woman who was serious about teaching. She didn't like to waste time. She said we were too far behind in education, so we had to make every minute count. She gave me homework every night, a book report twice a month, a spelling test every Friday. She demanded that each child's parent be present at all P.T.A. meetings. You know, a lot of parents were also afraid of her, but she was a great teacher. She said I would thank her later, and I do. There were thirty-two students in my fifth-grade class but only eighteen passed on to the sixth grade. She refused to pass a student if he or she were not qualified. By passing her class you knew you were ready for anything.

In the sixth grade I won first place in the school science fair and third place in the school district science fair. I did an experiment with two baby hamsters. I was trying to find out "Do vitamins take the place of fresh food?" I fed one hamster vitamins and the other fresh food (lettuce, carrots, spinach, etc.). I don't remember the result but it was a great experiment.

Now I was in the seventh grade, attending Henry Horner School with my first male teacher. He was concerned and cared, but it was hard for him to teach because this was the seventh grade and the girls start to become a little "fast," if you know what I mean. He did okay and I learned a lot from him. My eighth-grade teacher used to sit on her desk and tell the class that she got her education and that we would not be anything in life but welfare recipients. This was no trick or ploy to get us motivated, she was just a dream killer. She could squash all the aspiration we had. Even though she was very negative, I learned what I could by keeping my mouth shut and my mind open.

I knew at an early age that the mind was a terrible thing to waste and that knowledge was power. I also knew I had to escape the ghetto stranglehold. I had to be educated. So I studied, read and studied more, until reading and learning became fun to me. That made my mother proud because she always wanted me to be something special in life. My grammar school graduation was held in a church. I was so proud and happy. I was proud because my mother and father were in attendance, showing much pride. I was happy because I was in the House of God once again. School and Church should go together hand-in-hand.

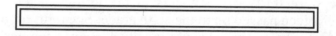

After graduating from grammar school at age fourteen, I went to Paul Lawrence Dunbar High School on the South Side of Chicago. At first, I didn't want to go there because all my brothers went to DuSable High School and it was a family tradition. I was so upset I couldn't go to DuSable that I cried like a baby and the whole thing worked on me mentally. In my freshman year I didn't do too well: I was only a member on the FroshSoph football team. I was not outstanding, like I was supposed to be. It took me until the last three months of my freshman year to snap out of it. Then I told myself, now that I'm here at Dunbar I might as well make the best of it.

I entered Dunbar in September of 1966 and left in June of 1970. Within those four years, I was City Wrestling Champ for two years straight at 165 pounds. I held the record for the fastest pin, which was seven seconds . . . that's right, seven seconds.

I loved wrestling. I would practice an hour before everyone else and an hour after everyone else. We were scheduled for three hours a day, but I would practice five hours a day. I had to lose 35 pounds in order to wrestle at 165 pounds. A lot of days I couldn't eat; I was afraid I would gain weight. I made up my mind that I was gonna be the best wrestler in Dunbar's history, and I was. No doubt about it. I would train, practice, and psych myself up. I lived wrestling, I ate wrestling, I slept wrestling. I was never absent from practice.

Even when the girls would try to keep me from wrestling practice, I said "NO." I remember one girl, who was my girlfriend at the time. I say "at the time" because she didn't stay my girlfriend too long, because she began to crowd me and I didn't like to be crowded. One day she said to me, "Let's go over to my house, there ain't nobody home and you can wrestle me instead of going to practice." Then she said, "You don't have to practice, everybody know you are the best. Can't nobody beat you." I said, "That's right, I am the best and do you know why can't anybody beat me? . . . Because I practice every day!" She said, "You make up your mind what you want—me or wrestling." I told her, "I'm going to wrestling practice, I'll see you around," and left her standing there.

I knew that there is a time and a place for everything and I wanted to be something. I wasn't going to let anything stand in my way. I was gonna be a champ. I was a proud wrestler. I had so much confidence. I didn't believe that there was a wrestler alive who could beat me. When I finally lost, I didn't cry, I was not mad. Why? Because I gave a 100 percent performance, I gave it all I have to give. I tried, but I still lost. So, I shook the hand of the man who beat me and told him, "You are the best." It was a moment I will never forget. We hugged each other in the center of the mat and he told me, in my ear, "Tero, I have heard so much about you. You are all they said you were. A tough competitor; a very clean wrestler, and above all, you are a great champion." While we were hugging in the center of the mat, the capacity crowd in the fieldhouse at the University of Illinois, Champaign/Urbana, were giving us a standing ovation. My eyes began to get watery, not because I lost, but because of what he said and felt in his heart. I shook his coach's hand and told him, "You have a great wrestler there," and headed for my dressing room. As I was walking, I could hear the crowd chanting "TERO, TERO, TERO." I waved to the crowd and said, "Thank you," and continued walking. Several kids caught up with me and asked if I would sign their programs. I signed my name and said, "Thank you," to each of them. After taking my shower, I began to get dressed when an old man came into my dressing room and said, "I just want to shake your hand, and that's all right, son. Today the victory goes to the other fellow, but tomorrow it's yours again." He patted me on my shoulder and left, with me right behind him.

Yes, I had a glorious wrestling career at Dunbar; I won many medals, trophies and awards. Every tournament I was in, I won at least two trophies—one for first place and the other for most outstanding wrestler, fastest pin or most valuable. It got so that I would be winning everything and I became the most feared wrestler in Chicago. They soon started barring me from tournaments, saying that I had won enough; give someone else a chance. In my two years of wrestling at Dunbar and AAU tournaments, I had a record of ninety-one wins and two losses . . . not bad, huh? I never got pinned, I never had a close match, and I never hurt an opponent.

But I did begin to lose interest after a while. The challenge was not there anymore, the thrill was gone. Why? Well, I became so feared that guys who found out they had to wrestle me got scared and went home. That was cool for one or two times; naturally I would win by forfeit. But I didn't want to win by a forfeit (not having an opponent show up). When my opponent did show up and if he was halfway good, it would be an exciting match. I put the "grunt" and "groan," the "slam" and "bam" back into high school wrestling. You may think

I'm bragging, but I'm just telling the truth. Before I started wrestling, there would be no more than twenty-five people watching a match at Dunbar. Then I came on the scene. I was colorful, exciting and had style. I used to pack the whole school in the gym to see me wrestle and do my thing. I would meet my opponent at the center of the mat and stare at him, then go to my corner and hold my hands and pray. I had this penetrating look, this hypnotizing look, this intimidating look on my face, and I was a vicious wrestler. Mean and brutal but never dirty. I would pick the other guy up over my head and strut around the mat with him, then throw him down and pin him. If a wrestler thought he was bad or tough, I would torture him; I would pin him but also punish him. That's how I got my reputation and that's the reason nobody wanted to wrestle me. I would like to repeat that none of my matches were ever close. Either I dominated the guy or I lost, and I only lost twice in two years of wrestling.

They called me "Tero the Terror" on the mat. The spectators in the gym would start going wild when they saw me getting off the bench and moving toward the mat. They would holler, stomp, chant, clap and throw paper in the air. The noise would continue until I got ready to pray, then all of a sudden, the whole gym would be silent. When my prayer was over, the noise would begin again.

I didn't wrestle in my senior year and let me explain why. When I took the City title in my sophomore year and went downstate to wrestle for the State title, I won my first match and lost my second. I had gone further than any other wrestler from our school. We had to vote to see who was the Most Valuable Wrestler . . . and I won. It is understood that the wrestler who goes the furthest is the most valuable player.

In my junior year I took City again and went downstate, but this time I won third place in State, the first time any wrestler from Dunbar ever placed downstate. But this time, we did not vote to see who would be most valuable—the coach just gave the trophy to someone else. The coach said he gave the trophy to this senior because he came crying to him, telling him how much he thought he deserved it. So the coach gave it to him without a vote. I cried; there was not a wrestler in the city better than I, even though I lost one time and took third place. Every member on the wrestling team knew it. But the coach told me, "Don't worry, you got next year." But I was hurt, disappointed and embarrassed. What made it so bad was I didn't find out until the sports banquet. Everybody from the school was there, teachers, principal, students, fellow athletes, guests and reporters. I will never forget those words of my coach, "And now for the Most Valuable Wrestler award," and everybody turned to look at me, then all of a sudden the coach called someone else's name. My eyes got watery and glassy. I was stunned. I couldn't believe I hadn't won the Most Valuable Wrestler award, which was a very big trophy. Man, I was hurt.

So I did not wrestle in my senior year. Everyone tried to talk me into coming back, but I said, "NO! I don't want to be disappointed again." I told the coach that words couldn't express the sadness I felt in my heart.

I learned to discipline myself and I learned to be a good sport. But most important, I learned "It's not who wins or loses, but how you play the game." Sports are a way of life. To be the best in any sport, you must train and train and do more than the next guy. In life, if you want to get ahead, you must work harder than the next fellow. I knew I would be a success in life because I was a success in sports. I paid my dues to be the best in wrestling. Being the best wrestler in the city of Chicago was no accident.

□ ■ □

At Dunbar, I not only wrestled, I played football for all four years. I was on the FroshSoph football team in my freshman year, but in my sophomore year I was moved up to the varsity team, which was mostly seniors and a couple of juniors. There were only two sophomores who played and I was one of them. Not only did we play, but we started every game—including the first one. That was back in the fall of 1967 and that year Dunbar won the championship of the public league, but lost 37–0 to the Catholic league champs, Mt. Carmel.

In my sophomore year, I only played defense. I was a defensive halfback, but I saw a little action on offense. I was not a star yet, but I soon got known as a hard hitter and a hell of a defensive back. My only claim to fame in that year was that I started on a championship team as a sophomore. I made five interceptions and I got a lot of offers from colleges and universities (as a sophomore). At the end of the 1967 season, we started to rebuild for the next year, and one thing I had in my favor was that I had a whole lot of experience under my belt. Besides being a born leader (which the coaches found out and made me co-captain in my junior year), I became a good ball carrier, a good kicker and passer. I was fast becoming a household name in high school because in my junior year I played offense and defense. I ran back punts and kickoffs, I made picture-book catches. I would carry two and three guys on my back at one time. I can truly say that one man never brought me down in a game.

I knew of only one guy who could tackle me and bring me down by himself. He was Ricky "Ju-Ju" Fisher. He was the other sophomore who started with me on the championship team. He played defensive guard and he was good, too. The other team would put two and three men on him and he would still get through and tackle their quarterback. Ju-Ju and I were good friends. We had gone through grammar school together and we became Dunbar's one-two punch. The other teams couldn't run because he would stop them, and if they tried to pass, I would intercept. Ju-Ju and I did a lot of things together, especially chasing girls. We became known as the "Gruesome Twosome" and "Mr. Outside and Mr. Inside." I gave us that name because in the middle of the football season, the coach switched Ju-Ju to be a fullback because they needed someone like Ju-Ju to spring me loose. When he hit you, you knew you had been hit. He would hit two guys, straighten them up and hit them again. They would fall back about five yards. Once we taught him how to hold the ball, he became a darn good runner. He was about 235 pounds then, and he had an explosive takeoff, quick like lightning. And he was not easy to bring down either.

We had a dream backfield: Ju-Ju at fullback and me at halfback. Ju-Ju could block and run real good, but couldn't catch that well. Matter of fact, he couldn't catch a pass at all, but he recovered a lot of the other team's fumbles. Now I could run well and catch well, but I was not too good a blocker. Matter of fact, blocking was my weakness. So our styles complemented each other! He would run the ball up the middle for the tough yards and I would run the sweeps for the long gainers. So Ju-Ju was "Mr. Inside" because he ran up the middle, and I was "Mr. Outside" because I ran wide. We both made all-city and all-state in our junior and senior years. We got so many offers from colleges that the coach would hide the letters and not tell us about them. He figured we would get "big heads" and think we were too good.

Well, I have news for him: I knew I was good, and yes, I had a big head (I wore size 7¾ hat). I was cocky and I was conceited. But I averaged at least two touchdowns a game, and was called "Touchdown Tero." I wore jersey #14 with tape around my wrists and I ran around in white shoes. When I scored a touchdown, I would run in the end zone holding the football over my head. I was just exciting to watch. When the students at Dunbar came to the game, they knew I would put on a show. When I would make those picture-book touch-downs—catches and slides in the end zone—the crowd would go wild, and they loved to see me drag a couple of guys for ten yards, then dump them off. I wore white shoes because they would make me stand out. I always had to be different. I always had this flair about me, this showmanship. I had to be the main attraction, center stage, and I was. I got a lot of press coverage. I was written up every week in the papers and got some TV highlight coverage also. Once, they asked my coach, Lou Tortorelli, to describe me and he put it best. He said, "Tero can do it all."

Sure I used to brag and boast, but when game time came, boy, did I come through! You see, talking is my style. I remember one day we were having a pep rally in the school's auditorium. We were getting ready to play our archrivals, Phillips High School, which is ten blocks away from Dunbar. Nobody figured Dunbar had a ghost of chance to beat Phillips. I was called to speak because I was the captain. I heard some cheers and boos because the coach had just told them we were gonna beat Phillips. The crowd said, "That's a laugh." Well, I will tell you that it wasn't a laugh. I told them, "We're gonna win, and I'm gonna score three touchdowns myself." Can you imagine me telling the crowd we were gonna beat Phillips, who hadn't lost a game all season? They had a record of 5–0 and the last three games they had won by shutouts. At Dunbar, our record was 2–3, and we had been shut out twice. Some people said it took a lot of nerve to say Dunbar was going to beat Phillips, but the crazy part was saying, "I'm gonna score not one, or two, but *three* touchdowns myself." Was I crazy, was I high on drugs? No! No! None of those. I just knew what I had to do and felt it, so I said it. I made a prediction and a promise I had to keep.

Of all the games that I have played in, this game with Phillips was the biggest. At Dunbar, we used to say, "If we lose every game in the season, it don't matter as long as we beat Phillips." Of the four years I was at Dunbar, I played against Phillips twice. The first time was in 1968. It was a practice game, but you couldn't tell that to all those people who were there. You see, when Dunbar and Phillips played anything, a huge crowd was going to be there watching. The first game with Phillips I was a junior. We played to a 6–6 tie and I think that was the way it should have ended between the two schools. That tie set the stage for the big game one year later, the one I'm going to tell you about. This game with Phillips was sold out the day the tickets went on sale. Everybody was coming: old alumni, teachers, relatives, grammar school kids, college scouts, newspaper reporters, photographers, TV cameramen, neighborhood bums, dropouts and people who just heard about the game. All that week, tension was mounting between the two schools.

What makes Dunbar and Phillips such rivals is that they are so close to each other. Some of your best friends go there; your brother or sister might go there, while you attend Dunbar. Your girlfriend might go there; your next-door neighbor might go there and vice versa. It was a must that every first-team member be in good shape. I was the captain, the leader, so I had to be ready, and besides I had a big mouth. I told a packed house what I was gonna do.

The coaches were nervous, teachers in school were trying to give me tips on winning. They gave me time off from class to get ready for Phillips. I tell you, I'd never seen anything like it before. Every day that week when we practiced, the whole school would turn out and watch us. Signs were made saying, "Go Dunbar, Beat Phillips." Our nickname was the "Mighty Men" and the Phillips team were the "Wild Cats." You should have heard me going around school promoting the game; telling everybody what I was gonna do. And I wasn't by myself either. I was with my right-hand man, Ju-Ju, and the new member of our group, Jerry "Mole" Johnson, who was the center on the team. We stuck together; we knew what we had to do. We were very loose; we were psyched up for the game because we needed the respect and we hadn't had it. By beating Phillips, we would get respect and lots of other things too. Parties were planned all that weekend, victory parties, of course. We had just come off a big win, a come-from-behind 12–8 victory over CVS (Chicago Vocational School). That was our homecoming game, and we were riding high for Phillips.

Couch Lou Tortorelli had Ju-Ju and me in for our weekly private conference, but this time he put more stress on winning. He told us, "You guys have been around, you are good ball players. You are leaders, the young guys look up to you for guidance and they respect you. That's why it is so important that we score first because if we score first, I think that will break their backs a little and shock them. While they are stunned, we will start pouring it on. We can beat Phillips, I know we can. When we score, don't let up; keep the pressure on them.

"Tero, you are a very confident young man. I hear how you've been going around school talking about the game and what you're gonna do. Well, that's fine and it's all right to be cocky. Keep the other guys' spirits up and get a good night's sleep." Just before Ju-Ju and I left the room, I told him, "We're gonna win tomorrow," and he replied, "I know we are."

□ ■ □

Saturday morning, the day of the big game, I got up at 8:00 A.M. and carefully started putting my football gear in the bag. The game wouldn't start until 1:00 P.M., but the coaches wanted us there by 11:30 because we had to be taped up. I had bad knees and ankles. Ju-Ju had a bad shoulder that had to be taped. About 10:30, I had everything packed and ready to go. I had a fresh coat of white paint on my football shoes and I always hand-carried them carefully. While I was sitting at home waiting for Ju-Ju and Jerry to come by and pick me up, one of my older brothers, Gus, was giving me my last pep talk, which was very important. He said, "Okay! Truck, you have been running one and two touchdowns some games, but this one you have to break loose like you never have before. You need three or four touchdowns today. A lot of college scouts will be there; this is a big game and they will be watching you and you've got to do it. The whole family will be there. You got a name, reputation and pride you must defend."

Ju-Ju, Jerry and I left. We went by a store and bought three real big cigars and three rags to tie around our heads to make us look tough, rough and rugged. We also ate raw onions so our breath would stink and that made us mean. When we arrived at Gately Stadium at 103rd and Cottage Grove Avenue around 11:30, it was already crowded. People were outside in the parking lots, and people were still coming by buses, cars, cabs, bicycles, and some came walking.

At last game time arrived. It was a perfect day, not a cloud in the sky and about seventy-five degrees. I lined up the ball on the kicking tee, raised my hand to tell the ref that I was ready, and took one last look at Lou. I nodded my head and ran up to kick the football. I kicked that football so hard and far, I kicked it out of the end zone and over the fence behind the end zone. The Dunbar fans loved that and I called a defense huddle and said, "Phillips ain't that hot, we can beat them!" We had to wait a couple of minutes for them to get the football back. We were fired up and we held Phillips' explosive offensive to no gain in three downs and they had to punt. We had the ball on our own thirty-two-yard line. The first play for us offensively was a "220 swing," that was me carrying the ball to our right side. I picked up nine yards on that play and we were ready then. The next play, Ju-Ju got the call to go up the middle on a "231 quickie." He ran to the left side of the center (with help from Jerry, who did some fine blocking all during the game). Ju-Ju gained twelve yards on that play because the whole defense was keying on me so I faked like I had the ball and ran wide. A lot of guys on the other team ran after me and when they found out I didn't have the ball it was too late. Ju-Ju had already gained his yards. The coach decided to run that play again so we did, and this time Ju-Ju got seven yards. It was my turn to burn, so I got the ball two times in a row. The first I ran for thirteen yards, and the ball was on Phillips' thirty-yard line.

I felt a touchdown coming and the whole offensive line felt the same way. Our quarterback, Curtis Walker, called his own play. He said, "Let's run that play again and all day long." We broke the huddle with big smiles on our faces. Now we would be a little fancy. We would do like the Dallas Cowboys—a lot of shifting to confuse the defense. We lined up on the ball and Curtis called the signal. The snap was on "One." He shouted, "Down. . . . Set. . . . Hut, one," and Jerry, the center, snapped the football to Curtis. Curtis took one step backward, turned around and gave me the ball going around the right side. In front of me were Ju-Ju, Jerry and Curtis, the two pulling guards and the right end. They cleaned the path. I mean, they knocked everybody down in my way and I just ran thirty yards for the first touchdown of the game. I congratulated the linemen and everybody else. Then we got ready for the extra point try. The ball was snapped. Curtis held it and I kicked it through the goalpost to make the score Dunbar 7, and Phillips 0. That only took four and a half minutes.

The Dunbar fans went wild and the place went up for grabs. the band started jamming and everything seemed unreal. I had to try to keep everybody cool because the game had just started and we hadn't won yet. I kicked off to Phillips again and one more time the ball went out of the end zone. So far, everything was all Dunbar; that must have been our day.

Phillips had the ball but couldn't get a first down. So they had to punt it again. The football exchanged sides a couple of times. Then, in the second quarter, with about six minutes remaining before halftime, Phillips was about to punt from their fifteen-yard line. I wasn't prepared to receive the punt and then all of a sudden I saw the football in the air coming right at me. I caught it on my own forty-three-yard line and started to run straight up the middle. Then I looked to my right and saw my team setting up a wall for me to run down. I ran over there and who was leading the way? None other than Ju-Ju. I followed him up to the eighteen-yard line where he hit two guys and went out of bounds with them. I was still running. I could hear the crowd hollering, "Go, Tero, Go!" I was running real hard and fast toward the end zone. Standing at the goal line was Phillips' last man to try and stop me— Larry Murray. He was a good athlete and he stood there waiting on me and I'm coming with speed, power and force. When I got to the five-yard line, I lowered my head and ran over him. He was slow getting up and I lay there in the end zone looking up at the referee to see if it was a touchdown. The referee raised his hands and I rejoiced. Some fans ran into the end zone and helped me up. We lined up for the extra point try, but this time we ran for it and Ju-Ju made it and the score was Dunbar 15 and Phillips 0.

We kicked off to Phillips and they decided to down the ball in the end zone, so the play started at their twenty-yard line. To our surprise, they began to move the ball on our defense. I told everybody to tighten up and they did on the next play. One of Phillips' backs was running with the ball when Ju-Ju came right up to him and took it out of his arms and started the other way before he was tackled. A couple of plays later, we ran out of time; it was halftime.

We came out for the second half with intentions of blowing Phillips off the field. It didn't take me long to score my third touchdown. Now the score was 21–0 in favor of Dunbar. At the end of the third quarter, Phillips finally scored a touchdown, making the score 21–6.

In the fourth quarter, I almost scored again. I ran thirty-three yards and stepped out of bounds at the Phillips two-yard line with eight minutes left in the game. I took myself out and told the coach to let the young boys have a chance. A junior

In the third grade at Forrestville School, age nine, 1961

In the sixth grade, the Edward Hartigan School, 41st Street and State, age twelve, 1964

My favorite—cake and ice cream— at a birthday party for one of my sisters. I was eleven years old.

In the seventh grade at Henry Weller School, 41st Street and Michigan, 1965

Senior class portrait, Dunbar High School, 1970

Senior at Dunbar High, 1970

Opposite: Sophomore wrestling champion at Dunbar, 1968
Inset: Wrestling in my junior year at Dunbar, 1969
Above: Me and Ju Ju at practice

Above and right: Playing football for Dunbar
Opposite: Football practice, my senior year at Dunbar
I was number 14

At Prairie A & M, my freshman year

Fort Jackson, South Carolina

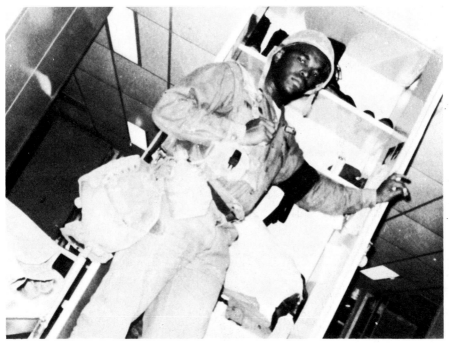

Just back from marching, a pack on my back

Above: MP school, Fort
McCullum, Alabama
Right: Squad leader, basic
training

replaced me and ran two yards for the touchdown. The final score was 27–6. We beat the unbeatable Phillips! We made believers out of everybody.

The following week, we played Morgan Park High School and beat them 38–0. I scored two touchdowns and ran twice for two extra points for a total of sixteen points that day. It was now time for the playoffs and we were pitted against Englewood High School. You know it's funny—they shouldn't have been on the same field with Dunbar, but they beat us 8–6 and we were eliminated.

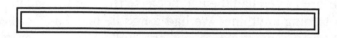

I had a wonderful time at Dunbar for the four years I spent there. Now, it was time for me to decide which college I was going to. I had over thirty-six offers, from the Big 10, Pac 8, Ivy League and all over. But I chose Prairie View A&M College in Prairie View, Texas, which was in the same conference as Grambling, Jackson State, Alcorn, Texas Southern and Southern U in Louisiana. It was an all-black college. I decided on Prairie View A&M because I thought they played a tougher game of football down there (and they did). I had always wanted to play against Grambling and their coach Eddie Robinson; I thought he was the best coach around but didn't get enough recognition because he was black.

When I first arrived at Prairie View in August of 1970 for football summer training, the coaches never quite understood me, coming from Chicago, wearing suits to class all the time with temperatures averaging eighty-five degrees and up. They were just not used to someone like me. I was still cocky; I told the coach that I didn't come all the way from Chicago to ride the bench. At first, the coach totally overlooked me until he put me against his first-team defense. I was on the Zu-lu team, the kind of team that one week you are Grambling offense, the next week you are Jackson State offense. Well, I said to myself, this is my big chance because I'm playing his best defensive team and I'm playing on the worst offensive team. I had a halfback playing tackle, a split end playing center, and the other tackle and two guards were small and very scared. I was bigger than some of my linemen, but we scrimmaged away.

Seems that all the plays were designed for me to carry the ball and I liked that. I began running, but the defense began tackling me and, man, were they hitting! They were getting to me before I even had the ball because the line we had up there wasn't doing anything. We had a huddle and I asked them to at least give me time to get the ball. I got closer to the quarterback. When he got the ball from the center, I was there to get it. I carried the football like a loaf of bread, with one hand instead of two. The coach told me after practice, "You're a good runner, strong, and can take a lot of punishment, but I want you to practice covering the ball. Tomorrow report to the first-team offense."

That night, I had to get my head shaven. It was traditional for all freshmen football players to get heads shaven bald. I cut all my hair off and I liked it, so I've been wearing it bald (or semi-bald) ever since. I made the traveling team and then the first team as a halfback. At 215 pounds, I was the biggest halfback Prairie View had. They wanted me to be a fullback because they only had two fullbacks; one was 190 pounds and the other was 225 pounds. I didn't want to play fullback because the fullback didn't get the ball enough for me, all he did was block. I never was that good at blocking, but give me the football at least twenty times a game and I can guarantee you at least two touchdowns for the day.

My biggest thrill while playing football at Prairie View was coming home to Chicago to play against Grambling at White Sox Park in October 1970. Needless to say, we lost 57–6, but it was fun to come back home again. After the season I was nominated for president of the freshman class. I won the election, but I was not just a dumb football player and class president. I made the honor roll also, with a 4.0 grade average. I had six A's.

□ ■ □

When I enrolled at Prairie View A&M, I changed my first name to Mohammad and demanded everyone call me by that name or I would not answer. I had a big confrontation with my English instructor because he didn't want to call me Mohammad. So we had to work something out, and we did. He would call everyone else by their first and last name, but when he got to me he would say, "Mr. Tero," and then I would reply, "Here, sir!"

When I was in college, I was sort of militant—that is, I was a militant from the authorities' point of view. I just didn't take no stuff, that's all. Besides, I was class president so I had some power and I voiced my opinion. I was later told that was a mistake. I always said what I felt and I didn't fear what would happen to me for saying it.

Now you must understand, when I was in college back in 1970, there was unrest all around the country, at many colleges and universities. On February 24, 1970, violence struck Prairie View. I didn't start it, and I wasn't a participant either, but I was blamed for it. The night it happened, I was . . . well, with a young lady, one I had wanted to be alone with for a long time. I heard all the noise, saw the students running and screaming, buildings burning, windows being smashed. The college bookstore was looted, and everybody was running and grabbing what they wanted. The campus police car was turned over and set on fire with a fire bomb. I mean it was a nightmare, I couldn't believe all this was happening at an all-black college in a small town. Whatever reasons made these students riot, the situations must have been brewing for a long time because I never saw so many angry students at one time in one place before.

Prairie View burned all night. Stores, dormitories, even the dean's two-story office building burned to the ground. There were so many fires going on at once that the fire department couldn't handle it. About a thousand students marched a mile and a half up to the college president's house, knocked on his door and woke him up. They demanded a number of things that they had written down on a list.

The next day a big meeting was called at the administration building for 11:00 A.M. that morning and the majority of the student body was there. Some were sitting on the lawn, some in their cars, and some looking from their dormitory windows. I was in the background listening to what was being said by one of the administrators: "I need all responsible and concerned students who want to work with us in bringing this problem to an end." They called the student government leader, all class officers, the president, then my name was called and a big roar went up. As I began to make my way through the students, my girlfriend said to me, "Don't go because if you go, all they will do is write your name down and kick you out later. That's the way they do it, that is why you don't hardly see anyone going in." I told her, "I will be all right."

Me being always outspoken in everything I had ever done and president of the freshman class and all, I couldn't hide and not come forward. Now before the meeting I even talked to a couple of deans who told me, "No, you shouldn't get involved in that." But I'm the type of guy when you tell me I *shouldn't*, I don't like that—I got to be my own man, otherwise I just burn up inside. So I spoke up. I'm not going to be afraid of the consequences. I'd be less than a man if I didn't stand up for certain things. I couldn't look myself in the face, or look my mother and my father in the face.

Anyway, later at this meeting, all the students had to stand up one by one and state their name, year in college, where they were from and what dormitory they stayed in. I didn't think about what my girlfriend had said until I was in there and noticed that the instructors were writing down everything we were saying, especially the students who spoke against the college. I also noticed something funny when it was my turn to stand up and introduce myself. I said, "My name is Mohammad Tero and I'm president of the freshman class. I stay in Alexander Hall and I'm from Chicago, Illinois." I was about to sit down when an instructor asked me, "Aren't you a football player on a scholarship?" I said with force, "Yes sir, I am!" Nothing really happened at that meeting, but the college was closed the next day and it stayed closed for a week. The administrators said they would weed out those responsible. Every student that was in that meeting was suspended, mostly the out-of-state students and Muslims (only seven of them on campus). I was a Muslim and I was out-of-state.

If you were suspended, the only way you got back in school was to admit to the charges they had against you, sign a statement that you did those things even if you really didn't do them, and you had to tell on someone else. Well, I was suspended and I was charged with about twenty-three different things including inciting a riot, stealing, breaking curfew, trespassing, failure to prevent a riot, burglary and many other crazy charges. I was suspended without a hearing. All my rights were violated. I never got a chance to confront my accusers. Why? Because there weren't any. All the charges were trumped up. I had two college hearings in which I had no chance at all. The only thing the board wanted to hear was the names of other students who participated in the riot. I refused to tell. If that's what I had to do to get back in college, well, I didn't want an education there.

I went to court trying to get back into school. I appeared on TV and radio shows, spoke at other colleges and universities, went to Austin, Texas, to see the politicians and then spoke to state senator Barbara Jordan, who was planning an investigation of the disturbance. I really stirred up a lot of attention. When I got suspended they thought I would just pack my clothes and leave, but not me. You see, I have always been a warrior. I stayed in Houston fighting for my cause, to make sure all those false charges would be dropped and my name cleared. Then I sued for defamation of character. I was for real. They didn't think I would fight back, but I did. Prairie View wanted to keep the whole thing quiet, but I have this big mouth and I got to tell it like it is, and I did. A lot of people called, sent telegrams telling me to hang in there, go all the way, don't give up. I was fighting my case so tough that a dean at Prairie View asked me to "go home, you have proven your point, you have nothing to gain." On the contrary, I did.

When I finally went home, which was in May, I left Prairie View in a state of shock. Some of the students who had been reinstated were kicked back out again, three deans lost their jobs, eleven instructors got fired and many other college employees were dismissed. Many students left Prairie View and didn't return the following semester. When I finished what I had to do, I left Houston to come home to Chicago.

BACK
IN CHICAGO

FTER BEING HOME FOR A WHILE AND RE-grouping from my experience at college, I began looking for a job. Finding a job was not easy, especially a decent-paying job. I looked in the newspapers, called places, filled out applications, got up early in the morning to look—but no job. I would do the same thing the next day until I found something, because any kind of money is better than no money at all.

Finally, I got a job at one of the hotels downtown, as a houseman in the housekeeping department. I would set up rooms and chairs and tables, ashtrays, and water bottles. Then after the meetings were over, I would stack the chairs and take them out. Once in a while, I would get a couple of dollars in tips for doing something small for one of the guests. They would say, "Hey, boy, come here." I was nineteen years old, old enough to vote and go into the army and die for my country but still they called me "boy." I was getting plenty tired of that "boy" shit. When those white folks called me boy, I would really move slow even though they were going to give me a tip. I wasn't going to be bowing and scraping for it, not like the older black guys. They were fifty and sixty years old and the white guys were twenty and thirty years old but still they would call these black men "boy." "Hey, boy, come here," or "Boys, could you get us more chairs in this room. . . . Hurry! Hurry!" To see old black men running as fast as they could carrying all those chairs was really sickening.

My supervisor, who was a black man, did not like me because I was young, strong and didn't take no shit! He used to ask me why I didn't run or move fast like they did and I told him, "When I applied for this job, they didn't tell me I had to be a track star to get it." He then said, "You're a smart-ass nigger, aren't you?" I said, "Yes, I am, I just left college," and I walked away.

When I got off work that day, I started to look for another job in the evenings and I found one. It was perfect—the hours, that is—and the pay was all right. I was now working two jobs. In the day, I was at the hotel from 7:00 A.M. to 3:30 P.M., then I would walk around downtown for a while before it was time to go to my second job, which was at the First National Bank of Chicago. I worked as a janitor for three years. I quit the hotel after three months.

It was at this time (1972) that I changed my name to Mr. T. Why? Because I got tired of white people calling me "boy." You see, a lot of whites have this problem of calling all black men "boys." It doesn't matter how old they are, it's still "boy this" and "boy that." And when your second name is boy, your first name is nigger. Now, when I am addressed, the very first word that comes out of a person's mouth must be "Mister." It's a sign of respect. As a black man growing up in a white society, I ask you: What does a black man have to do before he is given respect? When I was eighteen years old, I was old enough to fight and die for my country in the United States Army, but still, I couldn't live where my money afforded me. It was at that moment I knew I needed respect. So I started with my name. Mr. T. I don't allow no one to call me just "T." My first name is Mister, my middle name is that period and my last name is T. Sure, that name doesn't appear on my birth certificate; more importantly, "nigger" doesn't appear on my birth certificate either, but I have been called nigger plenty of times.

Some white people don't like to call me Mr. T. They ask

me, "What is your real name?" But they never ask John Wayne his real name, or Rock Hudson, Cher, Liberace, Tiny Tim or Boy George. And what about Pope John Paul II? Nobody asks him, "What's your real name, Pope?" My point is this, if you don't ask all the white people who have changed their names, don't ask me. White folks play double standards: "If you're white it's all right, but if you're black then get back." So if we're going to play this name game, let's play it fair or not at all.

If I say, "My name is Mr. T," then call me Mr. T. When I am referred to as Lawrence Tero, I don't answer or respond. When bills come with that name on them, I say, "That person doesn't live here anymore." When the phone rings and someone asks for Lawrence Tero, I say, "Wrong number." So pretty soon people got the message and started acting accordingly as far as my name is concerned.

☐　■　☐

After I quit working at the hotel, I had to get another job because I wanted more money to buy a new car and an apartment building. I had this idea since I was very young of owning real estate, because real estate would pay for itself and I could retire early. I wanted to become a millionaire by age thirty-three. That was a special number to me because that's the age Jesus died. You see, I was always thinking bigger and faster than the average kid in the ghetto.

By this time I was already developing my style, which was *sharp*. I would wear these three-piece suits, my derby, my spats, my cane, my hair style (I was bald then, and sometimes had a Fu Manchu mustache and beard). I used to save my money and buy things on lay-away, 'cause I knew I had to play the game. I was living in the ghetto but I used to go downtown and be treated like a millionaire because I played the part. They didn't know what I did, but I looked like money. Sometimes I didn't have more than five dollars in my pocket, but I'd buy the *Wall Street Journal,* go to some posh place and get a cup of coffee and sit there. Playing the game.

I was only twenty but I made people with money gravitate toward me. I use to crash $250-a-plate dinners and just walk in there. People would come up and say, "Who are you? Come on in." I'd say "Mr. T," and they still wouldn't know anything, but they were impressed. And we'd chitchat and stuff, and they'd say, "How interesting, you must come back." You see, I wanted to be a gentleman, and get respect, and it all played together and it was catchy: "Mr. T."

I found a job working as a guard for $1.95 per hour at one of those agencies. I worked there for a couple of months, saved my money and quit. Then I found another guard job; this time the pay was $2.10 per hour. I was still at the bank at night. I worked the guard job for five months and then quit to work for the Board of Education as a gym instructor in a government-funded program called Operation Impact.

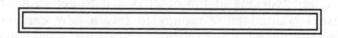

Operation Impact was a pilot program set up by the Board of Education. It was a school for boys, seventy to eighty per year, ages twelve to sixteen or once in a while seventeen. These boys had all sorts of problems: some were real slow learners; some just didn't want to learn; some had attendance problems, some used to fight and beat up teachers; some had personal hygiene problems and some liked to smoke and curse in class. Well, I was hired as a gym and health instructor. One thing I knew for sure: they could not have found a better man for the job than me. I knew what these boys were going through and what they were faced with every day. I knew because I just came out from there. They were very poor, they came from broken homes, and I came from a broken home. Many of them lived on welfare and so had I. Therefore, we had a common bond that united us, even though I was doing pretty well by the time I started at the school. I had a message to tell and a lesson in life to teach these boys. I didn't come with that everyday textbook jive. I studied their homes; I got to the root of the problem. You can't expect a boy to learn if he hasn't eaten in a couple of days, or if he lives with his mother and hasn't seen her all weekend and when he does see her, she doesn't have time to listen to him. She's only at home to change and get back in the streets to go to a lounge with another man. All of that works on a young boy's mind. It's hard for him to think about school with all of that on his mind. I really got into that program; it meant so much to me to try and save all of those young boys from going into a life of hell, and I *know* that is where they were headed if no one caught them in time and tried to help.

I started working at Operation Impact back in 1972. When I first started working there, I wanted the boys in the school to know that I was a no-nonsense type of person. I wanted them to know that I was hard but I was fair. I wanted them to know and understand that I did not play favorites and I would not have a teacher's pet. They understood what I meant but didn't like it, and that was good because I was not there to be their buddy, I was there to teach them. If I became their buddy, it would have been totally impossible to control them and teach them.

I did not trick them or play games, I just told them the hard, cold facts about life in a way they could deal with. I did not butter them up, pat them on the back, smile at them or say something nice if they didn't deserve it. I rarely gave compliments. I was very strict and I hated excuses. I was a firm believer in discipline. I didn't cut any slack. If I caught one of the boys smoking a cigarette, I would hit him with my paddle. Every puff he took off the cigarette cost him a lick from the paddle. If I heard one of the boys cursing, that would be more licks, plus he had to write a composition on the curse words he used.

Yes, I was challenged, threatened, cursed at, rocks were thrown at me and my car was scratched many times in the beginning. So I pulled out the leaders, the tough guys, the real bad ones, and the ones with the big mouths. I took them all to the gym—there were three of them. As they stood around, I told them, "I eat three punks alive for breakfast every morning with my cornflakes." I then said to them, "If I can't beat three snotty-nosed kids, I shouldn't be here." I knew that would make them mad. Now these were real tough boys who had a record of beating up teachers—and some had even beat up their parents. But there I stood, calling their bluff and looking them straight in the eyes, daring them to jump.

I am sure they had never seen anything like that before. I walked up to them and grabbed one, then said, "Listen, punk, if you ever disrupt the class again, threaten any teacher, be late to school, miss your homework, or if I catch you with your shirttail out, I'm gonna bring you down here and mop the gym floor with your butt, you understand?" At the same time lifting him in the air. By that time, one of the punks ran out of the gym screaming, "I'm gonna get my gang on you." He stayed away from school for three days until I went to bring him back. He didn't even have a gang, he only said that to save face in front of the other guys.

After a number of long chats with the boys, things began to get better. For once they found out school was a place of learning, not fighting. They would sometimes fight each other, so I would allow them six minutes to fight in the gym, and after the six minutes, win, lose or draw, the fight was *over!* No more! That really worked because the boys didn't take the fighting from school into the streets of their neighborhoods. Also if one of the boys that was fighting said, "I give," or "I quit," that was it, the fight was over! Sometimes the boys would fight in the morning and be friends by lunchtime. That was good because I wanted them to concentrate on learning instead of fighting.

Impact school started at 9:00 A.M.; I was there at 8:30, downstairs playing with the boys in the playgroud. That helped me establish a one-on-one relationship with them. School let out at 2:30 P.M., but I stayed much later sometimes, talking to some of the boys. Sometimes I would drive them home or park my car and walk with them through their neighborhoods. I made three home visits a week. Sometimes I would take them to the movies, football games, baseball games and basketball games, or dinner and swimming. I gave them another outlook on life. And if you think I just took the good students or the smart students, then you are mistaken. I took the worst, the baddest and the extremely slow learners. Why? They all needed to feel loved and wanted. I gave my phone number to every student at the school so they could call me and talk if they wanted to, and they all did at one time or another. At Impact, we would keep each student for at least two years, then they would graduate and go on to regular high school. I would like to say, "We didn't work miracles at Operation Impact . . . we just cared."

I gave that program all I had and when the day was done, I was truly exhausted. But I felt good because I was giving of myself totally to the kids. I was more than a teacher. I was everything to those boys because they trusted in me and they believed in me. I was a father to the fatherless. I was their only true friend. I was their big brother and, sometimes, I was their mother. I worked in that program for three years and I'd just like to say, of all my thirty-two years in life, those three years I spent working with those boys at Operation Impact were the most rewarding. I never got a trophy or a big pay raise for my work there, but I got self-gratification and satisfaction in knowing I did my best.

You see personally I didn't and still don't believe that there are children who can't learn. There are some children in the ghettos who thrive on learning, they miss the luxuries of good foot to eat and decent clothes to wear, but their minds are sharp. But too many teachers in the projects are afraid to teach because they fear rape and hostile assault. That is one of the main reasons black children are so uneducated—their teachers take on an apathetic attitude. Then there are those teachers who tell the children that thcy will never be anybody and brag about how they got their pot of gold. So the kids are discouraged, lose hope and self-confidence, turn to crime and drugs and head for the streets to find themselves. The schools today are a reflection of society. I think the schools must cure society's ills. As the educators and administrators, you teachers have an awesome responsibility for the development of an individual, and you have a massive influence in the shaping of society. So, teachers, you must teach. Students, you must try to learn. And parents, you must get involved and do your part. So let's put the blame where it belongs. The way I see it—everybody is at fault. Since we are all at fault, let's get together and straighten this mess out once and for all. Perhaps the dwellers in the projects can find themselves with the help of others. And those of you who live in the projects have got to want, need and have the desire to *be* somebody and *believe* you can be somebody. You must make your breaks and not wait for them. God only helps those who help themselves.

Do you as parents blame the schoolteachers for your child's bad habits and misbehaving? I stated that the problem and the solution is right in the home, but you teachers can help also by doing what you get paid for, and that is teaching and educating the children. You see, when a child is growing up, every adult plays a key role in developing that child into a good, productive citizen of the community. Sure, it's easy for any parent to say, "My children wouldn't do that." Now, you as parent and as an adult are in the wrong: You should tell that child when he is doing wrong and counsel him, that's what you should do. If you can't and don't help, don't be the first to criticize, okay? Also, remember that every time a child has committed a crime, it should affect you indirectly, if not directly, because I am sure that child has crossed your path at some time or another and you had a chance to mold that child into something respectful and responsible. Whatever becomes of them has something to do with us; if they go bad, it's our fault, and if they go straight, it's because of our patience, understanding and counseling.

A lot of kids are not given a chance, they are pushed into the background; they are thrown out of the house; they are misused, mistreated, misguided and misdirected. After all of that, how can you expect a child to grow up? How can you expect a child to respect the law and other human beings when he has been forgotten? If you really want crime to go down, start working with these kids today. Start helping them, spend some time with them, get involved and show them that you care and I guarantee you will see some improvements. Everybody must join this war against crime. We don't have any room for conscientious objectors. You teachers must teach and stop just collecting paychecks, stop watching the clock, stop doing your nails in class. You men teachers, stop rapping to the women teachers or vice versa. You community leaders, let's start leading, make yourself more visible to the community. Form block clubs, have neighborhood meetings, get to know the person across the street, make yourself known to the teenagers in the area. You church leaders and preachers, start practicing what you preach. Stop riding around in your big Cadillacs, Lincolns and other fancy cars and start walking down and through the neighborhood. Go visit the jails, talk to the inmates, go to the foster homes and detention centers, show these kids that you love them and maybe we can stop this contagious, cancerous disease of crime in children. If we can help them go straight while they are young, then we don't have to worry about them growing up in a life of crime. My father used to always say, "From small acorns, large oak trees grow." I'm sure that saying is self-explanatory. My challenge and plea to you parents, teachers, preachers, judges, lawyers and social workers is: Reach out, reach back, reach down and grab the hand of a confused child. Lift that child up to where he ought to be. Don't leave him alone in this mean world because he might not have anybody to turn to. And if he does, they might not love him or want him, so we must care for him. Yes, you and I.

You see, it's totally unrealistic and stupid to rely on the juvenile justice system today; it's out of date, especially in the ghetto. The juvenile system was created for kids who don't exist anymore; because of communications and television and everything else, the teenagers are much more sophisticated than fourteen- to eighteen-year-olds once were. I think that people are making the mistake of thinking of today's juvenile criminals by the old term "juvenile delinquent." You remember the "juvenile delinquent." He was a young creature who existed many years ago. He liked to break school windows, steal hubcaps from cars, stand around street corners and talk tough, sometimes shoplift at the neighborhood five-and-dime store, and even form a gang that would have fistfights with the gang from the next block. He smarted off to teachers, spent a lot of time in the principal's office, skipped school to go to the movies or bum around the street, and was a chronic headache to his parents and to the local juvenile cop. But in general, he was a harmless pain in the neck.

Sorry, that's not today's modern juvenile criminal. He doesn't smirk and lip off to a teacher. He's more likely to break her jaw with one punch or corner her in the supply room with a knife. When he joins a gang and the gangs fight, it's not with fists. The bullets fly and the blood flows. And if the people in the neighborhood treat the gang with disrespect, their houses are likely to be burned down. Instead of standing on a street corner talking tough, they hide around the corner and wait for you to walk by, so they can skull you with a brick, strip you of your clothing and entertain themselves by conducting a gang rape.

Today's juvenile offenders are bigger, tougher and meaner. And the crimes they engage in are bigger, tougher and meaner. When you talk about rape, armed robbery and murder, it's irrelevant to the victim that the person who did it to them is a juvenile under the law. You bleed just as much. I don't trust juvenile criminals, whether they know what they are doing or not. I also realize that older people will try to capitalize on the young by getting them to do their dirty work. But still, they are criminals because *they* committed a crime. How should the courts try them? As adults, which means maybe a stiffer sentence if convicted, or as children which means maybe reform school and supervision?

Now the only problem is that we really don't know any more about the use of punishment than the ancients did thousands of years ago. We can still find nothing better to do with transgressors than lock them up, hang them by the neck or burn them to death. Nothing that we do seems to work, but we keep on doing it anyway. Prisons make men worse and parole releases incorrigibles as well as people who never should have been put in prison in the first place. Penitentiaries don't make inmates penitent; reformatories don't reform; capital punishment has no effect on the crimes punishable by death. The reason for this, it seems to me, is that we keep looking upon "crime" as an individual act, when it really is a reflection of the society itself. We are quick to blame a family if its children are delinquent, but we are unwilling to put the responsibility on society for its criminal offspring. We are also extremely reluctant even to admit to ourselves that the moral climate of a community is a big factor in the crime rate. Rather, we blame the rot on the plant, not on the soil in which it grew. And this relieves us of any obligation to nourish the soil.

All you have to do is care and try. Now it's true that some of the boys fell by the wayside, some didn't graduate and some went back on the street. One got killed; I attended his funeral. I visited one in jail; I went to a hospital to see another. Whatever happened to them I was there, caring and concerned and still trying to do something. When one went to court I was there, pleading his case before the judge. If a child failed and went astray, I figured that I had failed and I didn't do enough. I took my job personally. When one of them got hurt, I felt pain and cried.

My mission at Impact was to teach the unteachable, to reach the unreachable, and to wait on the late bloomers. I told all the students not to get sidetracked because we were in a school with broken windows or cold classrooms in winter. We read from old beat-up books, but I tried to instill in them pride, self-worth, dignity, and responsibility. I told them the story about the ugly worm inside the cocoon, but that same cocoon produced the most beautiful butterfly in the world. I asked them what difference does it make if you have old books or new books if you open neither? I told them not to worry about the architectural structure of the school, but the value of education that they received while inside.

So at this time, I want to say to all the teachers and would-be teachers of the world,

I challenge you to *teach,* I mean teach like you can't help it, I challenge you to become the ultimate in a teacher. Teach your students as if they were your own children. I challenge you to become a great teacher. Great teachers are not known by what they know, but by what they share. The final measure of a great teacher is not merely how high you score, but how high your *students* score. Great teachers are characterized by service, sacrifice, sincerity, sensitivity and sanity. Great teachers go the second mile because great teachers—I'm not talking about qualified teachers, I am discussing great ones now—great teachers know the law of contentment leads to collapse, but the law of sacrifice leads to greatness. They are patient, understanding, caring, and in love with their jobs because they see teaching and the classroom as the pinnacle. A great teacher knows that there are no jobs nobler than teaching. Teaching isn't a steppingstone to another job; teaching is the highest calling. Great teachers, I mean *great* teachers, really survive on psychic income. They know that the real reward is a satisfied spirit that comes from knowing you've done your job well. Great teachers are never limited by legalese, by "what all I don't have to do," or by materialism, "how much I can make." They must fight to earn a livable wage, but you know when you start learning to teach, this is not a profession that will ever attract luxurious compensation. If a teacher is ever paid what that teacher is worth, that teacher is not worth what that teacher is paid. Your work is infinite, your work is immeasurable, your work is divine. Reverend Jesse Jackson said, "Teaching is a test of immortality." If you choose to really be great, don't get trapped coming to school as late as you can, leaving as early as you can, making as much as you can while sitting on your can without a lesson plan. Be a real great teacher. Be the truth of that which you teach. Teach with moral authority, teach 'cause you can't help it. Believe deeply in *what* you teach and *who* you teach. Make yourself indispensable, make yourself necessary. Great teachers know that there are values in values. You must be on fire to give off heat. We *can* teach our children, it is possible. We *ought* to teach them, it is the moral thing to do. *We must teach them,* it is the imperative of now.

That is my challenge to all teachers and would-be teachers.

□ ■ □

I worked at Impact for three years and for three years Impact held graduating ceremonies. Now two of those three years, Pastor T. L. Barrett was the guest speaker at the graduation ceremony, but in 1975 I was the guest speaker because that was Operation Impact's last day of existence (our funds were cut out) and there was something I wanted to say to the students, parents, friends, relatives and staff. I will never forget that day. It was filled with emotion, hugs, handshakes, pats on the back, joy, sadness and, yes, tears. That year thirty-five students graduated from Operation Impact, and they marched into the school auditorium wearing their caps and gowns, looking proud. I stepped up to the podium and all the graduates took their seats. The place was packed, it was SRO. I remember standing there speaking as if it were just yesterday. I didn't prepare a speech because I wanted the words to flow from my heart to theirs, and I remember that message. It went something like this:

I am so very happy and moved today, words are inadequate for me to express the deep joy that comes from my heart this afternoon. I congratulate you graduates of Operation Impact. All of you, each and every one of you. This is history in the making, because I was told we couldn't teach you anything and that you would learn nothing. I was told that we would be wasting our time. Then I told the nonbelievers: Bring me your tired, your weary, et cetera, whoever will, let them. I don't know what they do at those other schools, but here at Impact WE LOVE YOU! Here at Operation Impact we have armed each student with the sword of knowledge, the shield of education, the breast plate of truth and sat them upon a horse called confidence. Every student is ready and prepared to do battle against ignorance and illiteracy. At Impact, we realize that many of you boys—or young men, I should say—have come to us motherless, some came fatherless, while others came homeless, but the important thing is that you came to us. Now, I say to you parents and to you, my fellow teachers, I know these young men might not be all they ought to be, but I thank God that they are not what they used to be. I got to be honest with you all.

Now, as I tried to continue my message, I got a little choked up. My eyes got watery, my throat got dry, my heart started pumping faster, my voice lowered, and then the tears began to roll down my face—I had to stop. I just couldn't continue because my emotions had gotten the best of me. But when I took my seat the students and their parents gave me a standing ovation, and I was deeply touched. Anyway, the graduation went on as scheduled and the students graduated and continued on to high school to further their education and training skills. All in all, Operation Impact was a success and I was honored that I had played a part in the program.

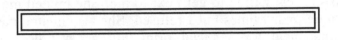

During the summer of '75, I sort of took it easy. I had money in the bank and a brand-new car and I had recently bought a four-unit apartment building. Let me tell you what I went through being a young, single, black landlord. Now I got this building at a steal because the neighborhood was changing and the man who was the previous owner (a white man) figured it was time to get out. So I came along just in time, with my pockets bulging with money. The man wanted $1,500 down, but I gave him $5,000 down to show him I meant business. I bought the building when I was twenty-three years old, but I couldn't really take over until they thoroughly screened me, checked me out, and everything else they had to do. You know they had to be sure, and why not? I was young and black, so they thought I wanted the building for a big house of prostitution or for drug sales. They just couldn't understand that I had bright ideas, plans and big goals. After all the paperwork was done, the building was now mine and mine alone.

Wow! I said to myself, it's a dream come true! At twenty-three years old, a landlord, and collecting rent too. All those years of working two jobs paid off because I was able to save so much money, and it surprised me. I tell you, when I introduced myself to all the tenants personally, they were shocked, startled and outright in disbelief. Two white families moved out after they told me, "Mr. T, you probably want your own kind in this building." I replied, "No, sir! I just want good tenants; the ones that will pay their rent on time." One white man said, "That's nice," but he still moved out, and other families moved in; some good, some bad.

One lady told me that she was married, but when she moved in I found out that she was single and loved to mingle. I mean she really tried to get next to me. She invited me over for dinner many times but I refused. She also invited me into her apartment for a social drink but again I declined. I remember when I used to go and collect the rent, when I got to her apartment she would come to the door with this see-through lingerie on. I kept my mind on business. You know, that lady was a very good tenant but she was a little lonely.

Some days after I would cut the grass at the building, I would get a lawn chair and some orange juice and sit out on the grass and enjoy life. I was really trying to let everything soak in. To be truthful with you, that was my "high." I mean, just thinking about my building I would feel good all over. Some days I would drive around the block saying to myself, "That's my building." I was very proud and happy.

I felt like a millionare for once in my life. That year was a very good year for me. Nothing was too good for me and I spared no expenses. The summer of '75 . . . I had so much fun that summer it was hard for me to readjust myself and think about working again. But summer was ending and fall was beginning, so I knew it was time to get back to work.

I had big plans and I had this goal in front of my mind—to become a bodyguard, to become the best bodyguard in the world. Everybody's got to have something to reach for, some reason to get out of bed in the morning, something to keep them going, and I had this dream of becoming the world's greatest bodyguard.

6 THE BODY THAT GUARDS

I DECIDED TO BECOME A BODYGUARD. WHY? BECAUSE I liked the danger, the excitement of it, the satisfaction I got out of saving someone's life. As a bodyguard, I found my self-worth in life. Being a bodyguard was something special: I'm saving a life. It made me feel good when my clients told me how safe and secure they felt with me. That meant more to me than the money I got paid. After all, I grew up in a violent society, a violent neighborhood, why not put myself to something useful? What could be more useful than being a bodyguard, or being a doctor?

And I can truthfully say, "Mr. T was the best bodyguard in the business, the best money could buy." The best description of me was "the body that guards." I had this drive to do my job so well that the living, the dead, or the unborn couldn't do it any better.

□ ■ □

As a bodyguard, every client I have protected I have vowed to die for. My life belongs to them. I like to think of myself as a kamikaze pilot. I am a human shield. If there's a gun, I'll take the bullet. If there's a knife, I'll get stabbed. You just got to be ready to die. Why did I like being a bodyguard? Well, it's like this—I like danger. The challenges, the pay, the travel, and most of all I like the reward of self-gratification and satisfaction that I get when I know I have saved my client from bodily harm or death. Dr. King made a statement once that summed up how I feel about my chosen profession, and I quote: "If a man hasn't found something that is so dear, so precious that he will die for it, then he isn't fit to live." When I choose to bodyguard someone I lay my life on the line for that person. I will protect them with all my might. I belong to them and I am all they need. Therefore, when someone's life is threatened I am called into action. I become their bodyguard and protect I do, I cover them like a blanket on a bed, like ugly on an ape. I protect all my clients that way. I have to, because I always work alone. You see I don't work with an army of security people like the secret service. Therefore when I work I do the work of at least three or four good men. As a bodyguard I cannot tell you in words exactly what I look for when protecting my clients. But I will tell you this, I don't chance anything. I don't leave a stone unturned, because when someone hires me that means that they believe in me, they trust me, and most of all they need me. I do firmly believe that I have personally saved a lot of people from death. I know those are some big words; well, I am a big man. You see the thing that makes me so good at what I do is this: I simply do not fear death. I am not afraid of dying. I fear no man, no monster, no anything, because "The Lord is my shepherd and I shall not want. . . . Yea, though I walk through the valley of the shadow of death, I will fear no evil, for thou art with me."

I have studied long hours, I have trained intensely, I have watched the President's Secret Service agents protect him. I have watched special security personnel guard heads of state and I have watched other bodyguards protect their clients. I train two hours a day, seven days a week. I run three miles a day, I do six fifty-yard sprints, a hundred jumping jacks, a hundred push-ups, a hundred sit-ups, fifty squats, I punch the heavy bag for twenty minutes a day, I jump rope ten minutes, and then I meditate or pray. I trimmed down from a bulky 255 pounds to a lean, mean 208 pounds.

With all the money he may get, a good bodyguard is still underpaid for the work that he does. It's true, the job is dangerous and God only knows the trouble I've seen. I realized that one day I might not return home from an assignment, but I understood that. One thing you must understand about me is that I am no stranger to danger. Matter of fact, the harder the job the better I am. When it came to the safety of my clients, I knew I might be killed one day in order to protect them. I knew all of that when I decided to become a bodyguard, it comes with the territory. But take it from me, you have never lived until you have almost died. For those who fight for it, life has a flavor the protected will never know.

I also realize and know of my faith and belief in my God whom I serve, that life is a corridor and death is a transition. I wasn't put here to stay, I was just passing through trying to do God's will. I was put here for a purpose and when I have done my job, my time will be up.

I really liked the responsibility of knowing that someone's life lay in my hands. In order to really ensure the safety of my client, I had to think like a killer. When I did that, I always stayed ahead of the game. Confidence radiated all around me. I was in complete control of the situation and I was ready for anything and prepared for the worst. Bodyguarding was a way of life for me. I slept it, I ate it, and I drank it. What separated me (the best bodyguard in the business) from the rest? I knew what I was doing and no one did it better . . . no one. If it sounds like I'm blowing my own horn or patting myself on the back . . . I am. If I'm not for myself, then who will be for me? If it sounds like I'm cocky or conceited, it's because I am. I just have to be the best in whatever I do. I have certain motivating factors and one of them is the Bible. My Bible tells me, "Whatsoever a man thinketh in his heart long and strong enough, so is he." You got to believe in yourself before you attempt anything or the battle is lost. I must do my job so well that all the Host of Heaven and Earth would have to pause and say, "Mr. T did his job well."

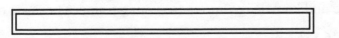

But I knew that before I became a bodyguard I had to have a lot of security experience and background. That's why I worked so many guard jobs that paid nothing—the experience was invaluable and it looked great on my record. I started going to law enforcement schools and writing letters to security organizations for more information. I sent off for books about police work, I went to seminars and workshops, I visited police stations and courtrooms to see the professionals at work firsthand.

I saw an ad in the paper about security guards at one of the local hospitals and I put in an application. I was interviewed three times, given a polygraph test and a physical examination, and was hired on the second shift. I worked there six months and got promoted to sergeant on the third shift.

□　■　□

At that time, I decided to sign up with the National Guard Military Police to further my education in the security profession. I knew National Guard MP credentials would look good on my résumé when they asked for background experience or special skills. In November 1975 I took a military leave from the hospital and left for Fort Jackson, South Carolina. While at Fort Jackson, I got into better shape than I had ever been in. I enjoyed the discipline and the hard work; the exercises were strenuous on me but nothing I couldn't handle. The physical part was no problem, but getting up at 4:00 in the morning, making my bed a certain way, running around saying, "Thank you, Drill Sergeant, for making me do a hundred push-ups"—that was a problem.

But I did my job so well that I was made Senior Squad Leader. I would march my platoon, lead them in exercise, lead them to the mess hall and lead them off the base for relaxation. It was a challenge and it was fun. I became a highly motivated soldier. I tried to instill some of my confidence and knowledge into these young trainees because often they couldn't cut the mustard. They joined the army at sixteen, seventeen years old, and most of them had never been away from home before.

There were a lot of white guys who had never been near black men before. That caused problems for them because they had to sleep in the same room with blacks! This was unheard of where a lot of them came from, and it was one of the reasons why some of them wanted to get out of the Army. And others got discharged because they couldn't adjust to military life. Those who stayed in my squad, I think, learned a valuable lesson in human nature from me. You see, I have this certain something about me that makes people stop, look and listen to what I have to say. Aside from being a big black brute, I am a very intelligent man and my drill sergeants soon found that out. I was one hell of a soldier and I knew it. Soon enough my drill sergeants and the company commander found that out also.

A couple of weeks passed and I found myself the talk of the fort. Everybody was watching me, from generals all the way down to other trainees. Sometimes officers or other sergeants would stop me when I was on detail, just for small talk. Most wanted to know where I came from. One day the senior drill sergeant pulled me aside and said, "Private Tero, you have been doing a real fine job here, and I want you to know that all the other drill sergeants feel the same way, so we have elected you the 'Trainee of the Cycle.' When you graduate from basic training, you will be given an award by the general during the ceremony."

That ceremony was a very important and special moment in my life. I was the top trainee out of about six thousand men and I stood up on the platform with captains, majors and generals. I stood at attention during the whole ceremony. All the other trainees' eyes were upon me: parents, guests, friends, and most of all, my drill sergeants. My uniform was starched stiff; my shoes were shined the best that they had ever been. You could see your face in them. Then the general came up to me. I gave him a sharp, snappy salute and he returned it, shook my hand, gave me the award and said, "Private Tero, you are a good soldier, keep up the good work." I said, "Thank you, sir," and we saluted again. He walked back, but I remained on the platform. We all stood there while the six thousand trainees passed us on the reviewing stand. I tell you, it's hard to try to explain to you what I felt standing there, knowing I was the best trainee—number one—in my training cycle. I wished my whole family could have been there to see me looking good, standing tall, not moving for one and a half hours in all that heat. It was a day and a moment I will never forget. I was so proud.

I also received a letter of recommendation from my drill sergeant and some of the other drill sergeants wanted me to enlist in the army. They said I had drive, determination, motivation and desire, plus I had what it took to be a good leader. But I had other plans. After graduation at Fort Jackson Basic Training Center, I was sent to Fort McCullom, Alabama, for AIT (Advanced Individual Training and Military Police School).

At MP school we had to be sharp because we were policing other soldiers. We had to be in order ourselves; that's why we had inspection every morning and sometimes during the day. It was really fun and rewarding. I learned a lot during my stay there. I had one sad moment, in our judo and self-defense class, which we had to take for two weeks. Judo and karate and all other martial arts I don't fool around with, and I was paired with a guy who was scared and tried to resist the attack. I was not trying to hurt him but when I went into action, I guess I must have forgotten where I was momentarily. Before I knew what had happened, he had been flipped over my shoulder and was lying on the ground holding his leg. I had broken it. He stayed at camp until his leg healed and took the class again two months later.

MP school was just that, a school. You go to class, the next day you are given a test and if you pass, you go on to the next course. If you fail, you remain there until you pass. You get only three tries to pass; after that, you get kicked out. Once you are in MP school, you must have three security clearances to graduate. If you don't, you will never get a diploma. I enjoyed MP school because it reminded me of college so much. I had classes from 7:00 A.M. to 4:00 P.M. and after class, your time was your own.

When we finally got an off-base pass, our drill sergeant (who was white) told us (the black guys) to watch where we were going because in some places we might go, the people were "rednecks" and there might be trouble. I remember my first day away from the fort; I had a three-day off-base pass and I got a room at a motel in town. This motel had a swimming pool and it was real hot that day, so I decided to take a swim. I think I was the only black in the motel besides the maids. Anyway, I came to the pool and got on the diving board and was getting ready to dive. All of a sudden, all the white people in the water got out and all those sitting or lying around the pool area got up and disappeared. I was left there all by myself. I said to myself, "I don't like crowds anyway; if they were stupid enough to leave because they hate blacks, let them go and sweat in their rooms. I'm gonna stay here and cool off in this pool." I know the motel was glad to see me check out; and do you know, all the while I was at that motel, a state police car was always on the scene. My pass had run out and it was time for me to get back in my army clothes and on base, where I was glad to be by now. I had gotten used to all the classes and studying. I was passing my courses really fast so I could graduate early, by late June, which I did. Well, almost—I got out of the army on July 1, 1976, which made me very happy.

I arrived home on July 3, just in time for the holiday and the family picnic. Two days later I had to pack my gear all over again because I had to go away for two weeks' summer camp at the National Guard Annual Training at Fort McCoy, Wisconsin. One week we slept in the barracks, the next week we slept out in the woods in our sleeping bags and tents. I remember one time my platoon sergeant thought he was punishing me by putting me on a detail chopping down trees. I asked him, "How many should I chop down?" and he said, "I'll let you know." I started to swing the ax and trees were falling everywhere. I must have chopped trees for four or five hours. I was given the job right after breakfast, which was at 6:30 A.M., and by 10:00 A.M. it was hot as hell out there with bugs, insects, mosquitoes flying all around. But I kept on chopping. You see, every time I was put on a dirty detail, I would use reverse psychology. They thought a detail like that would break my spirits but I would take the job and smile, do it, then ask if there was anything else they wanted me to do "because I just love hard work, it makes me strong." They couldn't understand me, they thought I was crazy.

I must have chopped down about seventy-five trees, no little trees either. I was chopping so hard that I didn't see or hear the major coming up the hill to where I was until he stood in front of me. When I saw him, I dropped the ax and stood at attention. I gave him a salute and said, "Good morning, sir." He said, "At ease, soldier." I said, "Thank you, sir." I was standing there, muscles shining, heart pounding, bald head gleaming, no shirt, and a white handkerchief around my head. He asked, "Why are you chopping down so many trees?" looking around at the same time and then adding, "God damn!" I said, "Sir, I was told to by my platoon sergeant." The major then asked, "Where is your platoon sergeant?" I told him that he was down at the end of the hill. He then said, "Carry on, soldier." I saluted him and he left. He went down to our camp area, chewed out my platoon sergeant and told him to take me off that detail. I heard my platoon sergeant calling my name but I acted like I didn't hear him. So he had to run all the way up the hill and tell me to stop. I said, "How could I hear you calling me when I was busy swinging this ax?" My platoon sergeant then asked me, "Why did you chop down so many trees?" I told him, "You told me to chop down trees until you told me to stop," with a big cheesy grin on my face. After that I didn't have any more trouble. I wasn't put on any more dirty details.

Those weeks went by *very* slowly, especially when we were in the woods. We had to stay out there in the rain and everything. Two days it rained on us. One night they threw tear gas on us while we were sleeping. We later learned that it was all part of army war games. That wasn't funny at all because I couldn't find my gas mask. It was very dark out there and the only thing you could see was the blue and white smoke from the tear gas canisters. After I couldn't find my gas mask, I started to run, trying to hold my breath at the same time, but I ran right into a big tree, head first. Boy! Did I have a headache after that, and a real big bruise on my head. I put ice on it and kept ice on it until the ice melted. After that, I rubbed some cocoa butter on the bruise and scar. At that point I was going to grow my hair back because I couldn't deal with scratches all over my bald head. Whenever I was off duty I would sit in the sun with my head covered with cocoa butter because cocoa butter is supposed to remove scars and it did. My head was healing pretty good.

One Thursday my buddies in the barracks bet me fifty dollars that I couldn't run through the barracks door. One of them said, "Big T . . . you might be big, strong and crazy, but you can't go through that door." Actually, it was two doors. A thick, hard wooden door and a screen door with some wood in it. I said, "You are right. I couldn't run through the door . . . well, not for fifty dollars. But if you made it one hundred dollars, I might go through the door for you." I said that with a confident grin on my face, with my hands behind my head, lying in my bunk with my legs crossed. Everybody looked at one another, puzzled. Then I said, "Well?" My buddy said, "Okay, I got the extra fifty." To be truthful about it, I would have run through that door for free, just to be destructive, but since money was involved that made everything a little nicer. I told them I wanted the money first, before I went through the door. They obliged. After one of the guys handed me the money, I got ready. I got down in a football stance and I said, "Down, set, hut one!" then took off running for about ten yards. I made a charge like a bull and I hit the door with so much force that the whole barracks shook. Wood was flying everywhere. It sounded like an explosion. I made it through the door all right, but not unmarked. I must say that I was lucky because I was cut between the eyes and had a deep cut under my nose. I also had cuts and scratches on my arms, and to this day, I still have the scar under my nose.

The next day our company commander was passing by and saw the door broken. The screen was busted out, wood was all over the ground and some pieces of the door were still hanging on. He came inside and said, "Who did this? How did this happen?" I told him, "Sir, some guys came in last night and jumped on me. I think they were drunk or something and look what they did to my face." I showed him my face with all those cuts. He told me that he'd get someone to take me to the hospital for treatment and he asked, "Can you identify any of them?" I said, "No, sir, it was dark and besides, I think I hurt some of them pretty bad. I don't think they'll be back." He said, "Okay, Tero, as long as you're satisfied, but we still have to get the door fixed." He left the barracks and everyone started laughing. My buddy, Mosely, said, "Damn, T, you are somethin' else!"

Besides the tear gas, the tree incident, sleeping in the woods for five nights and the bugs, I had a great time in Uncle Sam's army. I learned a lot and I enjoyed the experience. It was fun and educational living in the barracks with all races of people, especially in South Carolina and Alabama. I think I made a lot of friends.

□ ■ □

I arrived home on a Saturday morning from camp and had to report to work that night. I started work back at the same hospital in the same position that I had left, which was a sergeant in security. I was working on the third shift from 12:00 A.M. to 8:30 A.M. Some people call it the graveyard shift, but I called it the sleeping shift. Most people who worked that shift were old, and I do mean *old*. We also had three women on the shift, and one of them was my superior. She was strict on me and two-faced. I was a threat to her; she feared I was after her job. She would criticize me for making a bad choice and stay on my back instead of showing me how to be a good supervisor. You know, I honestly felt sorry for her because she was caught up in this web of begging, kissing behinds, bowing and scraping, skinning and grinning, trying to do anything that would give her brownie points.

Aside from all the personality conflicts and all the bullshit that was going on in the department, I was a hell of an officer and sergeant. I was involved in fights, arguments, patient restraints, and many rundowns of escaped mental patients. I saved many officers from getting the shit beat out of them. Sometimes it would be a psychiatric patient or an alcoholic, a visitor or just the general public. I never chased a person without catching them. I was so good at calming down mental patients that I thought about becoming a psychiatric social worker. I would calm them down by talking, not always by force. I have taken knives, sticks, bats and other weapons away from mental patients. I even talked four of them out of committing suicide.

The thing that made me so effective at the hospital was that I really loved my work. I loved to help the old people into wheelchairs, get them cabs, walk them to their cars at night. I had to count my blessings while working at the hospital, because I saw so many sick people and that really saddened my heart. I saw little babies die; I saw a man being brought into the emergency room, a big knife in his stomach with only the handle sticking out. I helped in delivering four babies and assisted in delivering six more. Of all the emergencies that I faced at the hospital, and I must admit we had a lot, I never lost my head or blew my cool. We had blackouts, floods, nurses getting raped, doctors getting robbed—one doctor was shot and killed by one of his psychiatric patients. I was in charge of the security detail when the President's wife, Rosalynn Carter, visited the hospital's psychiatric department. I was in charge of the security detail when Mayor Michael Bilandic's mother was in the hospital, twice, before she finally died there.

I was soon moved to the second shift, supposedly to help and assist a new lieutenant they had just promoted, a white boy who had race hatred all over his face. The deck was truly stacked against me. I had more experience as a sergeant and could help the new lieutenant, but he saw it as an insult. Why? Because he was white and didn't need any help from a black. He had a degree from college and I didn't. Therefore, he knew more than me, so he thought. What he failed to understand, and many others also, was that college can't teach you courage, it can't teach you bravery, nor can it teach you to overcome fear.

I was put on this second shift to help the new lieutenant, but not once did he ask my opinion. I was being completely phased out. If it were not for my exceptional ability in dealing with wild patients, I guess I would have been gone a long time ago, but they couldn't find anyone to replace me. The department was very ill-trained and all out of shape, and old too. Don't get me wrong, I'm not a chauvinist, but we had women in the department who didn't weigh over ninety-five pounds and weren't a good four feet ten inches tall. What could they possibly do with one of those psychiatrics or alcoholics who were going berserk in the emergency rooms? What made it bad was that we averaged about two psychiatric patients a day on the second shift. We had some pretty women in the department who should have been in the beauty salon instead of security work. They didn't want to break their nails or ruffle their hair or get their makeup smeared. That type of thing pissed me off. If you wear a uniform, you do the work, and if you didn't want the job then you're a handicap to me. I'm not downing all women; I'm just talking about the women I had the unforgettable pleasure of working with. I also know that there are a lot of mean, tough, strong women in the security business. I know there are some women that are hard as a rock, ugly as hell, who would rather fight than cook. We didn't have any of those women working in our security department.

Most of the men in the security department were a lot of sissies to me. Frightened nonprofessionals with a badge. I didn't like the hospital criteria in hiring, which were if you passed the polygraph test (which just about anybody can beat) and you passed the physical exam (and all they had to know was that your heart was beating). We had one guy in the department who had had two heart attacks, another guy who couldn't walk up a flight of stairs without wheezing and breathing hard, one guy whose stomach was so big he couldn't see his shoes, another guy who was three years from retirement. Now suppose I was getting my behind kicked, do you think any one of those guys could help me? By the time they arrived, I would have been dead for an hour. I know I'm a very harsh guy, but when I work, I give 100 percent to my job. I expect everybody to do the same thing. I don't care if you are woman, man, sissy or lesbian. If you wear the uniform and carry the title, then damn it . . . do the job!

We had some guys in the department who were well educated, but they had too much book sense and not enough street sense. Therefore their book sense wasn't worth a damn. See, I was born in the ghetto, raised in the ghetto, educated in the ghetto and I also learned the white man's ways. I guess that's why I was so effective in my job. I knew the street lingo. I knew how to rap to brothers, Mexicans, Puerto Ricans, whites and Latinos. Not only was I big, but I had smarts, the kind you can't learn in any classroom. I knew I made a lot of people mad, especially the educated ones and the ones who were over me. They wanted to find fault in my work but they couldn't. So they started nitpicking, saying I was playing favorites because I would eat lunch with one fellow officer all the time. I was told to stop doing that by my new supervisor.

One day I came to the aid of a fellow officer who was fighting a man trying to enter the hospital without permission. He called me on the radio with a code that meant he needed assistance. I arrived on the scene just as the man had thrown the security officer to the ground and started running away. I ran after him, caught and tackled him. But my elbow hit the concrete really hard and it felt like I'd broken my arm. I got up with my right arm dangling in much pain, picked up the man with my left hand and brought him back to the hospital. Then I went and saw the doctor about my arm. I had some X-rays taken and got a prescription for some medicine for pain. The doctor said there were no bones broken but that I was badly bruised and I should stay off work for a week to ten days. I had to take medication for four days to stop the throbbing pain. My arm was swollen so big that it looked like two arms. Do you know that while I was hurt and under the doctor's care, my lieutenant was saying that I was faking and there wasn't anything wrong with me? The officer I saved called me just about every day to see how I was doing and to say thanks. Hearing his voice made the pain bearable because it was nice to know that someone appreciated my efforts.

I stayed off work for a week and a half. When I returned, I was put on disciplinary probation not for the usual three months, but for six, by my white superiors. The whole thing was a shock to me. First the probation, then the length of time. I wasn't given due process of law. I was supposed to have been given a verbal warning, then a written warning, and put on three months' probation. You see the reason I received six months was that it was easier to make a mistake in six months than in three, and they wanted to get rid of me and needed all the evidence they could get. The six months they gave me was actually illegal.

While I was on probation, I received four letters of commendation and did superior work that made the front office really mad because they didn't have a case against me. Never did this lieutenant or anyone else have a bad thing to say about my work during my probation except once. And that was when they wanted me to stop arresting people. See, while I was on probation, I made seven arrests by myself, for stealing, robbery and trespassing, and that was making me look too good. So word came down: "Tell Sergeant Tero not to make any more arrests." Even if I was the one to catch the suspect, I was to turn him over to another officer and let him make the arrest. I mean they were really on me. I was checked every day for mistakes.

One day in May, out of the blue sky, the assistant director called me into his office. He told me that I wouldn't make it to the end of my probation, I just wasn't doing it. I just didn't quite work out. He stated that I was a hell of an officer but I just couldn't cut it as a sergeant. I then asked him, "What did I do wrong?" He said, "You didn't do anything wrong. But it's such a big step from officer to sergeant, and you didn't handle it too well." Ain't that something? Now, I worked there for three years, two and a half years as a sergeant, and all of a sudden, he tells me I can't do a sergeant's work? So instead of demoting me back to an officer, he was firing me and finding me a job at another hospital on the other side of town. That way it would look like I quit and went to work somewhere else. He said that he was doing me a favor by getting me a job at this other hospital, and that he didn't do this for everybody. He also said that whatever time I need to get another job, I should take because I would still get paid by the hospital.

Instead of going to the hospital that he had sent me to, I went to the Equal Employment Opportunity Commission and also retained a private attorney to sue the hospital for racial discrimination and unfair employment practices because the assistant director said he would not put me back as an officer. But there were two white guys who were working as officers and both had been sergeants but were later demoted to officers. That happened on a Thursday and by Monday, the hospital received two letters, one from EEOC and the other from my attorney. The assistant director and the director tried to talk me out of the lawsuit, saying we didn't need any outside help, we could work this problem out among ourselves. I told them, "This time you have messed with the wrong black man." They said, "What do you want? We can compromise." I said, "I want my sergeant's job back; I want my raise; I want that cleared from my record; and I don't want to be harassed anymore. Also, I want all of the above in writing." Right after that, I was given my two weeks' vacation and three holidays (which I had requested four times previously and been turned down). They were trying to pacify me but I was used to that old trick. I took my vacation anyway because mentally I needed a break from the hospital. I needed to get away from all the Uncle Toms, all the white racists and all those jealous people. While on vacation, I continued to do bodyguard work, something I was doing all along while I was at the hospital.

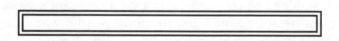

I was in the security business off and on for nine years and in that time, I have protected a lot of people. In the early days, I made a lot of mistakes that could have been very costly. But since I'm a fast learner, I quickly corrected them.

For instance, I have been to a lot of security seminars and

never have I heard anyone stress total first aid. When I used to go looking for a job as a security guard, never once did the interviewer ask me about first aid. The first thing that the employer wanted to know was did I have a weapon and a blue card. First aid was not a requirement in the security field, one man told me. One employer told me to "shoot to kill, that's the only skill. The times that first aid is needed are very few and besides, we don't run a hospital." Please take it from me, first aid is a must and it ranks number one on my priority list. A bodyguard should know the difference between a person under the influence of drugs or alcohol and a person having an epileptic seizure. A bodyguard should know what to do in each case. He should know how to treat a person for shock; how to make an arm sling; how to stop the bleeding of a wound. A bodyguard should be compassionate and understanding enough to know how to deal with a mentally disturbed person because they need help too. A bodyguard should know how to treat snake bites, dog bites, insect bites and gunshot wounds. He should know how to administer artificial respiration, how to carry and transport an injured person. He should know how to treat someone who is choking on food or the victim of a heat stroke or frostbite, what to do in case of fire and how to treat burns. He should know CPR. He should know what to do in case of poisoning, whether it was accidental or attempted suicide or planted purposely to kill. If a bodyguard doesn't know the correct answer to all those questions, he should quickly get out of the protection business, because it takes more than being tough to be a good bodyguard.

When I was hired to protect someone, I did everything except guarantee them their lives. I didn't give them a guarantee because to do that would be trying to play God and I can't do that. But I did tell my clients that I would give them the best possible protection a human being can render, because next to God, there is no better protector than I.

Now I did give them a guarantee, but the guarantee was

this: "I guarantee you that I will give my life protecting yours." I do that for my friends and when I protected someone they automatically became my friends. The Bible says, "Greater love hath no man than this, that he would lay down his life for his friend." When it comes to bodyguarding or personal protection, I was in a class all by myself. If you say that I was not the best bodyguard in the world, that's because I never protected you. Then you would understand when I say the rest are frauds, fakes, phonies, pretenders, actors and so-called bodyguards. They are really stand-ins and substitutes for the real "body that guards," which is myself. If you've ever seen me in action, then you too would know why I was the best. Just ask some of my clients whom I've protected.

Ask that West Side mother on welfare with those five children who called me up at 3:30 in the morning asking for help. That case I will never forget for a number of reasons: (1) She told me that for the last three months every time she cashed her welfare check, she was robbed of her food stamps and cash. She also told me that one time she was robbed right in front of the currency exchange and nobody tried to help her. (2) She told me how she was mistreated and abused by the neighborhood thugs. (3) She told me that her children hadn't had new clothes in a year because every time she got some money, she was robbed. (4) She then told me how much she needed me and added that she could never pay me for my protection. She started to cry on the phone, saying that everybody had turned their backs on her . . . even the police who, she said, she'd "called about a thousand times." They said they didn't have manpower to supply personal protection for every citizen. I told her to stop crying because I would help her and I would be over there first thing in the morning. After I finished talking to her, I couldn't sleep any more for thinking about her situation.

I went over to her house that next morning. I didn't make a fanfare out of it. I didn't tell the press, I didn't arrive there in my limousine and I didn't take a cab either, because the cabs would not go into her neighborhood. So I had to take the bus and walk five blocks to her house, or apartment I should say. When I got there, that welfare mother was so glad to see me and I was glad that I came, really I was. Her apartment was no palace, she had no furniture and the children were running around—some naked, and the others crying. But I was not there to inspect or criticize. I was there to protect her. I wasn't wearing a suit, but I was dressed the way the local thugs dress. A rag around my head, gym shoes, army pants and baggy shirt half open to reveal my chest, and most important, I was packing my heat (a .38 caliber snubnose pistol). I sat down and she told me everything that was happening. I told her what I was going to do and how it would be done.

For about a week and a half every day I was with her wherever she went with her five children. You know, it didn't even bother me when people would look at me funny walking down the street with this lady and her five children. Matter of fact, I felt proud. Soon the thugs got the news of me being with her every day and they thought I was her new boyfriend. They didn't know who I really was, so that was cool. I remember the morning of the day that her monthly check was due, I arrived at her house at 7:00 A.M. I wanted to be there real early, even though the mailman wasn't due to arrive until 11:00, so we just waited and waited. Then finally the mailman arrived with her welfare check. She got the check and I told her to do what she usually does. She put the check in her bra, fastened her blouse and buttoned her sweater. I didn't want to take any unnecessary chances. I told her to take the same route to the currency exchange that she usually did and the streets looked okay. No thugs hanging around that I could see.

We made it to the currency exchange with no incident; she said they never bothered her going into the currency exchange but always after she cashed her check. She cashed her check, bought food stamps and was ready to leave when she looked in the envelope that contained her money and food stamps. She fondled through a couple of bills and tried to give me some money, but I told her, "No, I couldn't." So she put the money and food stamps in her bosom and we started out the door of the currency exchange. The currency exchange was a good six blocks from her house, so we had a little walk ahead of us. As we walked and talked, I noticed this four-door dark blue Chevy, about a '68 or '69, cruising about with four guys in it. Every time I would turn around the car would stop and the guys would duck down. I told her to stop and we would talk for a while, which we did. Then the car took off, ahead of us. So we started walking again.

Just before we got to the corner, which was a vacant lot, we were approached by three guys—tough-looking guys, too. Two of them were about my size and the other one was much smaller. As they approached us, they tried to pretend they were friendly. One of them said to me, "What's happening, brother?" I looked at him and said, "Everything's cool," but never turning my back on them. That's when the short one said, 'Why are you looking at us like that? Are you scared?" I said, "No." Then the lady said, "The short guy is always with the guys who've been robbing me." I said to her, "Okay, step back to the wall out of the way." Then the short guy said, "Who do you think you are?" I replied, "It's not important who I am, but don't bother this lady no more, you understand?" The short guy got mad and said, "You must don't know who we are!" Then one of the big guys said, "Nigger! You think you're bad, huh?" I replied, "If you are looking for trouble, then you are calling my name." Then the two big guys got to arguing, saying to each other, "Let me fight this motherfucker, he think he is bad!"

I said calmly, "One of you guys won't have a chance against me, all of you better jump on me, that might help."

You see, I challenged them, and their manhood was at stake, their egos were insulted; that was a blow to their macho image. I out-psyched them momentarily. They started arguing to see which one of them was man enough to take me on by himself. I said to them, "First, I want to show you all something." I picked up a brick and laid it between two other bricks on the low broken-down wall running along the sidewalk. I told them to watch closely. Now can you imagine this whole scene? First we are getting ready to fight, then they stop completely in their tracks watching me. After I told them to watch closely, I began to do my thing. I put my hand on this brick a couple of times like I was gonna chop it in half, then I started making hissing sounds. After that I brought my head down real fast and hard, like the crack of a whip. I brought my head back up straight, spun around and looked those thugs in the eye. They were shocked, stunned and amazed. I had broken the brick in half with my head! I told them, "That's why one of you won't have a chance." Then they said, "Fuck that, we ain't gonna fight you! Shit, man, you are crazy!" The two big guys kept asking, "Who are you? What's your name? Where are you from?" I said, "If you really want to know, I'm Mr. T." And I took the rag off my head and put my earring in my ear. Then the short guy said, "Yeah! I seen you on TV a lot and I seen your picture in the papers all the time. You are that mean motherfucker that be protecting them rich people. Hey man, we are sorry, we didn't know who you were, and if you give me a chance, I will get a hold of them guys who took her money before and get it back in a week."

I then accompanied her to the grocery store to do her shopping and went with her to buy her children some clothes. Then I escorted her back home. I told her before I left, "If you ever have a problem again, don't call the police. Call me instead, because nine times out of ten I will get to you before the police will, even though I have to come all the way across town. Besides, I won't come here saying this is a routine incident, and most important, I don't do anything half-ass like the police."

The lady called me a week later and said the thugs came again but this time they had two big boxes of new children's things and $417. They told her she would get the rest before long. She called me again and said everything was fine and that her kids were doing well in school. She also invited me to dinner one Sunday, which I accepted, and that was my pay. A good family dinner with all her children.

□ ■ □

Of all the bodyguards that I've seen, and I have seen a lot, there is one group of bodyguards in particular that is outstanding—the Fruit of Islam, the bodyguards of the late Honorable Elijah Muhammad of the Nation of Islam. The Nation of Islam is now headed by the fiery Minister Louis Farrakhan and his security men do not play. When Reverend Jesse Jackson's life was threatened and the secret service seemed a little lax in their duties, Minister Farrakhan assigned members of the Fruit of Islam all over America to protect Reverend Jackson. Minister Farrakhan made a statement to all those people who hate Reverend Jackson: "Don't harm this brother [Reverend Jackson]; if you do, you will never harm another." Then the secret service told Minister Farrakhan, "It's *our* responsibility to watch Reverend Jackson!" Minister Farrakhan replied, "It is, but you didn't do too good of a job watching Kennedy. You didn't do too good a job watching George Wallace. You didn't do too good a job watching President Reagan. We know you mean you're gonna watch him, but we are gonna watch you and the people too. We are gonna watch all those people who claim to be listening and if anybody comes out with the wrong stuff, we're gonna come out with the right stuff, and deal." The Fruit of Islam bodyguards are strict, alert, well conditioned, well trained, highly educated, very serious, dedicated and always clean. You can feel their piercing eyes looking all over you. I found no loopholes in their security.

The Fruit of Islam is very respectful. They move with plenty of authority, they never speak, they stand like statues—tall and strong and so confident. They make sure no harm will come to their leader. When someone enters the mosque or temple, he is thoroughly searched by at least six or seven Fruit of Islam brothers. It's like going through an automatic car wash. Each man is detailed and trained to check certain parts of the body and clothes. Then the last two search you all over. Women, children, everybody who comes in is searched and if you go outside the door just to spit, believe me, you are searched all over again. Anything that looks like or could be used as a weapon is not allowed in with you. It would be checked and you could pick it up on your way out. Just to see these men standing there in their expertly tailored Fruit of Islam uniforms is a sight to behold. There is no clowning or joking in their ranks. There is no "give me five" BS.

I don't know if you have ever been to their "Savior's Day Services" at the old Coliseum on 14th and Wabash or the Amphitheater on 43rd and Halsted or the Armory on 52nd and Cottage Grove. Well, I went to the one at the Amphitheater and I never saw so much order and control. I mean everybody knew what they were supposed to do and they were doing it. Muhammad Ali was there. He was one of the featured speakers. The day of the event, the Fruit of Islam security force was there early. Some had stayed there overnight to make sure the place was well secured, looking for anything out of the ordinary. When it was time to let the public in, we were only allowed in at certain doors. Before the public started in, each member of the Fruit of Islam was searched himself by other members. (I told you there were no loopholes.) No cameras were allowed, no chewing gum, no smoking in the washrooms and no talking. During the course of the program, if you had to go to the washroom, you would have to let one of the members of the Fruit of Islam know and they would accompany you to the washroom. They would wait for you, not outside but inside the toilet, and when you finished, they would return you to your seat. They didn't leave anything to chance. They really take care of business and that's why I admire them so much.

□ ■ □

I was probably one of the most famous and highest-paid bodyguards in the business, simply because I did my job so well. My business card read, "Mr. T Bodyguard Extraordinaire. Next to God there is no better protector than I." If you can build a better mousetrap than your neighbor, the world will beat a path to your door. You know everybody wants the best in everything, and since it's protection we're talking about, you can imagine what it was like for me. Yes, I brag and boast of the fact that I have never lost a client and I have never had a client who was not pleased with my work. I have protected a lot of people in my time—here is a partial list: eight bankers, nineteen actors and actresses, seventeen male and female entertainers, eight airline stewardesses, forty-two millionaires, five preachers, three politicians, four store owners, eight housewives, fourteen secretaries, seven clothes designers, six athletes, seven judges, four attorneys, five models, ten schoolteachers (male and female), sixteen prostitutes, four stockbrokers, nine welfare recipients, ten executives, and eighteen children. I have protected all kinds of people because everybody needs protection. As soon as I finished with one client, I was protecting another. They would be waiting in line . . . really. That's the main reason why it didn't really bother me when the hospital tried to fire me. You see, I had so much going for me. In fact, I had more than I could handle.

Now a lot of interesting things happened during this time, but part of my profession is to be confidential; like a doctor or lawyer, a bodyguard doesn't tell all he's heard. As a bodyguard, I have been called upon to do a lot of things. Some men called me to find out who their wives' lovers were. I have received calls from large firms to collect past-due payments from individuals (by force if necessary). I have been called to find three runaway teenagers. I was paid to find a husband who deserted his family and who was behind on his alimony payments for six months. I guess my funniest case was the time when I was called to find a dog. That's right, I said dog. This dog was with the family for ten years and I was hired to track him down. I told those people that I was a bodyguard, not a detective or private investigator. I told them that I didn't handle cases like that, but they persuaded me and I took the case. What the hell, it's a challenge, and it only took me four weeks to find the mutt.

I got a lot of calls from people who wanted me to beat someone up, break an arm, give someone a black eye or just knock out a couple of teeth. I have even had a few calls to kill someone. That's right, rub them out, put them to sleep forever. I have had three women call me to say that they wanted me to kill their husbands because they were tired of getting beaten by them. At first I thought it was all a joke and the women who were calling me were disguising their voices each time, but soon I found out that these women were real each time. They were serious, too. I made it clear to each woman that called: "I save lives, I do not take them." I also tried to talk them out of that idea, but it was all in vain. They all insisted that death was the only way out because they had tried everything else already. Well, naturally, I refused to handle the cases but, before stepping down, I was offered and tempted with large sums of money, anything I wanted—half of the insurance claims, and the women, all of them, offered their bodies to me sexually whenever I wanted it. One woman begged me to kill her husband; then she started crying when she told me about all the horrible things that her husband had done to her. She was so afraid and frightened she asked to move in with me but I told her no. I told her if she wanted me to protect her I would, but I would not kill for her, at least not that way. Then she screamed at me, "I don't need no protection; all I need is for you to kill that bastard!" When she finally realized that I wasn't gonna kill her husband, she told me in a very angry voice, "I'll get somebody to kill you then." Man, I thought to myself, how in the world did I get in this mess in the first place?

I remember one case in particular; this time it was a man on the phone. He wanted me to kill his best friend. Well, this case was very strange and unusual for me, everything was a mystery. First of all, I never met this man who wanted me to kill his best friend. I talked to him once over the phone and it was only for thirty-five seconds. He stated in the conversation that he liked my style and admired my dedication to duty. He also said that he would never call me again but all future contacts would be made by mail. Then the mystery man hung up. I was a little puzzled and confused but I figured it was just another clown on the phone. Well, two days passed and on the third day there it was, a large envelope with a little note, typed, of course. In the note was a P.O. box number with this message: "All future business will be done via this P.O. box and you should check the box every day for instructions." Well, I did check the box every day, and every day there was a letter or note in it, and this went on for six straight days. That whole thing seemed like "Mission Impossible"; I couldn't believe it. I did notice on each envelope that there was never a return address and each was by express mail, but from a different city and state. The first letter was sent from Denver, Colorado; then Portland, Oregon; Green Bay, Wisconsin; Atlanta, Georgia; Austin, Texas; and the last one was from Miami, Florida. It all seemed like a big chess game or something. But the message was clear—this man wanted me to kill somebody. Why? He really didn't care to explain and I had no way of contacting him.

I must admit he was a smart man and a smooth operator. He

offered me $75,000 to kill his friend. The last envelope and letter contained a round-trip airline ticket, first class, United. Plus there was $5,000 wrapped in a little package (fifty- and hundred-dollar bills). I tell you the honest truth, when I saw that money I didn't believe it was real. I thought it was phony and that I was only dreaming. I said to myself, "This only happens in the movies, fairy tales and spy thriller novels." Well, it wasn't a dream. It was all true and the money was right before my eyes, plus a file on my target or victim. It showed pictures of him, his beautiful home, the cars he owned, phone numbers of his home and office and his daily routine, from the food he ate to his favorite TV program. I tell you, somebody had done some extra homework on this man . . . he was marked for death.

The letter stated that I was to use the $5,000 for shoeshine money. I was told once I reached the town where my target lived, I was to receive the $75,000 in advance. But I turned the money down and refused the offer. I guess I have to be for real and tell the truth: I have killed, but I don't kill for money. I did try to warn the "victim" that his life was in danger, but it was too late. He was killed in a car accident. Well, I don't know if it was an accident or not, but he was killed. I can only say that the person or persons unknown wanted that man dead very badly. I put the money back in the P.O. box but when I returned the next day the money was gone and the combination was changed. I have never been on a merry-go-round ride in my life, but I swear, I was taken for a ride in that case.

I got a lot of other calls too. I got calls from a lot of women who wanted me to come over and stay with them at night because they were lonely. Naturally, I didn't have time for that, even though a lot of them were willing to pay my fee to have me with them. I sometimes received calls from homosexuals who wanted me to come over to their houses and beat them with rubber hoses or wet towels. I tell you, requests for my services had no limits. I sometimes wondered, do people really know what a bodyguard is and what he does?

They say everybody's got their price, right? Well, not me. I have been offered a lot of money by some people to be their protector but with all of their money, they still didn't have enough. When I chose to protect someone, I didn't take into consideration their bank account. Well then, Mr. T, just how did you choose your clients? Well, it's like this: first of all, a client can't lie to me. Second, I required all potential clients to shop around in the protection field before coming to me. I always try to give my competitors a chance, and besides, most bodyguards don't give a damn what you have done just as long as you pay them. I don't work like that. I have principles, morals, pride in my work and, most important, an unwritten code that I will never violate. Like I said, some bodyguards will protect anybody—drug dealers, pimps, rapists, thugs, hitmen, arsonists, whoever can pay them. Those are the bodyguards who bring discredit and dishonor to my profession. For them, I am ashamed. They give all us hard-working protectors a black eye. My conscience would not allow me to protect people like that. That's another reason why I was the top bodyguard, because I simply couldn't be bought and sold like cattle. See, I don't let money rule me, I know it's a means but it don't have to be my end.

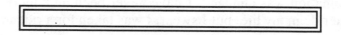

Now, while I was on vacation from the hospital, I was called to protect Leon Spinks, the heavyweight champion of the world. Leon Spinks and his entourage came to Chicago the last week of June 1978. He was preparing to fight in an exhibition against a guy named George Mostradini. While he was in town his attorneys, Judge Ed Bell and Lester Hudson, and his trainer, Sam Solomon, felt he needed a bodyguard, and I was highly recommended for the job. I was called to the Conrad Hilton Hotel and I met the heavyweight champion of the world. I told Leon Spinks, "Whether you hire me or not, I am the best bodyguard you will ever find." Leon replied, "I like T." I was instructed to protect him while he was in Chicago.

□ ■ □

The first week passed with no incident and everything was going smoothly. It was already June 30, 1978, the day of the exhibition fight. I was the first one up, so I quickly showered and changed clothes. The suit I wore that day was a three-piece number with a blue vest and pants and a multicolored blue jacket. I wore a pair of blue and white shoes, two gold earrings dangling from my left ear, a gold pocket watch and chain, and I also had on my diamond rings. It was early in the morning and people started knocking on the door seeking Leon's autograph and the phone began to ring . . . mostly women who wanted to see and talk to him. Leon wanted breakfast in his room and I went downstairs to the kitchen to watch his food being prepared. I watched the cook very closely as he mixed and stirred, cut and sliced. When the food was ready, I followed room service back to the room. After Leon ate, he rested for a couple of hours.

While he slept, I paced the floor thinking about the big job ahead of me . . . that job was getting Leon safely in and out of the Amphitheater where the exhibition was going to take place. I thought to myself, this is and still will be my finest hour. I knew a lot of people would be there. I tried to watch TV for a while, but that didn't work. I was really beginning to feel like a fool, because everybody else in the room was asleep or relaxing. Well, (1) they were used to that, and (2) their jobs didn't call for them to protect Leon, they were just there mostly as leeches or parasites.

Time had closed in on us now. It was almost 5:00 P.M. and the phone rang. Sam was on the other end and he said, "Wake up the champ, it's almost time to go." I went to Leon's room, shook him, and told him it was time to get ready. He looked up at me and said, "Okay, T." Everybody in the other room was packing Leon's equipment. I looked out of the hotel window and saw two big limos and two other cars (apparently our escort). By the time Leon finally got ready to leave the room, it was 5:50 P.M. Leon always made it a point to be late to everything.

Anyway, we were soon on our way to the Amphitheater. "Leon must not get hurt while he is here." Those were my instructions. "We've got a big fight [over $5 million] coming up in September" (the rematch with Ali). I was the last one in the limo and after I gave the signal to move out, we started. We drove off at a somewhat slow pace and it took us about twenty minutes to arrive at the Amphitheater, where the crowds were still piling in. When the kids saw those two limos, they started screaming, "Leon Spinks! Leon Spinks!" Leon waved to the crowd as the limo made its way through the police barricades.

To avoid as much of the crowd as possible, the limo drove all the way inside the Amphitheater, right beneath the dressing room Leon was going to use. I quickly got out of the limo and opened the door for Leon, and we went upstairs to the dressing room. It was only 6:30 P.M. and Leon wouldn't fight until around 8:00. He didn't want to wait in that dingy, uncomfortable place, so he decided to take a walk around the inside of the Amphitheater. As Leon walked, I tried to stay either on his right or left side, never in front and never in back, because if something happened I could handle it from either side. As we walked we drew a crowd. Some people wanted to shake his hand, some wanted autographs and some wanted to take his picture. Then some people saw him and starting booing him real loud. Now the people who were booing were, obviously, his opponent's followers (all white people). I could tell by that scene that we were in for a rough night and that it would be a racial bout. It really seemed crazy—the people in the crowd were acting as if it were a fifteen-round championship fight; it was only a four-round exhibition bout where no one wins or loses, but those whites, and especially the Italians, didn't scc it that way.

People began to get a little rowdy, so I told Leon we should get back to the dressing room. We made it back without any trouble except some bad words directed toward Leon. The dressing room was now crowded with people who, to my knowledge, did not belong there. When I asked who they were with, they would reply that they were with somebody else. Then I started to put everybody out, because this dressing room was beginning to get filled with smoke from cigarettes and cigars, and Leon doesn't like cigar smoke. When he smelled it he said, "T, get that man out of here with that cigar." And I grabbed the man and put him and his cigar out. Leon continued to get dressed while more people came in from the press with their tape recorders, cameras and note-pads.

After the press left, Leon started shadow boxing. Man, when he began to sweat, his muscles started gleaming and shining. He was bobbing and weaving and walking forward. Everybody in the dressing room was awed by his warmups and his seriousness. Then someone ran into the dressing room and said, "You've got twenty minutes, champ."

Now Sam begins to tape Leon's hands very carefully and Leon starts loosening up his neck at the same time. After his hands were taped, Leon put on his protection cup, which covers his privates in case of low blows. At last, Leon was dressed, a white towel over his head and more towels around his neck under his velvety silk robe. His robe had the letters "L.S." embroidered on the front of it and on the back, "Heavyweight Champion of the World—Leon Spinks."

It was decided earlier that Leon would march out behind the U.S. Marine Color Guard but before we left the room Leon asked, "Who has my belt?" (meaning the heavyweight championship belt he was awarded for beating Muhammad Ali for the title). Sam replied, "We have it." Now we were ready to go to the ring. I asked who would be guarding the dressing room and one of the officials told me, "We will have two guards—one at the door and one downstairs." I said, "Okay," and Leon look at me and smiled.

We were downstairs now, waiting to walk down the aisle, but the aisles were all cluttered with people. We wondered whether it was accidental or on purpose. We had to choose another aisle, and by that time Leon's opponent, George Mostradini, was already in the ring dancing around and warming up to the roar of the crowd. His crowd, of course. I didn't see too many black people seated on the main floor; they were all in the balconies looking down (really the best seats in the house).

The moment had finally come. It was time for us to make our way to the ring. At the time, I didn't pay any attention to the noise, I was busy watching Leon's every step. As we inched closer and closer to the ring, I heard screams, boos and cheers. I heard the word "nigger" a lot, but I kept going. We went down one aisle and could hardly get through, but I was determined. The crowd of white folks began laughing because we couldn't get through. I heard one white man holler, "Dumb-ass nigger, can't even get to the ring! No way he can be champion!" The crowd applauded and another man hollered, "You ain't no REAL champ, nigger." Some yelled, "Leon, you ain't shit!"

Through all of that we kept walking until we came upon these two white guys who deliberately put their chairs in the aisle, trying to block our way. I said, "Excuse us, gentlemen, we are trying to get through." I didn't have to be nice, but I tried to be. And guess what . . . it didn't work. I looked around at Leon and he was beginning to get annoyed by all of this. So I turned back to these two guys and said, "I have asked you politely. Now if you don't move and move quick, I am gonna break every bone in your bodies!" They got up like they were going to do something, but took a good look at me, sized me up, and then they wisely decided to move. When we got to the ring, some people began to throw their empty beer cups at us. Leon's sparring partner, Leroy Diggs, had jumped in the ring to part the ropes to let him and other members of his entourage enter. I jumped up on the ring apron, holding on to the ropes and looking at the crowd.

I say to you, I never ran into so many angry, hostile and mad white folks in my life. I couldn't figure it out . . . why were they so mad at Leon? What did he do to them? He didn't try to move into their neighborhood! He served in the U.S. Marines and he represented the United States proudly at the Olympic games in 1976 and earned a gold medal in the process. The only thing I could come up with was that old saying, "Success breeds hatred." Also, those white folks didn't like to see a black man out of the ghetto making all that money. They were envious, apparently.

Leon began to walk around the ring, bouncing up and down and waving to the crowd. They hated that and Leon knew it, too. They got even more angry when Sam placed the championship belt around Leon's waist and the press began taking pictures. The ring announcer kept saying, "Ladies and gentlemen, the heavyweight champion of the world, Leon Spinks." It took about ten minutes for everybody to clear the ring and for the announcer to make the official introduction of the fighters, which went something like this: "Ladies and gentlemen, the main event of the evening, a four-round exhibition bout, featuring Chicago's own George 'The Italian Assassin' Mostradini." And the crowd applauded for five minutes. Then the announcer said, "From St. Louis, Missouri, the heavyweight champion of the world, Leon Spinks," and the crowd booed for another five minutes. Leon did have some loyal fans in the house, but they were drowned out by the Mostradini crowd, and some were just too scared to say anything because Mostradini fans have been known to fight every time he fights.

After the announcer gave the introduction and the referee gave the final instructions, the bell rang to start round one. I was excited and thrilled but I had to remind myself that I was there to protect Leon, not to watch the fight. Leon started off by feeling out Mostradini. Neither man gave any ground to the other. Then Leon threw a couple of jabs. Mostradini blocked one and threw two body punches that Leon took with no problem. Then, all of a sudden, Leon opened up with a flurry of blows and a couple of stiff jabs to Mostradini's face that busted his nose. The blood began to pour from it. You guessed it, those white people didn't like that, not one bit! More paper cups were thrown into the ring. Leon stayed on the attack, throwing combinations, jabs and upper cuts. Then the bell rang to end round one.

Over in Mostradini's corner his people were working hard trying to stop his nosebleed. In Leon's corner, Sam told him, "You're the champ, just keep showing them." You know, Leon never sits down in his corner between rounds. He stands up, looking across the ring at his opponent. Then the time was up, and the bell sounded for round two, and it's almost a repeat of the first round, except that Leon somehow sensed that he could knock his man out, so he sort of backed off to give him a break. When he did, Mostradini thought he was getting tired, so he tried to take command of the fight by charging Leon; then they tied up. The referee moved in to break them.

Leon started pounding Mostradini in the body with a devastating power that left his ribs red and sore. Then Leon tried a couple of quick shots to Mostradini's head, which made his neck snap backward. The bell sounded to end the round.

The crowd was beginning to get a little restless and more

hostile. It is true, we were outnumbered fifteen to one (white to black, that is) but I was not afraid, I was ready. Someone threw a beer can at me, but I saw it coming out of the corner of my eye and ducked. I was about to charge into the stands and get the person responsible when some black guy touched my arm and said, "Forget it, they do that all the time at Mostradini's fights." So I told this scared brother, "If you're afraid, you'd better leave now because someone is going to get their ass kicked before I leave here tonight. One more thing, brother, don't you ever put your hands on me again unless you want to fight." Some people in the seats right by the ring were making racial remarks to Sam and began throwing beer at us. By this time, I was really pissed off and when I get pissed, I get mean. I was ready to fight, and when I'm ready to fight, my opponent has a better chance of surviving a forest fire wearing gasoline drawers. Just before the bell rang to start the third round, I told Leroy Diggs to get ready. He replied, "I can't wait," smiling and cracking his knuckles.

The third round had begun and Leon started putting together a few more combinations that Mostradini could not defend himself against, mainly because Leon hit so hard and he kept coming. Mostradini's corner kept hollering at him, "Stay away and punch!" Mostradini looked at them as if he wanted to say, "It's easy for you to say because you ain't in this ring getting your behind kicked." The crowd began to get mad at Mostradini, but the main person they hated was Leon. Leon didn't care, he just kept the pressure on. Sam was hollering, "Leon, take him out so we can go home early." Leon went to work on Mostradini like a programmed missile, exploding with every punch. When the third round ended, Mostradini's face was all puffed up and bloody even though he had headgear on. His body bore the marks of Leon's punches, and his eyes said, "I have had enough," but the crowd said, "You've got to get him!"

In between the third and fourth rounds you could feel the

heat and tension rising in the place. I looked around for the police, but didn't see *one* in the house. I did see a lot of scared security guards who were ill-trained and unprofessional. One guy threw a lit cigarette in Leon's water bucket, then popcorn started coming at us. Somebody even threw a shoe. Sam did find a policeman and asked him if we could have a little protection in our corner. The white policeman turned and walked away.

The final round began and Leon went for the kill. He wanted to knock Mostradini out. Meanwhile, Sam was talking to another policeman about our protection when some irritated fan who thought he was bad—he must have been the leader of the mob—tried to hit Sam. He was a fool for trying to hit Sam Solomon, Leon's trainer. As a matter of fact, the guy reached over a police officer, who didn't do anything to stop him. So I went to work. I was at my natural best that night; I don't believe anyone could have beaten me that night.

When this fool took that swing at Sam (even though he missed), I hit him with a hard twisting right hand that sent him reeling backward a couple of rows of seats. People started to run and scream. The whole section rushed at us with the intent to do us some serious bodily harm. But boy, did we have a surprise for them! Now you know that I was carrying my piece (gun), but I would never think of pulling it if someone else didn't have one. Let me tell what all I did that night and to whom. After I hit this guy in the face, I started punching and kicking everybody who was standing up. I just grabbed a couple of guys by their hair and hit them in the eyes, noses and mouths until blood was all over my hand and their clothes. While I was fighting, I never took one step back, I kept moving toward them. One guy, I picked up and threw back at the others. Three guys tried to stop me with chairs in their hands, swinging wildly, but I kept coming and they began to back off. One of them threw his chair at me and I caught it in the air. Then I ran after him, but he got away. His two friends, however, weren't that lucky. They thought two chairs could hold me off, but *no way!* I got hit with the chairs, but they got the worst end. I'll take one lick and give fifteen hits any day. After they hit me, I was on them like a wild man showing no mercy. When I fight, I fight to the death and, no doubt, I would have killed somebody had there not been so many of them.

Now, I wasn't afraid of their number, but I wanted a lot of them to feel my wrath and the pain I was dishing out. I wanted everybody to get some. I grabbed those guys who'd had the chairs by their necks and cracked them in the mouth, then I kicked them to the side. I looked around to see how everyone else was doing and spotted Sam with his hands full. So I rushed over there and took a big swan dive into the crowd, landing on about ten guys who didn't know what had hit them. As I got up, I was punching everybody. I would help them up and then knock them down. Some of them I hit in the back of the necks with karate blows, disabling them. You see, I don't believe in fighting over five minutes and I don't believe I should have to hit a guy more than three times to finish him off, unless I want to torture him. I was hitting guys in the throats and they were running away screaming in pain, their color turning from white to red and blue.

One guy had managed to grab me by the leg, trying to bring me down, and a small crowd of five rushed me. Two of them I hit and knocked out cold. They fell in their tracks, and that scared the hell out of the others. So I spread my legs apart for more balance and continued to punch the other three while this other guy was still on my leg. Those three guys did hit me, but not like I hit them. Actually, they were hitting each other more than they were hitting me. They made a mistake by trying to wrestle me down. I put one in a headlock that almost killed him, but he fainted. So I let him drop, then I picked up another and dropped him down by his head, then kicked him. When I turned around, the third one ran off, so I punched the one on my leg in the head a couple of times until he just fell off.

By this time, the crowd was yelling, "Watch out for the baldheaded nigger, he's crazy!" I just had gotten warmed up and I started to talk to the crowd, saying loudly, "So you like to fight, huh?" and running toward them at the same time. When I ran into the crowd, I managed to pull away with one more victim to see if he could survive "Terrible T's Torture Test"—being thrown to the ground from over my head, then hit with two or three smashing forearm blows to the head, then kneed in the chest a couple of times, and for the grand finale I would ram his head into the wooden steps of the ring and toss him back to his buddies. Yes, that's right. I did all of that to the last guy and I'm not sorry, I'm not ashamed, nor do I feel any pain. You know why? Because I know that if I had lost and couldn't handle myself, I would be in the hospital today, if not dead. Remember, it was at least fifteen whites to one black. I know that it was a brutal, vicious, harsh, inhuman and downright sickening thing that I did, right? Wrong! I say right because that's what you think. But I say wrong because that's what I think. I know that every man should defend himself. I am not sorry and I don't apologize for my actions. I know I hurt that guy badly, but that was the price he had to pay. It was either him—them—or me. I tried to spread the pain and divide it equally, so I gave him some and them some. I know that some of those guys had to go to the hospital and some were seriously hurt. I beat that last guy the way I did for one reason, and that was to let everybody in the house know, "Don't bother with Mr. T and his clients." I used him as an example so that the word would spread. "If Mr. T comes in peace, let him go in peace, or else!"

That night I came in peace, but, you see, I have this split personality, something like Dr. Jekyll and Mr. Hyde. I am nice and kind if you let me be, but if I am crossed, you asked for it. Actually, I did so much fighting that night because my

Working out in the basement of my apartment building on the
North Side of Chicago, 1979

Left: With Leon Spinks in the
lobby of the Hilton Hotel, New
Orleans, 1978
Above: When I was working I
wouldn't say nothing to nobody,
not even Howard Cosell (who
finally gave up and started talking
with our police escort).

Standing guard for Leon at a press conference a couple of days before the championship fight

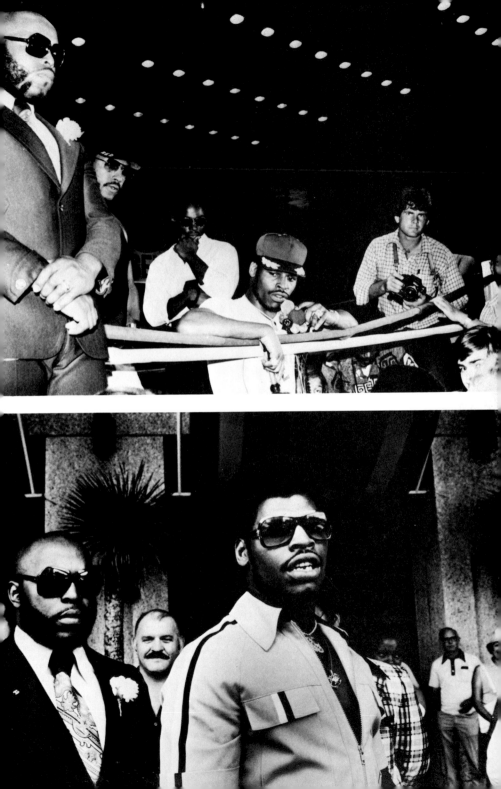

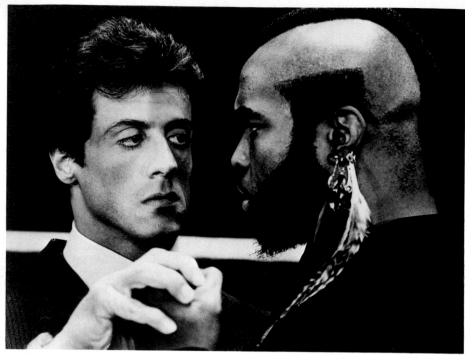

Publicity photo for *Rocky III*

Above: Publicity photo for *D.C. Cab*

Right: At a press conference for *D.C. Cab* at New York's Rivoli Theater, 1983

Above: Speaking at a neighborhood gathering on the West Side of Chicago, 1982.

Left: Speaking at an ex-offenders' program for people who had just gotten out of jail, trying to help them get back into the mainstream of society, Chicago, 1979

main concern was Leon, and he was in the ring watching it all. When I finished taking care of business, I jumped into the ring and put my arms around Leon, trying to cover him from the flying debris that was being thrown at him. I signaled to the ref and the other corner that it was enough, we would not fight anymore because there was not enough security protection.

The police finally came—I think because someone called them on me for beating up that crowd of people. The police hauled away the injured and badly hurt. I called the rest of our entourage to the corner of the ring to stand around Leon until the confusion cooled off. We waited for ten minutes while the police were trying to evacuate the area after they found out that the only people who got hurt were white. I asked a policeman if he was going to do anything about the aisle so that we could get out and he gave me a dirty look and kept walking until I said, "I've got your badge number and I will report you to your commanding officer." Then he began to tell the people to leave the building.

When the aisle was somewhat cleared and I figured that we could make it, I decided to start walking toward the dressing room. We were almost upstairs when this white guy came running behind us. I saw him and told everyone else to go ahead, then I yelled to the police to stop the guy before he got any closer. But the police didn't listen and this guy tried to make it up to the stairs. That's when I let him have it with a kung-fu kick that sent him flying back down on the police, who were standing around doing nothing. Then I told the police, "I don't want to get mad, now," so they grabbed the guy and put him in handcuffs.

I went upstairs to check on Leon to see if he was all right. I pushed everybody aside in the room until I got to Leon. I gave him a big hug and said, "Are you all right, champ?" Leon replied, "My man, T, you know, you're bad! I know that when you're around me I will never have any problem." Then everybody in the dressing room gave me a hand. Sam said to me, "Mr. T, I didn't know you were that mean, you are definitely our man." We all sat around the dressing room talking about Leon's fight with Mostradini and how we took care of ourselves against those unruly fans.

I eased away from everyone else to go to the washroom and tried to wash the blood off of my shoes, pants, hands and head. Now, this blood was not mine, it was from the other guys. The blood on my shoes was from the guys I kicked in the mouths and noses. The blood on my head was from a guy whose skull I butted. You see, I grabbed his head and held it still, then I rammed my head into his. I know he had a headache for days. I tried that with another guy also, but he didn't hold still, he moved his head some, so I hit him on the nose. I saw the blood running and tears flowing.

Finally a police captain came up to our dressing room and asked a very stupid question—were any of our people hurt? Did we want to press charges against the guys they arrested? Everybody in the room started laughing and told the police to check on the white people because they were the ones who needed medical help. Lester Hudson told the police, "No, we don't want to press charges because I think those guys are in enough pain already from the beating Mr. T gave them." The police left. As they were leaving, the press wanted to come in for an interview, but Leon said that he would talk on his way to his limo. We packed all the gear and were ready to leave when someone asked where his championship belt was and Sam's assistant ran back and found it.

We started down the steps and were met by the press with their TV cameras, microphones, tape recorders, the works. Everybody was asking Leon questions. One question I will always remember was, "What do you think of that riot, champ?" Leon replied, "It's just like any other city. If you've been in one riot, you've been in them all." Then a reporter asked him, "Were you ever worried that you might get hurt out there?" Leon said, "No, because I can deal with anybody in the ring and my man was here." The reporter asked, "Who is your man?" and Leon put his arm around me and said, "Right here—Mr. T." By that time, we were at the limo and I pushed everybody away, opened the door for Leon and then closed it. I walked alongside of the limo where Leon was sitting. The limo rolled along very slowly until I got into the car and everybody was smiling and happy, including me, because I knew deep down inside that I had done a hell of a job. Everybody was talking abut how we kicked those white guys' asses and had them running from us. The limo was noisy as hell with everybody running off at the mouth. Leon was sitting back there smoking a cigarette and smiling at the same time.

I was beginning to get a little sleepy and tired, but when I looked in the back seat at Leon he seemed wide awake and ready to go some more. I just couldn't understand it. He had been in a fight, I had been fighting, everybody had been fighting, and the only one of us that was tired was me. I know I did more fighting than anybody else, so something was wrong. I started to smell marijuana coming from the back of the car. I told myself that I would not look around because if I saw Leon smoking that would have destroyed the image I had of him. Well, I knew he was no saint, but you have a certain image you have to keep up when you are in the public eye all the time.

LEON SPINKS ... THE MAN I KNEW

WOULD LIKE TO SAY THAT ALL I AM I OWE TO LEON, because it was with him that I got universal exposure in the media. I am very grateful to Leon Spinks for hiring me. But I still think it is important that we try to understand the truth about Leon, because his story is like a dark mirror in which we can see how the evils of the ghetto can destroy even the greatest success. And I don't think this is breaking any confidentiality, because most all these things were in the papers. So before I take you into the glorious and glamorous but short-lived success of the one-time heavyweight champ, Leon Spinks, I want to take you back a little. I want you to know the kind of childhood he had.

Leon had it rough coming up. He was born into poverty, raised in it, and he spent his early years in the projects. This is one of the reasons it was so hard for Leon later to adjust to overnight success. When he was young, no one wanted to take the time to help him along. Everyone told him he would never be anything because (1) he was black, (2) he was born poor, and (3) he had an inferior education. So the only thing left for a ghetto kid to do was to rob and steal, hang out on street corners, snatch purses, steal cars, pimp, gamble or get hooked on drugs. Don't get me wrong, I am not saying that Leon did these things, but he sure did some pretty bad things, as you'll hear in this chapter. And what he didn't do was at his fingertips. Crime in the ghetto is contagious. It spreads throughout the black community like maggots on a dead dog.

When Leon was living in the ghetto slums of East St. Louis, he had to deal with stuff like that every day. Did he have a dream or fantasy? Hell, yes! Doesn't everybody have desires, wishes, wants and plans for life? Leon Spinks was no different. He had a dream of becoming the boxing champion of the world. The minute he let his dream be known is the minute everybody started telling him he would never be a boxer, let alone champ. Leon knew what he wanted, but it was so hard for him. He never was the brightest kid in the class, but he loved to fight. He would fight classmates, friends and anybody else; it didn't make any difference to him, so even though the odds were against him, he didn't listen. You see, Leon had a hard head. Leon made a sacrifice. He sacrificed his education to become the champ and it paid off. Or did it?

If you get out of the ghetto, any ghetto, alive and healthy, thank God for that. Leon escaped the ghetto alive, but not healthy. On the outside he looked like a perfectly sculptured young African warrior, but on the inside he was deteriorating. His mind and his spirit were damaged by the early use of drugs, and once started that's hard to stop. So the drugs were one of Leon's bad habits, one that grew with him and left the ghetto in him. Years later, it would come back to haunt him and Leon wouldn't know what hit him.

After Leon's school days (he dropped out in the tenth grade), he decided to join the U.S. Marines to become a real fighting man. Once in the Marines, he learned discipline and found out what it meant to be in top condition and in the best of shape. Leon didn't go to war; instead he got on the boxing team as a light heavyweight. In the Marines, Leon paid his dues. He tortured his body into shape. He ran and ran, he boxed and boxed like nobody else. Once Leon was in the gym, he would stay there for hours, even when it was closed for the day, until the coach had to make him leave.

As soon as Leon understood the rules, he was on his way. Leon had a streamlined body, not muscular, but well conditioned. He also had a punch like a mule's kick—hard as hell—that put you in dreamland. If you sat in Leon's trophy room you might mistake it for the Hall of Fame, he has so many trophies, medals, ribbons and pictures. The most prestigious medal of them all is the gold medal he won in the 1976 Olympics. Leon's brother Michael also won a gold medal. What a glorious moment it was for the Spinks family, as well as black people, and the whole United States. After his triumphant victory at the Olympics, he soon turned pro and so did his brother Michael. But before turning pro, Leon had compiled an amateur record of 178 wins and 7 losses (133 KOs) at 175 pounds. In 1974 Leon won a bronze medal at the World Games in Cuba. A year later, at the A.A.U. championship, he was light heavyweight champion for three years in a row: 1974, 1975 and 1976.

I remember when I first took notice of Leon Spinks. On July 31, 1976, I was at home watching the Olympics televised live from the Forum in Montreal, Canada. There was so much talk about the Spinks brothers (Leon and Michael) and the mystical "Spinks Jinx" they would put on their opponents. The Spinks brothers were about to do something that had never been done before in the seventy-eight-year history of the Olympic games—they both won gold medals in their respective divisions. I will remember Leon's fight for a long time; he was fighting a tough Cuban opponent by the name of Sixto Soria, but Leon wasn't afraid of him. Earlier, at the Pan Am Games in 1975 in Mexico City, he had lost the championship fight to another Cuban named Orestes Pedrozo. And that loss to Orestes in 1975 made Leon even more hungry for the gold medal and a chance to even the score against the Cubans.

Both Leon and Sixto Soria were ready and sharp. Leon's opponent was fast, quick and well disciplined, but Leon took his time trying to "feel" his Cuban opponent. That was Leon's mistake. An exchange of punches went by and all of a sudden, Leon was on the canvas and Sixto Soria was standing over him. Leon got up a little surprised and stunned, but he was ready to fight like he had never fought before and he did.

By the third round he had Sixto Soria dazed. Leon applied more pressure on his opponent with very hard blows, and Sixto Soria was through. He was out on his feet and the referee had to pull Leon off the Cuban. The winner, Leon Spinks! He had won the gold medal, the light heavyweight title, respect from the Cubans, and recognition from fight fans nationwide.

Boxing promoters everywhere figured that as a result of his outstanding performance, especially against Sixto Soria, he was definitely ready for the pros. After his Olympic victory, parties and celebrations followed. Leon quickly turned professional and was trained by a man named Sam Solomon. Leon had his first pro fight on Dr. Martin Luther King, Jr.'s birthday, January 15, 1977. His opponent was Bob "Lightning" Smith. The fight was held in Las Vegas and Leon knocked Smith out in the first round. Leon had four more consecutive knockouts. The first three were in the first round and the last one in the third round. Then on October 22, 1977, Leon and Scott LeDoux fought to a draw. After that, he fought Alfredo Righetti of Italy and won a ten-round decision. Leon was on the move. Now things were beginning to fall into place for him. He was preparing himself mentally and physically to fight for the championship title against his idol—none other than Muhammad Ali. The boxing world was shocked that Ali chose to defend his title against Leon, an unknown, unranked rookie with only seven pro fights and one of them a draw. Leon accepted the contest graciously, saying, "I'll do my best." When Ali was asked why he chose to fight Leon Spinks, he replied, "I just want to give this brother a chance."

A chance, yes, that was mighty big of Ali to give Leon a chance, nobody else would have done that. A chance is what Leon needed. A chance to be somebody, to make his mother proud. A chance for Leon to show the world his talent. A chance for Leon to make a dream come true. Leon Spinks, an unknown, unskilled bum, a nobody, was getting a shot at the crown. Just think, all of this happened to a kid from the ghetto of St. Louis, a kid they called "Mess Over," who was born on July 11, 1953, and who had weighed in at only three pounds because he was premature.

Leon was a product of a broken home because his father left his mother to raise seven children on her own with nothing but that monthly welfare check which amounted to about $135. Later on, Leon was too busy being big time to remember the times he had to eat peanut butter spread on cornbread, navy beans, or sometimes no food at all. How can you stretch $135 a month when you have rent to pay and food and clothes to buy for a family of eight?

By the time I knew him, Leon was showing all the signs and symptoms of Project Paralysis. The first sign was he forgot where he came from; he forgot his cause. In St. Louis, Leon was raised in the Pruitt Igoe housing projects, where he contracted Project Paralysis. You know what happens to someone when they are paralyzed—they get stiff, there's no mobilization. The same thing goes for Project Paralysis: it stiffens and scars the soul, it deteriorates discipline, it confuses the conscience. Project Paralysis makes the family welcome welfare. Project Paralysis limited Leon's vocabulary and left him living low. Insecurity and incoherency are other signs of Project Paralysis and Leon was certainly another one of its victims. Leon's whole boxing career started at age thirteen, when he decided to go to the gym and learn how to box. By the age of fifteen, he was ready to fight his first amateur bout. At that time, Leon had Project Paralysis, but he didn't know it. His mother knew something was wrong with him but didn't know exactly what it was. It grew with Leon and he became possessed by it. You could tell by everything he did and said, it wouldn't be long before Leon fell back into the same hole he once climbed out of.

□   ■   □

Anyway, back to the fight with Muhammad Ali on January 15, 1978. Leon was going to fight the man he had admired all his life, and Leon was gonna try to take the title. Leon was ready; he had trained hard, run a lot of miles in the snow every morning. No disco, no drugs, no women, no nothing. On the other hand, Ali was not himself; he appeared tired, worried, sad, lost and—oddly enough—speechless. It just wasn't Ali, he was so quiet. Ali did no fight build-up, he had no poem for Leon, he just didn't have anything to say. It was rumored that Ali was gonna retire after the Spinks fight, win or lose, but we all had heard that before.

At fight time both fighters were ready. In Leon's dressing room were his mother, sisters and brothers, plus the hangers-on all crowded in. Leon kissed a small crucifix, and placed it on his right ankle under his sock. Leon's mother said a prayer. Then everyone else said amen and started to leave the room. Leon was in the ring first, bouncing and dancing, then Ali came. He entered the ring and went over to Leon, shook his hand and said, "Good luck." He did the same to Sam Solomon and everybody else in Spinks' corner.

The fight was billed as another one of Ali's bum-of-the-month-club fights and Leon was the underdog ten-to-one. It was Leon's eagerness and youth versus Ali's experience and age. Ali toyed and played, but Leon was fighting for real. Ali danced and shuffled, Leon stalked and punched. Ali held, Leon wiggled. Ali talked to Leon while they fought, but Leon kept silent and piled up points. Ali tried to do his famous rope-a-dope but Leon jabbed Ali on his biceps and forearms until they became sore. Ali waited for Leon to tire but Leon never got tired. Everything Ali did was thrown back at him. His rope-a-dope failed, his shuffled got tired, his stinging right jab had no sting. He hit Leon a lot, but Leon kept coming. By the end of the fifteenth round both fighters were exhausted and barely on their feet. Over the boos and screams of the crowd, you could hear the ring announcer, Chuck Hall, shout,

"Ladies and gentlemen, we have a split decision." Then the announcer called the scores: first Art Lurie, who had Ali 143–142, then Lou Tobat, who had Leon 145–140. There were mixed reactions in the crowd after that score. The final score was Judge Harold Buck's, and he had Spinks 144–141. Leon Spinks had just beaten Muhammad Ali and the world would never be the same after that.

In Leon's corner it was the thrill of victory; in Ali's, it was the agony of defeat. Ali was dejected, he was embarrassed. Ali seemed let down and a lot of his entourage deserted him for Spinks. Ali had no words for the press nor comments for anybody. He went straight to his dressing room to be alone for a while. Now the press, the fans, the promoters and other fighters all wanted a shot at the new champ. Leon Spinks was finally on top of the world. Now he would do everything he used to only dream of doing. He didn't waste no time to party. Right after his victory, Leon went down to the lobby and started to gamble a little bit. Before he knew it, he had lost over $2,000, but he didn't care. He would have lost more, had it not been for his mother. She snatched a handful of money in order to make him leave the casino table.

Leon the heavyweight champion of the world was beginning to live a little. He soon bought three cars: a Cadillac Seville for his wife, a black Coupe DeVille for himself and a big long white six-door limo that cost $42,000. He bought diamond rings for himself and his wife, and by the time they finished buying jewelry, they had over $400,000 worth. He bought mink coats: a black one and a white one, with mink hats to match. He partied every night for about a month, celebrating, traveling, drinking, "getting high," discoing. Leon and his wife stayed in the Pontchartrain Hotel in Detroit for about a month and a half until they found a good home to buy, which they eventually did in a suburb of Detroit, Michigan.

But everything has its price. After four and a half weeks of being the champ he was stripped of half the title by the World Boxing Council for not fighting Ken Norton. He was being sued by his old landlord in Philadelphia for overdue rent, and why not? He's the champ, he can pay it! Then he was arrested for driving down a one-way street and he was handcuffed like a vicious criminal. He was released on $700 bond. After that, it was open season on Leon by the police and the press. Ali charged that Leon drank something from a bottle during the fight. Ali said, "The substance in that bottle gave Leon energy and strength." At first Leon tried to deny it, but the fight film showed the bottle. Leon was drinking something from a little brown bottle. What he was drinking, who knows? We can only guess.

Trouble became Leon's middle name, he was just a bad-luck guy. The papers made him the fall guy of the year. They talked about his manner of speech, they talked about his style of dressing and the type of people he associated with, especially women. It got to the point where Leon really thought he was a handsome playboy and women couldn't resist him. He didn't know that the women were only there with him because he was picking up the tab. I used to hear women talk about how ugly Leon was with his front teeth out.

Now, speaking of missing teeth . . . I spent a lot of time looking for his false teeth—in cars, hotel rooms, dressing rooms and just everywhere. We missed a lot of appointments because Leon would get high the night before and forget where he put his false teeth; we would have to turn the place upside down the next day to find them. While we were looking, he would be sitting in a chair or on the edge of the bed sucking his thumb—boy, what a sight! One time we had to disrupt the whole order of the hotel just to find his teeth. We had room service, housekeepers, doormen, bell captains, and busboys as well as the hotel manager running around looking for these teeth. We finally found them on his food tray downstairs in the kitchen about to be put in the garbage.

I didn't like running around looking for his false teeth, nor did I like telling him to comb his hair or wipe his mouth or blow his nose. Leon had the worst grooming habits, he had a problem keeping his personal appearance up, mainly because he really didn't care about anything, especially what people said about him. You see, Leon just didn't like making public appearances. He didn't like all the fanfare; he wanted to be plain old Leon, but no such thing. He couldn't understand that his time wasn't his own, that as the champ he had to respond to people, make appearances, sign autographs, take pictures, shake hands, hug old women and babies. Leon said, "I want to take the title to the people." He was going to places where people wouldn't ordinarily see a champ—small towns, the ghettos and the slums. Well, that much I admired him for, because that much I can appreciate. The problem was that Leon couldn't escape from the clutches of the ghetto. Like they say, you can take the man out of the ghetto, but you can't take the ghetto out of the man.

Leon was a troubled young man. He worried a lot, he never had peace of mind. He wanted to escape the hectic order of the day but he couldn't. He was out of place, like an elephant on an ant farm. Leon hated people trying to make him act like somebody he wasn't. He told me a number of times how bored he got when he was at those so-called important affairs. Leon had many invitations to be everybody's guest of honor. When they would invite him to an affair, Leon would tell them, "Okay, I'll be there," but he never showed up. Leon was hot—everybody wanted to see the kid from the ghetto of St. Louis who had beat the great Ali.

Now some things Leon did, I didn't blame him for doing because I could see the hurt he went through. What a difference a day makes, just twenty-four hours! On January 14, 1978, he was a bum, wild and immature. They said he should not be in the same ring with Ali. Now on January 15, 1978, after the fight, he was king of the ring. He had more people around him then you could shake a stick at. All of a sudden, he had more friends than a ghetto house had roaches. Everywhere he went, there were mobs praising him, honoring him and worshiping him. They were all there: pimps, drug dealers, whores, fight promoters, photographers, salesmen, you name them, they were there. All with their hands out. All with a gimmick. All with a scheme to get some of Leon's money. Even some of Ali's people had deserted him to come over to Spinks' side, because they knew since Ali had lost, he would have no further use for them. Actually Leon was used by the press, the public and everybody else. They only hailed Leon for beating Ali.

The public, especially white people, were tired of Ali fighting, winning, talking, preaching and bragging. They hated it when he refused to join the army, so they stripped him of his title and wouldn't let him fight for three and a half years. But he came back and won it again, still talking, still winning, still preaching, but this time he was more boastful and louder. So Leon was just an object to be used by the public until they got tired of him too. To make my point clearer, look at the time Joe Frazier beat Ali. The world fell in love with Joe. Sure, they fought for the undisputed title and Joe Frazier won, but it wasn't the title, it was the fact that somebody finally beat the unbeatable Ali. The same treatment was bestowed upon Ken Norton in March 1973, when he broke Ali's jaw and won the fight also. That fight wasn't a title fight, but when Norton won, everybody rejoiced. It really didn't matter who beat Ali, just as long as he was beaten. They don't like you as a person, they only like you because you beat Ali and they couldn't do it.

Every punch Leon hit Ali with, white people wished it was them throwing those punches. People hated Ali because they feared him, and don't you know that hate grows from fear. People were tired of seeing Ali make all that money and continuing to worship his God (Allah). I don't care how good a boxer or fighter you are, you ain't nothing—the people were saying—until you beat Ali. The strange thing about fighting Ali is this: if you beat Ali once and fight him again but lose to him, then you slide back into oblivion.

□　■　□

Let's back up a little and review Leon's case: "The Tragedy and Treasure of a Troublesome Guy." Let's go back and try to find his downfall. We already know about his rise, we must find his fall. Was Leon really that bad a champ? Did Leon have family problems? Was the title too much for him to handle? Was Leon really dumb? There's been so much written about Leon that I figured, as his bodyguard, it's time that I set the record straight by telling you the truth.

In my book, Leon had what it took to be champ for many years to come, but something happened to him. What was it, Mr. T? I figure I was the closest one to him—I saw a lot, I heard a lot and felt a lot. I saw Leon half training back in July of 1978 at Hilton Head Island, South Carolina, for the upcoming bout with Ali. I was there and I know. Sometimes he would run in the morning and sometimes he would not. That I could understand because he would be just getting up from some party at somebody's house that lasted until three or four in the morning. The weather was perfect at Hilton Head, ninety degrees every day. The grass was neatly cut, and the air was fresh and clean, unlike in the city. We stayed in modern condos, with every service. Leon had a cook who prepared his meals specially twice a day, one in the morning at 7:00 A.M. and then in the evening at 5:00 P.M. Now Leon really didn't eat that much—he had two or three eggs, sausage, vitamin pills and two bottles of beer after he ran. Leon didn't have a weight problem. He wasn't skinny but a little small for a heavyweight at 197 pounds and six feet three inches. He had a chest of 41 inches (normal), reach of 76 inches, waist 31, biceps 15, forearm 12, thigh 24, calf 15¼, neck 16½, wrist 7, ankle 12, and fist 9. He was only twenty-four years old with a birthday coming up soon (July 11), when he would be twenty-five.

The first week of training in July was very light, mainly because Leon didn't choose to work out that much. When he worked out, I enjoyed it very much because it was poetry in motion—to see the intensity, the sweat popping off him, his muscles flexing with every movement, and to hear his grunts, groans and growls as he put out 100 percent in each effort. I loved running, or rather trying to run, with Leon in the mornings but I just couldn't hang with him. He ran five to eight miles in the morning and I could only do two miles; but the more I ran with him, the better in shape I got. I kept running until I got up to four miles a day, and I thought that was damn good for a bodyguard who weighed in at 244 pounds. I remember Leon and I would start running together but before we reached the middle, he would be way ahead of me looking back, yelling, "C'mon, T!" I would holler back at him, "I will catch up, go ahead." Leon would run in big heavy combat boots, sweat pants, shorts, sweat shirt with a hood, and he would be moving too. When he worked out, he worked out. He was a sight to see. I was just honored to even be there, I was thrilled beyond belief by being with him.

After he finished running, he would shadow box for half an hour. My biggest job then was to keep people out of his way. They would try to interrupt his training just to get an autograph or picture with him. Some mornings we would run and then go chop down some trees, and believe me that's a job. It will definitely get you in shape. When we finished that, we would run to the gym, where he would box five to ten rounds, alternating sparring partners. And his sparring partners were good, too. I mean, you would think they were fighting for the championship or something. After every round there would be loud applause from the people who had gotten a chance to watch Leon work out. Some people would get up early in the morning just to get a glimpse of him. It was all unreal to me: the people, their reactions, everything.

I know what Leon was going through, because I tasted some of that fast-moving world just being with Leon. I would go into stores to buy something and the manager would come up and say, "Ain't you with Leon Spinks?" I would reply, "Yes, I am." Then he would reach for my hand and say, "Well, young man, you don't have to pay for this, it's on the house . . . anything for the champ." Then I replied to the man, "But this ain't for the champ." "That's all right, come back again." Well, I had to get used to things like that because more of it was in the making for me. Once I went into a restaurant to eat and I ordered my usual, which was six eggs, two steaks, three glasses of orange juice, eight pieces of toast, two salads, two pieces of apple pie with ice cream, and a strawberry shake. The waitress said to me, "I guess you need all of that to protect the champ?" Well, I didn't know that they knew who I was, so I didn't say anything. Then the head cashier came by and said, "How is the champ?" I stopped eating and said, "He's all right," then continued my meal. When I asked for my check, to my surprise, I was told, "Anybody with the champ don't have to pay, we are glad to have you all here." I got up and said, "Thank you very much, ma'am." That started to become an everyday pattern wherever we went. While this was going on in early July at Hilton Head, Ali was still in Russia rounding out his ten-day trip by meeting with Soviet leader Leonid Brezhnev and talking about peace and love for humanity.

Meanwhile, back at the Spinks camp, training was temporarily stopped because Leon said so; it was halted from July 3 until July 13, after his birthday celebration. The next day, training was resumed and Leon was involved in a car accident.

I am going to tell you the truth. Before I met Leon Spinks I had read in the papers, front page at that, that he had been caught with drugs (marijuana and cocaine) by the police. I didn't believe it! I said to myself that the authorities had put that on him to make him look bad. I never thought for one moment that he was guilty, even though Leon had beaten my idol Muhammad Ali for the title. After winning the title from Ali, he was charged with driving down a one-way street without any driver's license and possession of drugs. It was just a bit much for me to believe. I told everyone that it wasn't true. No way! Fortunately, the grand jury refused to indict him. Out of kindness the judge said, "I'm glad it turned out that way for you, Leon. Please be sure to bring that driver's license with you when you come back. And, Leon, could we have some autographs for the girls in the courthouse office?"

Drugs were Leon's weakness. If someone was smoking a joint and passed it to Leon, he would take a puff from it; the same with cocaine. Just mention dope and Leon would drop everything he was doing and go with you. He could be right in the middle of training but let someone whisper in his ear, "Hey, man, I got some good stuff," and in a flash he was there, and the same thing went for partying. The thing that made it so bad was that he would snort cocaine anywhere—in a car, plane, at a disco—it didn't matter. Now, I don't know too much about drugs (I mean, I don't get high), but I do know that it does more harm than good. Leon would buy and snort cocaine from anybody and I know about the streets, I know in the streets the drugs are cut so many ways that when you get some it's mixed with some of everything, and you don't know what you are getting. Also Leon was now getting a lot of pure coke, stuff he was not used to. It was expensive but he had the money because he was the champion of the world. So Leon found a good "contact" for the pure stuff and as long as Leon had the money, the guy had the right stuff. It was very hard for me to monitor Leon with drugs, but since I was his bodyguard it was my duty to try to protect him from all danger. I had grown to love Leon very much and didn't want anything to happen to him.

Now before he won the title, he was a very hungry, aggressive fighter with a purpose; but after he won it, he became a very complacent person . . . less training, a lot of disco, little sleep . . . a lot of drugs. A little time at home with his wife and a lot of time out on the streets with sluts. I mean the kind of women no champion would be caught dead with. Not only were some of them ugly, but they were the scum of the earth: whores, tramps, dope addicts and men chasers. He spent a lot of time chasing DABs—Dog Ass Bitches.

I don't really know why he didn't like to stay home, maybe it was because "the grass is always greener on the other side"; besides, you have to understand that Leon was not a very handsome young man. Therefore, when he was coming up he missed a lot of girls in his prime and now that he had fame and fortune, he was trying to make up for all that lost time by being with every woman he could. He wouldn't care if he had to buy them, get them high, or let them ride around with him in his big white limo. When you have money, a lot of women don't care if you're ugly or not. Yes, Leon did have a wide assortment of women and I said women instead of ladies because there is a difference. Not only did the women chase Leon, but he chased them too, and the more the merrier for him.

Now, speaking of car accidents and Leon's driving, well, personally, I think Leon should not have been driving in the first place. Sometimes he would fall asleep while driving or his mind would just wander off. Leon's mind was always heavy with thoughts and it was always something that was troubling him. He had trouble adjusting to different lifestyles, different cultures and different people. The only people Leon was comfortable with were the people who smoked pot and snorted cocaine. Those were his kind of people, and he would hang out daily with people like that. That's why it was so hard for him to keep his mind on training and the fight he had coming up.

There was no one thing that caused Leon's downfall, but a

multitude of things. The booze, sex, car accidents, too much partying and too little training. It was all in that order. The drug was sometimes 100 percent pure cocaine, the best. He would buy it by the pounds and just have a ball. He would wake up in the morning and blow coke; instead of eating lunch or dinner he would snort cocaine. Leon had these long fingernails, and he would put coke under his nails and snort away. Sometimes he would leave the cocaine that was left over from the night before all over his hotel room dresser. I had to check the room before the maid came in to clean up; I didn't want her to find that on the dresser. Some mornings, I would just tell the maids to skip Leon's room and come back tomorrow. I never saw a man snort so much cocaine in my life until I started working for Leon Spinks. He would be so high and spaced out that he wouldn't remember what he said to me from day to day. Sometimes he would forget what day it was and where he was at. He would get high some days and say, "I might not fight anymore after the Ali rematch." I mean working for Leon was really hard on me because every day it was a different story with him. The more cocaine Leon snorted the less he trained and the less he trained the more out of shape he got.

I didn't tell him how to run his life, I mean drugs and pot, et cetera. But it got to the point where I was the only one willing to tell him. Nobody else wanted Leon to stop snorting because most of his hangers-on got high too. When Leon snorted he would give them some. When I told Leon he should stop snorting coke and start training, he got mad at me and shouted, "Nobody tells me what to do!" When he said that, I shouted back at him, "That's your problem, Leon, you got a bunch of flunkies around you. A lot of poor-ass niggers beggin' you, asking for handouts, saying, 'Okay, champ, yeah, champ, anything you say, champ'! I told you, Leon, when we first met, I am not a leech nor am I a beggar. I also told you that I am the best bodyguard in the business. Therefore, I am not poor like these other suckers you have around you." As I was telling Leon my side, everybody in the room watched in shock and amazement. I continued: "Leon, you don't know a good thing when you see it. Here you are sitting on top of the boxing world and you are getting high every day. That's right, I've watched you in the morning, you smoke a joint or two, drink two beers, then back to snorting coke. You think your body can handle all of that and still stay in top shape? Leon, don't be no fool, for God's sake, 'cause I love you, brother. I wouldn't hurt you for nothing in the world and I wouldn't let anybody else hurt you either. But I can't stand by and watch you slowly self-destruct and kill yourself with marijuana, cocaine, late hours, reckless driving and drinking. Leon, if I wasn't your friend, I wouldn't care what you did. But I do care, and watching you destroy yourself like that makes me cry, it hurts me, brother, it just hurts. When I was asked how would I like to be the bodyguard to Leon Spinks, the heavyweight champion of the world, I said to myself, I would love it, I would do my best and it would be an honor to protect you. Well, Leon, I said that a while back, and since then you have let me down, let your mother down; she loves you and you don't even take time out to call or visit her. You ain't that busy or important that you can't stop everything and say, 'Hi, Mom, how are you? I want you to know, I am thinking of you.' But you would rather ride around in your Cadillac smoking reefers, snorting cocaine and driving like a damn fool. I mean, I have watched you real close, Leon, and I found out a lot of bad things about you, but nobody is perfect and there is still time for you to get your act together. I know you don't like me standing up to you, telling you what I think, but I couldn't hold it inside any longer. So, Leon, when it's time for you to figure out who your friends are, I want you to think about who always told you where the drugs were, the parties, the women, and then think about the person who told you to train. Leon, a true friend cares about you always.

Why? Because if you lose when you fight Ali on September 15, they won't need you then. For you would have served your purpose with them. I know it's hard for you to be mean and tell them where to go. I know you are a very soft-hearted guy, which is good, but they are taking kindness for weakness. They are draining you, Leon. They are like tentacles on an octopus reaching out and sucking the very life blood from your body. Leon, if you were to lose everything today, do you think they would treat you like you've been treating them? Hell, no! They'll disown you because nobody likes you when you are down and out. Leon, this is my plea to you as your bodyguard, your friend and your black brother—don't let these people down, little kids look up to you, don't mislead them. Give them hope and, for yourself, shake loose from the dope and give yourself a better start."

After my speech, I went over to Leon and we hugged. I then whispered in his ear, "Think about it." And I left the hotel room. As I was leaving the room, I looked at the expression on everyone's face and it was a sight to behold. Some had their heads down, some were confused, some sorry, some sad, some too damn high to know what was happening. But one thing's for sure, everyone knew I was right. You know, that was the only time it was quiet in Leon's hotel room. All the other times, the music would be blaring and the occupants in the other rooms would call the hotel manager and complain about the loud music.

Anyway, after my speech with Leon I left his room and went to mine, where I lay down and took a nap. Two hours later, Leon came up to me and said, "I really like you, T, nobody never came to me like that before and I wanna say the truth do hurt." He continued: "It's really hard for me to find real people, true friends, down-to-earth company; everybody is after what I got. That's why I need you, T, right by my side, taking care of business." I replied, "That'll work," and we shook hands. Then he said, "T, I am gonna start full training next week."

The fight date was closing in on Leon fast. There was a lot of talk going around the camp in regard to Leon's condition and his stamina. People were also saying that Ali would not be ready to fight Leon on September 15 because he was too big (235 pounds), too out of shape, and too old to train like he did when he was younger. One thing after another, there was never a dull moment at the Spinks camp. I remember one day when Leon's wife, Nova, came to training camp unexpectedly. Leon had a woman staying with him in his quarters. Everybody was trying to get to Leon before his wife did, but all our efforts failed. Nova went right to Leon's room and found him with a woman. That woman with Leon almost died from fear because Leon's wife was no lightweight; she's about six feet one, two hundred pounds or over and can be hellish when she wants to be. When Nova caught that woman in the room with Leon, she said to her, "Bitch, what the hell are you doin' here with my husband?" The woman didn't say anything, she just ran out of the room and I never saw her after that. One thing for sure, Leon's wife wasn't a fool and she took no mess from him or anybody else. She caught Leon with his pants down a lot of times but she always said, "I still love you, Leon, why don't you come back home?" You couldn't imagine the pain and sorrow, the heartache and the sleepless nights that Nova had to bear. I know you are saying, "She had it made being married to the champion of the world!" But if you only knew. She wasn't with Leon because he was the champ and had money. Hell, she had suffered the hard times, the lean days and the times when he was nobody. Therefore I think Nova deserved better treatment than what she got.

Another thing Leon didn't like was sitting down taking care of business with his attorneys. When they called him to the office to discuss some investments, business affairs, contract signing, or fight arrangements, he would take his own sweet time coming. If they needed him in the office Tuesday at 10:00 A.M., he wouldn't arrive until Friday at 1:00 P.M. Leon would always say, "They ain't got nothing to talk about." I remember a lot of times they called Leon to ask him to come in so they could explain to him what was happening to his money and where it was going, but Leon never wanted to come. Leon just didn't have a business mind. All he wanted to do was to boogie woogie and get high. When it was time for him to handle business, he hated it so much, he would sometimes go to sleep or leave the room. Leon's attention span wasn't long at all. I am sure Leon didn't realize that being champ would mean all of that, because he got very bored in meetings with his attorneys, fight promoters and accountants.

In fact, he was beginning to get bored with boxing—the training, the discipline, the crowds. He longed to be plain old Leon and live happily ever after, but that couldn't be because he was the champ and he had an obligation to fulfill. He belonged to the people and his fans. Somehow Leon just couldn't understand that, and for that reason he always tried to isolate himself from the outside world by going into drugs, alcohol and marijuana. That's why Leon hung out so tough back in the ghetto. He could find sanctuary there; he was at peace with himself. That's also the reason why he loved music and dancing, because he could momentarily escape life's troubles that way. Many people criticized Leon—and so do I—for hanging back in the ghetto where he came from. Now don't get me wrong, it's okay to go back in the ghetto to visit and try to inspire the young brothers and sisters, but to be there every day? No way. Well that's what Leon used to do and that's the only place he felt relaxed and comfortable. What Leon failed to realize was it is hard to relate to the ghetto after you've gone.

See, it is bad to waste your time but it is worse to waste your mind, and Leon did both. Leon lived in Detroit at 19300 Brenton Drive, a very wealthy part of town, but he felt very uncomfortable there, so he used to go across town to be with the junkies, pimps, whores, cutthroats and thugs. Those were his kind of people. Leon knew I didn't like him to be in places like that. I used to tell him about it too. I said to him once, "Leon, you are the champion of the world, not the champ of the block. Everybody in the world will be watching you, what you do and where you go. It's just like when you were a child you acted like a child, but since you have grown up, you put away childish things. Do you see what I mean, Leon? I am not telling you to forget your childhood either, but what I am saying is this, you can't go back to being a child, so why go back to being a ghetto dweller?" When I said that to Leon, he looked so confused and startled. Now Leon is the type of guy who has to have the last word, so he told me, "That's where I wanna go and I like being there. If you don't want to come, you don't have to." I said, "You pay me to protect you, how can I protect you if I'm not with you?" Then Leon replied, "You tell me."

You know, it was hard for me to understand Leon sometimes—his speech, his language, was just too much for me. He didn't speak with much clarity and a lot of times he just didn't make any sense. If you told him that you didn't understand, he would get mad and start cussing real loud. His language was fine for the ghetto but nowhere else. That's the reason he couldn't relate to any other environment.

It was really sad the way Leon was treated when he came back to the ghetto. The people resented him, they were envious of him too. Leon was trying so hard to make friends with the ghetto dwellers. He would buy people drinks, share his smoke and blow with them, then ride them around with him. You see, Leon had this habit of treating everybody, thinking he could buy friends. But they would eat his food, drink his drinks, sleep in his hotel rooms, snort his cocaine and still try to rob and steal from him. They still hated him and when the chance presented itself they would try to rip him off if I was not with him. Even Leon's ghetto friends said, "He's a damn fool using all those drugs and not training." They had lost respect for Leon and his name was mud. We would be in a bar and someone would come in and say, "Where is Spanks?" (not Spinks), and the bartender would say, "There's that motherfucker over there, fucked up." Sho' nuff, Leon would be slumped across a table with his mouth open, drunk as a skunk and high as hell on drugs. I used to tell Leon, "If you're gonna drink until you stink, if you're gonna smoke dope and if you must snort coke, don't, I say please don't let the whole world know what you are doing." Leon would tell me, "I don't give a fuck what people think." Well, there you have it, straight from the champ himself.

He didn't care about too much, especially when he drove. Now Leon very seldom drove when he was sober. Matter of fact, I don't think he liked to drive when he was sober. But as soon as he got high, Leon would say, "T, pull over, let me drive now." Then Leon the lunatic would be at the wheel. I used to pray that the powers that be would revoke Leon's driver's license permanently for the sake of all humanity. Because when Leon was driving, everybody's life was in danger, the other people on the road and myself in the car with him. People used to ask me, did Leon really have a driver's license? Yes, he did, but I don't know how he ever got it. One time, Leon was driving and I was riding on the passenger side and Leon told me, "T, you're gonna have to learn how to roll joints for me because I like to smoke while I am driving."

You know, I had the most fearful time of my life when I was in the car with Leon driving. He drove like he owned the road, he had no respect for anybody, he didn't know what road courtesy meant or how to yield the right of way, all he knew was his way. His way cost him a lot; he wrecked his Cadillac once, and another time it was stolen from in front of a drug dealer's house. He bought a Corvette, gray in color, and only had it three days before he wrecked it—he drove it off the highway and into a fence going about sixty miles per hour.

Then he wrecked two rental cars. One he smashed the side up by jumping lanes, the other one he drove into the back of another car. He also hit a lady's car that had stopped for the red light; he got out to see if the lady was hurt and she said, "No, I am all right." But the next day when she found out that it was Leon Spinks who had hit her, she claimed her back was injured in the accident and that she was going to sue. Leon couldn't win for losing.

One accident I will never forget, and it happened on December 21, 1978. We were in Elyria, Ohio, Leon's main hangout. All that day he had been drinking, smoking and snorting. Everywhere that he stopped he would have two or more double shots of Crown Royal and 7-Up, then go in the back room and snort some coke. It was about 8:00 or 9:00 P.M. when Leon decided to go visit one of his girlfriends who lived and worked in Loraine, Ohio, about five miles away. It was cold outside, the road had frozen ice patches in spots, and it was dark in some areas. Plus Leon was beginning to talk all out of his head by now and he staggered when he walked.

Finally, we were on the road that would take us to Loraine and Leon was driving fast, too fast for conditions. Actually, he was driving too fast for a dry sunny day, let alone a cold, slippery and dark night. Leon was driving eighty miles per hour, weaving in and out of traffic. Another guy from Leon's entourage was following us in the van; he was behind us blinking his lights on and off trying to get Leon's attention, but to no avail. So I told Leon, "That man is trying to catch up with you to tell you to slow down, we don't have to rush." Leon didn't reply, he just kept on driving wild; then he ran through two stoplights without even slowing down a little bit. I tell you we were really lucky, but I had a feeling that our luck was gonna run out, so I told Leon, "You're driving too fast and the roads are slippery with ice." Leon replied in a loud tone, "I know what I am doing, T, don't say nothing to me." So I didn't say anything else to him because when he talked to you he looked at you while he was driving and his head and eyes were off the road for long periods of time. When Leon drives, he never looks in his rearview mirror—he didn't even glance around. Really, I don't call it driving, what Leon does, I call it aiming the car. Anyway, back to the slippery road.

Leon had just put two hands on the steering wheel when the car tires hit an ice patch and you could feel the tires spinning, then the car started to fishtail and turned all the way around. The back end of the car was going in the same direction as the front end. We were moving fast too, and Leon was wrestling frantically with the wheel, trying to regain control, but no such luck.

Then the car turned around again but this time in a lady's yard. The car ran off the road past a little ditch and onto this lady's yard, where he drove over her shrubs and plants and right smack into this big tree that stood about seventy feet high and about eight feet around. I tried like hell to get out of the car before it hit the tree, but we were just going too fast. Just to show how out of it Leon was, after the car hit the tree, he was still trying to drive, he was still pushing the accelerator pedal in with his foot. I was shocked and in a daze. I looked up at the windshield and saw a big hole in it and a lot of cracks in the middle of the windshield. I sat there holding my head, momentarily stunned, when I saw this lady running from her house saying, "Is anyone hurt? I'll call the police and get help."

Then Leon jumped out of the wrecked car, staggering from being high (not the accident), shouting back at the lady, "Don't call the police, we don't need the police." But she saw me slump over the dashboard and ran back inside and called the police anyway. Leon's buddy finally caught up with us and he said, "Let's go, Leon, get in the van," and Leon said, "We got to get T." As I was getting out of the car I opened the glove compartment and took out the half pound of marijuana Leon had put in there. I also took the keys out of the ignition switch so that we could say that the car was stolen, but the keys wouldn't come out and the engine kept running, or grinding rather. We all got in the van and drove off to the lounge, where someone called the police and played like they were Leon Spinks and told the police that his car had just been stolen from in front of the lounge.

In five minutes the police came to the lounge and said, "We found the car." And Leon was so high it was a shame, he couldn't even talk straight. The police said to Leon, "You will have to come with us to positively identify you car." I said, "Okay, he'll be right out," and then I told Leon to take that big-ass hat off and wear my coat so the lady wouldn't be able to recognize him. The lady said, "I am sure it wasn't Leon who was driving, he had the big baldheaded fella with him, I don't know his name, but I've seen them both in the papers a lot together." The headlines in the paper read LEON SPINKS' CAR HITS A TREE, HE CLAIMS IT WAS STOLEN. The funny part is that in the papers the police accused me of driving the car into the tree.

That was another part of my job, taking the rap for Leon. I didn't want Leon's name to be smeared anymore. I was trying to be very protective of him. Yes, I had to lie a lot being with Leon and I really hated to lie to his wife. She liked me more than she did anybody else in the Spinks camp and I let her down when I lied to her. That's part of being a bodyguard—coverups, lies, taking the raps and getting hurt. Now fighting for Leon and getting hurt I didn't mind, but getting hurt in a car while he is driving under the influence of everything (drugs, alcohol, marijuana) don't make sense. That's when I told myself I had better think about quitting. I told Leon, "I can protect you from anybody, but I can't protect you from yourself." I also told him, "You are your worst enemy."

Meanwhile back at the training camp, Leon was working out a little more than he had in the past. But it really wasn't doing much good because the harder he trained the more he partied and the later he stayed out at night. Sam Solomon was still worried whether Leon would be physically and mentally ready for the big fight with Ali on September 15. Sam tried to get him into the spirit of training by reorganizing the camp and the training routine. Leon would run in the morning and do exercises, then go back to sleep, and in the afternoon he would spar. As the big day began to close in on him, more press people with cameras, tape recorders and notebooks and more curious fans and autograph seekers began piling in on the camp. Now everybody was getting fight fever and the camp was moved from Hilton Head to New York. After training in New York for a couple of weeks everybody was ready for the big trip to New Orleans. I had to go back to Chicago and then Detroit to help drive Leon's big white long limo.

We got A-1 treatment everywhere we stopped. When we stopped for gas the attendant would wash all the windows and check the oil, transmission fluid, and the tires. When we stopped to eat they gave us as much as we wanted in some places and didn't charge us. I said to myself, this type of life is all right! As we made our way along the highway, I really felt like the king of the road in that big car. People would get out of our way, trucks slowed down, cars moved to the side and police gave us escorts in some cities as we passed through. See, what made it so interesting and intriguing was that when I wasn't driving, instead of sitting on the passenger side in the front I sat in the back of the limo watching TV while Charles drove, and that really made me look like a big shot. Cars were running off the road trying to see who I was. It blew a lot of white people's minds to see a black guy driving (well, that was okay) but then to see a black guy in the back seat . . . well, that was just unbelievable.

Once in New Orleans we immediately went straight to the New Orleans Hilton Hotel. We checked in and I quickly introduced myself to the hotel security chief and manager. They pledged their full cooperation to me. The front desk gave me the room key and I checked it out. I really didn't like the setup. I mean, the room was fantastic and the hotel was just beautiful, but I didn't like the idea of everybody knowing in advance what room Leon would be staying in. That wasn't good security on the hotel's part, but then again, that's where I came in. In the hotel, I saw a lot of things that I didn't like and that I knew had to be changed before Leon arrived on September 1, Friday. So I had two days to get everything in order just the way I liked it.

I familiarized myself with the huge hotel and some of its employees, especially the room service and the cooks. I wanted the same people to serve us every day, and if there were to be any substitutes, I wanted to know about it in advance. Next, I drove around New Orleans for six hours trying to know the town a little. Then I went to the Super-Dome to check that out. Lastly I went to the auditorium where Leon would hold his workouts. By the time Thursday rolled around, I was a very tired soul, so I went to sleep early because Friday morning we had to be at the airport to pick up Leon. By Thursday afternoon, we had everything ready. The car was clean and spotless and ready to go. That night it was parked in a guarded garage. Twice during the course of the night, I went down to check on the limo. One night I slept in the limo because I didn't want anyone timing my security checks. I wanted to keep them off balance and guessing all the time.

On Friday morning, September 1, 1978, Charles and I got up to eat breakfast and get the car ready. We went into the café and Charles said, "I'll go check on the car." I said, "No, let me do that." I had little traps around the car to tell if it was tampered with, and only I knew where they were. I took ten minutes to check the car out. It was a security ritual I performed every time the car was out of my sight. I knew it was an eyecatcher, and that made it even harder to watch. We finally had breakfast and were en route to the airport with a police escort—four motorcycle cops in front of the limo and two in back. The airport was overflowing with people waiting to see the champ.

We parked the car by the main entrance of the airport and went in to wait for his arrival. We were about four to five minutes early, which was good. That gave me a chance to survey the airport and the police who were assigned to Leon and who reported directly to me. As we stood around waiting, the press people started pouring in, setting up their cameras and the like. The announcement came over the P.A. system that the plane carrying Leon Spinks was about to land and that everyone should try to keep the aisles clear. The plane landed and Leon came walking down the ramp with Leroy Diggs, his sparring partner, Lester Hudson and Judge Bell, his attorneys, and Sam Solomon, his trainer. I stood back momentarily, watching the crowds, the people, the police and the press. Then Leon started shaking hands, waving to people and hugging the ladies. When he saw me, he acknowledged my presence by saying, "My man T." We hugged each other and made our way to the limo outside.

We had begun to drive off when something happened ahead of us and Charles had to hit the brakes suddenly. One of the motorcycle cops couldn't react fast enough, so he ran into the back of the limo and fell off his bike. Leon got out, so I had to get out. Now Leon wasn't even worried about the limo, but he was concerned with the policeman's safety. Leon asked the officer, "Are you all right?" The officer said, "Yes, you all go ahead." I guess he was more embarrassed than anything. After Leon was sure the policeman was all right, he got back into the limo.

In the limo Leon said, "All right, give it here." This meant pass the reefer and light it up. It was funny; Leon was getting high and all those police were around us. Leon was smoking reefers and waving to the crowds of people who had lined the street waiting to see him. He stood up in his sun-roof limo, waving both hands now and smiling. The crowd loved him. People tried to run up to the moving car but the police kept them back.

The city of New Orleans belonged to Leon from that day up to the fifteenth. Whatever he wanted, wherever he went, anything, the city jumped to please.

I had Leon's room changed at the last minute for security reasons. Anyway, once in the room we turned on the TV and heard a reporter saying, "Leon Spinks can't seem to get away from the police. Leon's limo was hit from the rear by one of his police escorts and Leon cursed the officer out." That was a big lie and that lie ran in the papers all over the world. Anything to make the brother look bad. After that, Leon unpacked and took a nap while Sam discussed the workout schedule with fight promoters. The security plan was talked about again. I was introduced to the chief of police and the captain who was in charge of the police detail for both fighters. Each fighter had at least four round-the-clock police at their disposal. Nothing really happened for Leon until after the Labor Day holiday, so it was a slow weekend, except for Friday night, when Leon chose to disco and drink the night away. He was so drunk that night he didn't wake up until Saturday afternoon about 3:00 P.M.

Sam was upset because Leon didn't run that morning; he was too hung over. Sam came into my room and asked me how much did Leon drink and what time did he get in bed? I told him that Leon had six double shots of Crown Royal with 7–Up and he didn't go to sleep until 4:30 in the morning. Sam shouted, "Shit, this don't make any sense, it's too close for him to be doing things like this." And that wasn't the worst part of it. Leon had another one of his girlfriends in his room also. But when his wife came into town his girlfriend posed as the cook in the training camp. Nothing had changed with

Leon, he was still the same. The way he acted and carried on you wouldn't believe he had a championship fight coming up in less than two weeks. Leon still had his drugs and reefer with him.

The next day I was called down to the room of Leon's attorney for a secret meeting. At that meeting were Lester Hudson, Judge Bell and Sam Solomon. We discussed security, keeping the girls away, keeping the drug dealers away, how to get rid of the girl who was staying with him and how to make him stop drinking and partying. So the word went out to everyone in the camp whether you were on the payroll or not: everybody was told to try to keep Leon's mind on training and the fight. I said to myself, if this man's mind ain't on this fight by now, it will never be, and what we do say to him won't mean a thing.

Speaking of payroll and entourages; there were a lot of lies going around that Leon had fifty or sixty people in his entourage. That's a lie: I made sure of that. Leon had fewer than ten people on his payroll and they included: (1) his bodyguard, me; (2) Sam Solomon, the trainer; (3) Leroy Diggs, his sparring partner; (4) Butch, his personal aide; (5) his doctor; (6) his two attorneys; (7) his accountant; and (8) his boxing coach from the Marines.

Other people were always trying to hang around Leon, and as soon as Leon spotted them he would say, "T, it's all right, let him in." Then somebody else would knock on the door. I would open it and say, "Leon don't want to be bothered right now." Leon would hear the person's name and say, "T, let him in too." The next thing I knew, the whole room was filled with people. So instead of Leon resting, he was entertaining. Then Leon would say, "T, call room service," and he would ask who all was hungry, and everybody would say, "I am." If I had my way, I would have kicked everybody's ass in there and run them out of town.

Monday, Labor Day, was also an easy day because Leon

didn't train on that day either. It was really strange because if Leon didn't train one day, we would send our "spies" to find out if Ali had trained that day. That's how the hangers-on earned their keep, by doing shit jobs and running errands. They could not help but wear T-shirts with Leon's name on it because that was all they had. I mean, they came down there with no suitcases, no change of clothes, no toothbrush, nothing. Only their raggedy behinds and their hands out begging. They suckered Leon in. Man it was a shame . . . Leon should have filed them all on his tax return as his dependents because they were dependent on him.

At 6:30 P.M. Leon said, "T, get some sleep tonight, because you have twelve days of hard work ahead of you!" So I went back to my hotel room and tried to put the whole thing in perspective because the things that were happening to me were happening so fast that I thought I was on a merry-go-round. As I stared out my hotel room window at the Mississippi River and the boats that passed by, I thought to myself, "Is all this for real? Is it really happening to me? Am I really here?" So I lay down and tried to sleep but it was just too good a night to sleep that early. I tried to read myself to sleep—no luck. I tried to watch TV—no luck. Finally I took a shower for twenty-five minutes, and when I finished that, I was sleepy. Leon came back to the hotel about 11:00 P.M. to get a good start on Tuesday.

When Tuesday, September 5, rolled around, Leon, myself and two other guys ran a couple of miles. Well, I ran a couple of miles and Leon ran about six. He came back to the hotel to sleep until 1:00 P.M., then went to the auditorium for workouts. After that first day, Leon was a little tired; he had worked out hard. So he went back to the hotel and slept. Wednesday, September 6, Leon was up at 5:00 A.M., running again, but this time I was sleeping good, and boy, was that sleep good! Leon did the same routine as Tuesday, which was hitting the heavy bag about twenty minutes, hitting the speed bag about fifteen minutes, sit-ups, jumping rope twenty minutes, and shadow boxing eight rounds. Then he would sign autographs for about ten minutes.

Because it was so close to the fight and it was a very big fight, I couldn't take any chances as far as security went. Everywhere Leon went, it was noted by me. I took the names of people who cooked the food and prepared it for him. When he would go to a disco and start drinking, I would follow the waiter back to the bar and watch Leon's drink being poured. When he would dance, I would cover his drink with a napkin and hold his drink in my hands: one hand on the bottom and the other covering the top (so nothing could get in and nothing could get out). His drink would never leave my hand or eyesight. When it was time for Leon to use the washroom, I would be right there whether I had to use it or not. If he had to urinate or defecate, I was right there. As his bodyguard, I made it a point that Leon would never be out of my sight.

I didn't want anyone to know where we were going in advance, so when we ate out, we picked places at random and we would go in and I would introduce myself to the manager, and go into the kitchen while the food was being prepared. Of all the places we ate in, I never had any problems with the staff except one, and that was in the New Orleans Hilton Hotel. I had been told in advance, "If something isn't to your liking, let the manager know." Well, once Leon ordered some food from the hotel's kitchen and I went down to watch the food being prepared right before my eyes. Then this guy came in asking all the employees who I was, standing in the kitchen; "It's against house policy," he said in a very loud tone. Then I told him, "Sir, you made three mistakes, big mistakes: one, you failed to ask ME who I am; two, you failed to introduce yourself to me; and three, you spoke to me in a loud manner." I told him my job and reason for being there. He still insisted that I leave the kitchen. I then said to him, "Sir, you must not have heard what I said?" He replied, "I heard you but that don't mean anything."

When the food was prepared, I asked him his name and wrote it down in my little notebook. I escorted the food straight to Leon and then went to see the hotel manager to tell him what happened. He ran out of his office into the kitchen and personally fired that man on the spot. Before the fight took place, six male employees were fired and one girl. She got fired because she was up in the room dancing with Leon when she should have been in her room service office acting as supervisor. I told her, "You can't come in the room to see Leon right now." But she insisted and Leon told me to let her in. Now you can imagine how mad I was getting with all these people coming up to see Leon, knowing damn well he had a big fight coming up and he needed his rest. How can people be so inconsiderate?

So Thursday, September 7, passed, as did Friday. On Saturday, Leon ran in the morning and sparred in the afternoon—six grueling rounds with Leroy Diggs and two each with two more sparring partners. Now it was Sunday, September 10. I rested a little, prayed a little, then asked Leon did he want to go to church. "Well," he said, "not today." So we all went out to eat and drove around the city of New Orleans for a while, then hurried back in time to participate in the Parade of Champions, which consisted of all champion fighters and their opponents. It was a nice, long parade but the parade made it difficult to maintain a watchful eye on Leon.

On Monday, the workouts got more intense. Leon was looking like he meant business, ripping his sparring partners apart with his hard hitting. After the workout, Leon talked to the press, took pictures, signed autographs and danced a little. Also, all that week the press was trying to talk to me, but I declined to speak to them, saying, "They don't pay me to talk." So I became a controversial figure in Leon's camp—because no one had ever seen a man so dedicated, so serious, so mean and so for real. I was approached by a number of people who wanted me to protect them and let Leon go. Some asked, "Are you under contract with Leon? I'll pay you more money." One man said, "Mr. T, I have been watching you ever since you arrived and you are the best. How would you like to work for me? I am willing to pay you whatever Leon's paying, plus ten thousand dollars extra." I told him that it was a nice offer, but I was loyal to Leon and I wouldn't forsake him.

All of a sudden I was the talk of the fight. Everybody wanted to interview me but I said no, until Sam said, "Go ahead, it's good publicity for the fight." I told Sam, "I can't talk to them and watch Leon too." Then Sam said, "Maybe after the workouts." I said, "Okay." One reporter asked me, "Why do you stand out so much?" I said, "I can't help but stand out; I wear earrings, I am clean every day (with a different suit, of course); I wear a fresh flower every day; I wear dark glasses; I don't speak; I don't drink; I don't smoke; I don't chase girls; and I eat a ton of food a day." "Why do they call you Mr. T?" "Because I tell them to," I said. "Is Mr. T your real name?" "Why do you wear earrings?" "Where are you from?" All day long, questions. I found myself giving interviews to reporters who couldn't speak English and had to have an interpreter. Things were getting to be too much. I say it now as I said it before, I didn't want to give those interviews. I wasn't trying to steal the limelight from Leon; those weren't my intentions. I just wanted to do a damn good job of protecting him.

On Monday evening, during the halftime of the football game, Howard Cosell interviewed Leon and Ali. Tuesday, September 12, Leon ran in the morning and exercised in the park, but did not work out at the auditorium because he had gone to the dentist to have a tooth pulled that had gotten loosened in a workout the previous day. So we left the auditorium to pick up his wife, and that meant trouble for Leon's girlfriend; she had to go somewhere and quick. When his wife was in his hotel room, Leon's girlfriend, or rather cook I should say, waited her turn in the other room of the suite by pretending to be cleaning up the place. I couldn't believe what was going on, but it was happening and Leon was getting away with it! Then my concern was that Nova might get wise and jump on Leon or the girlfriend in the other room. Believe me, I had my hands full with Leon's women, his so-called buddies, the drug dealers, the press, the fans and the people that prepared his food.

The next day, Wednesday, September 13, was the last day for hard workouts. Leon came down from his locker room with me leading the way as usual and started to work. He jumped rope for twenty minutes, did situps, hit the heavy bag and the speed bag. Then he sparred for ten rounds straight, mixing it up with three different sparring partners, a fresh one every round, and the crowd applauded. They finally felt they were getting their money's worth—they had to pay three dollars each to watch the workouts. During the workout, Leon and his brother Michael had a little heated discussion and, as Leon continued to work out, he began to cry. Tears were flowing down his face and he cried for ten minutes. Michael had gotten on Leon's case because of the way he treated his mother and the rest of the family. After the workout Leon went to take a shower. No press or visitors were allowed in. Those were my orders. Then this man came up trying to get in the locker room. I said, "Sir, where are you going?" He said, "I want to go into the locker room to see my son, Leon." Well, I had never met his father before and I wasn't taking any chances either. So I told the man, "Well, you're just gonna have to wait out here until I find out who you really are." I kept him out there for about five minutes, then Michael came back and said, "He's okay, T, he's our father." Later, Mr. Spinks came back to me and said, "You're a hell of a soldier and you are on your job. Because suppose I wasn't Leon's father and you let me in?" Before the day of the fight arrived, I had won the respect of everyone down there in New Orleans.

Wednesday evening, Leon decided to take his wife out to dinner and relax a little, which he did. That night the mayor of New Orleans had a magnificent reception for both fighters.

On Thursday, September 14, we were supposed to be at the weigh-in at ten o'clock, but we didn't leave the house until ten. Before Leon left the house, he had a couple of drinks for the road. Once at the weigh-in, which was like a madhouse, we stayed in a back room until the reporters and the people had calmed down. Ali weighed in first. It was so crowded on the stage that it collapsed from the weight of the people. When the platform was fixed, I brought Leon through. I had to be rough that day because people just wouldn't move, so I started knocking people down, shoving them aside to make way for Leon to come through.

Leon weighed in at 204 pounds. We left to go to the auditorium and the people were cheering. Leon jumped a little rope, then he danced to a couple of his favorite tunes, "Boogie Oogie Oogie" by Taste of Honey and "Holding On" by LTD. He also said "Holding On" was his theme for the fight because he was trying to hold on to the title. Then the people started asking him questions, and the very first question was, "Are you going to use the brown bottle again?" Then everybody in the crowd said, "Yeah, tell us about that." Leon replied, "What bottle?" He answered questions for an hour, then he ran out to the limo and got away from the crowd.

There were pre-fight parties going on all over New Orleans. Peddlers were selling Ali's T-shirts, Spinks' T-shirts; you name it, they were selling it. Prostitutes were selling their stuff at skyrocket prices and some people were even selling tickets at enormous prices. Everybody was there to get over in one way or another. That Thursday night, Leon stayed in but he didn't rest. He danced, he talked, he yelled, he drank, he smoked and did a little coke, had sex with another girl while his girlfriend was getting mad in the other room. He engaged in sex just about every night. Leon stayed up until about 2:00 A.M. but didn't really get to sleep until about 2:35 A.M. I know because I checked periodically during that night.

The day had finally come. It was Friday, September 15, 1978. The day Leon meets Ali for the championship of the world at the SuperDome. The fight had been billed as the Battle of New Orleans and the SuperDome was sold out. Hotels were overcrowded, people were sleeping in cars and tents, and some were even sleeping on sidewalks. Bourbon Street was jumping and bets were popping. Everybody who was anybody was there. Movie stars, sports stars, politicians, entertainers, homosexuals, Muslims, Catholics, Baptists and a lot who didn't believe in nothing but luck. It was raining that day and the sky was dark but it made for easy thinking.

Leon got up at 11:00 A.M. and appeared to be somewhat troubled, so I didn't say anything to him. I was just silent until he said, "Good morning, T. How do you feel?" I said, "Fine, champ, what about yourself?" He said, "I'm ready," then he walked around the house, loosening up. Sam Solomon telephoned and said, "I want to speak to the champ." After Leon got off the phone he said, "We will leave at six P.M. Okay, T?" I said, "Sure, champ." Leon didn't eat that day, but he drank a couple of beers. He talked to his girlfriend for a while because she was very concerned with all his drinking and excessive sex, especially with other women. But he assured her that he was all right and that he would do his best against Ali. I kept walking back and forth checking on him.

Later in the afternoon about five people came over, one man and four women. Leon told me that they were all right and I let them in. They went straight to Leon's room in the back. The music wasn't that loud (this time) and you could hear everybody's voice clearly. They laughed, they talked and shouted. I continued to walk back and forth and Leon knew I was checking because I had that certain look on my face. That's when Leon said to me, "T, you don't have to worry. I'm not gonna do anything before the fight." I said, "Okay, champ," and walked away. Then Leon went back into the room and tried to lock the door, but the latch didn't catch and the door was open a crack. I came back about three minutes later and what I saw, I just couldn't believe. Leon was snorting cocaine and this was the day of the fight; 5:15 P.M., to be exact. I said to myself, "What is Leon doing to himself?" I was so mad at him. I wanted to burst that door open and kick everybody's ass in the room. I said to myself, "Damn! How stupid can you get?" I was steaming mad at Leon and he knew it. His guests left at 5:45 P.M. and we started to get Leon ready. We were almost ready to leave but I had to go back and get the Bible. I then said to Leon, "Let's pause and pray," which we did.

Now we were on our way to the SuperDome. It was still dark and raining, but we made it through traffic with the help of our police escort. When we got to the Dome, Leon told me to stop the car. He got out and gave away about fifty tickets (good seats, too) and got back in the car and drove into the Dome all the way up to our dressing room. When Leon got to his dressing room it was already filled with relatives, friends, police, and well-wishers. Outside the dressing room stood the Marine Corps Color Guard. As we sat around the dressing room talking, everyone was loose and relaxed. Leon was playful and a little concerned, but he kept playing with his sister's baby and his little brother. Nobody asked him how he felt. Everyone was kind of shy when it came to certain subjects that night. Just about every fifteen minutes, a man would run back to our room and say how much time Leon had to get ready. Then Frank Gifford from ABC-TV came in to interview Leon.

Leon began to get dressed but there was a problem, a big problem. Somebody forgot to bring Leon's cup, a device that protects the genitals from low blows and punches. Leon shouted, "Where's my cup?" Sam Solomon looked around and asked his assistant, "Did you bring the thing?" He said, "No, I thought you had it." Sam replied, "I told you to pack everything Thursday night and double-check this morning!" Then Leon shouted, "Just forget it, you won't be with me next time and you can bet on that." Somebody ran to Mike Rossman's dressing room and borrowed his cup, which was all sweaty and stinking after he'd fought a tough thirteen rounds with Victor Galindez. Now Leon was ready. Well, dressed-wise he was. I must admit, Leon looked good in that outfit, but outfits don't win fights. He was dressed in red boxing shoes, red velour trunks and a red robe. It was hot and crowded in that dressing room.

Just before we were about to leave, Mrs. Spinks said, "Everybody, let's bow our heads and pray." Now that prayer was very touching to me. It went like this: "Lord, let the victory go to the better man. Lord, I don't want my son to win because he is my son but only if he is the better man. Lord, teach my son to love and pray. Amen." Leon then kissed a small cross and put it in his right sock by his ankle. Just before we went out, I went quickly to a meeting with some state troopers and police who had their men posted over and around the walkway to the ring. I told them what I wanted and needed, then I left to bring Leon out.

We started out of the dressing room and you could hear the thundering sound of the crowd chanting. Ali was already in the ring doing his thing. As we were making our way down the tight aisle, people were reaching out their hands and I was knocking them back. Somebody pushed a man into me and I hit him with an uppercut that straightened him up and I kept moving. I had one arm around Leon and with the other arm I was knocking people out of the way. I hit so many people that night, I was tired and sore when we finally reached the ring. I jumped up and held the ropes for Leon and stood right in back of him as he moved around loosening up. I just couldn't believe the number of people in the SuperDome. I was awed by the huge crowd, which was over 80,000 people. From the moment you walked in the SuperDome, you could tell what kind of crowd it was—it was an Ali crowd. I told Leon before I left the ring, "Hang in there, champ." I told him to hang in there because after taking cocaine, there was little he could do anyway.

The bell sounded and the fight was underway. In the first round, neither fighter did much damage to the other, but there was a difference between the two men. The first time Leon fought Ali, Leon never sat down between rounds for the whole fifteen-round fight. But this time, at the end of round one, Leon waved to Sam to get the stool ready and when Leon came to the corner, he flopped down on the stool, exhausted. I knew from that it was gonna be a long night for him. As the fight wore on, Leon grew weary. His eyes were all glazed and he didn't even know where he was. He was just fighting out of instinct, his mind and reflexes were gone. Sam and Michael were hollering at Leon when he sat in the corner but he didn't hear them—he was in another world. The whole world watched as he stumbled around the ring trying to hit Ali. When the fight was nearing the end, Leon knew he had lost, so he just held on to keep from getting knocked down. When the fight was over, Leon was so glad that, if you didn't know any better, you would think he had won instead of Ali.

Well, it was only fitting that Ali won his title back, and you can rest assured that Ali would never disrespect the title the way Leon did. Once back in the dressing room all was somber and quiet. Leon's dressing room wasn't as crowded as it was before the fight. That's why his wife Nova said, "Leon, I hope you know who your friends are?" Then Leon walked away to take a shower. I waited, holding his towel, then I burst into tears. Yes, I cried like a baby and I ain't ashamed to say so. I didn't cry because Leon lost that fight, I cried because of what he had done to himself by snorting cocaine and smoking reefers. When Leon finished his shower, he reached for his towel and saw me crying. He said, "I'm sorry, T." I hugged him and said, "I still love you, brother," and walked away to finish crying. Leon's mother came in a few minutes later and said, "That's okay, son, you tried. We still love Ali because he gave us the title for a while so we gave it back to him. Today Ali was the better man. We want to thank Ali for allowing us to be here tonight."

At the press conference after the fight the news reporters asked Leon what happened. Leon said firmly, "My mind wasn't on the fight." Silence fell over the big room and you could hear whispers repeating what Leon had said: "His mind wasn't on the fight." The biggest fight of his boxing career and his mind wasn't on it? Why not? If you were high on cocaine your mind wouldn't have been on the fight either!

Then a couple of months later Leon said that the press tried to make him out something he's not. After Leon lost to Ali, his career and life seemed to stop. I mean he wasn't hungry anymore and he didn't care anymore. He made two and a half million dollars for his losing effort, so why worry? He said, "I got mine." Well, that was in September 1978, but by April 1979, he began to run a little short on cash. He was sued three or four times by people he ran into while trying to drive. He partied and partied, he drank and drank, he smoked and smoked, he snorted cocaine and boy did he get high. I mean, he would be so high that he would be foaming at the mouth and he was a sight to behold. Leon would have at least two big hotel suites and a private room in each hotel he stayed at, which would run him into big debt. Now let me explain something, he also had four or five other rooms for his so-called friends, and they would party every day for weeks. Everybody would order room service and charge it to Leon Spinks. Why not? He didn't care, and besides he was too high to know what was happening. I'll tell you the truth, I really wanted to quit protecting Leon so many times, but love brought me back. I knew that if I left Leon then or any time, he would be taken advantage of (maybe even robbed or killed) because of all the people trying to rip him off.

Soon all his big-time spending started catching up with him because Leon didn't know what was happening with his money and wasn't educated enough to know. Leon partied, drank and snorted so much that it was feared he would never fight again.

Anyway, by now protecting Leon had become a big game. I mean, hide and seek. Leon would hide in the next town and I had to go seek him out. Man! I started feeling like a babysitter. It got to the point that I just told Leon, "Look, man, you pay me to protect you and I can't protect you if you keep running away, so you make up your mind and tell me what you want to do!" Well, that talk only lasted two days, and he was back to his old tricks again and I was back chasing him, playing detective instead of bodyguard.

One day, he ran away from me for the last time and I retired from the job. I mean, I just gave up. I couldn't take it anymore, I had to start my own career. I just didn't have a bright future with Leon anymore, so I had to let him go. He was so high when I left, he didn't realize I was gone until a week later. It didn't matter, he kept on partying until one night some bitch set him up. He got high in a hotel room in January 1981 and she stole all his jewelry, his mink coat, money and drugs. He lied and told the police that he was robbed coming from a tavern. He said someone hit him on the back of the head and took his money and dragged him to a hotel, where they took all his clothes. I tell you, Leon couldn't even lie straight. Then Leon was given another shot at the title against Larry Holmes. He was flat broke plus he was out of shape. The fight was held on June 12, 1981. I arrived in Detroit on the tenth of June to wish him well and thank him for allowing me to be his friend and protector. When I got to town, I was told he wasn't training. He had been drinking and screwing all week long. When I finally caught up with him, we hugged and laughed. Well, it's all history and nothing new happened. I mean, Leon was late to the fight as usual and he got knocked out in the third round . . . so what else is new? One week after he lost the fight, he was arrested for carrying a concealed weapon, a .357 Magnum, in his glove compartment. The Detroit judge ordered him to report to a probation officer and stay employed for a year to avoid prosecution on a charge of possession of a concealed weapon.

It was all over—he had it but he lost it. He said it all happened to him too fast. I say that's a lie! Everything that happened to Leon, he brought upon himself. When I heard Leon crying the blues about society being on his case, that they expected him to be like God, how he wasn't ready for all of that success, I say sure he wasn't ready for it, but that's his fault. I get so tired of hearing about Leon being too young to handle all the fame and fortune. That's a bunch of bull. Leon lost his title because he took God's blessing for granted. God had left Leon and he didn't even know it. Leon only wanted the Bible when it was his last hope. Leon didn't use his God-given talent wisely, and if you don't use it, you'll lose it. No man is too big to take time out to pray and be thankful to God for what he has. Leon lost his title because he forgot that God giveth and God taketh away. Jesus said it best: "Your father knoweth what things ye have need of. Seek ye first the Kingdom of God and His righteousness and all those other things shall be added unto you."

The tragedy of Leon was that he sought the means first and in the process the ends were swallowed by the means. So there you have it, the rise and fall of Leon Spinks.

T TANGLES
WITH
TROUBLE

EVERYTHING WAS LOOKING GREAT FOR ME. I WAS an established bodyguard, a young businessman on my way up, a realtor, and all of that was just the beginning. But then trouble came. I mean big trouble. Trouble with the Internal Revenue Service, the U.S. Army National Guard and the Chicago Police Department.

First, let me deal with the Army. I am not the kind of guy you push around. I have no problem takings orders but don't give me no dirty deal. The thing that rubbed me the wrong way in this new company I was assigned to was they had too many chiefs and not enough Indians. Everybody wanted to give orders just because they had more stripes on their arm than me. I saw I was being misused by guys who outranked me.

A lot of guys were jealous of me, especially when they found out that I was Leon Spinks' bodyguard. I informed my platoon sergeant that as bodyguard for Leon Spinks, I would not be able to make all the scheduled drills, and I would make up all the ones I missed. I even requested a leave of absence and asked my sergeant to reschedule my drills, but he said, no, it wouldn't be necessary. But later I got the word from one of my trusted Army Guard buddies that the commander was trying to send me to the Army for two years—you see, since I never had prior military service, I could be reactivated into the regular Army because I had missed so many drills that they could consider me AWOL. My buddy also told me in early July 1979 that a warrant had been issued for my arrest.

If that wasn't enough to worry about, in July 1979, while

leaving my apartment building, I was confronted by two white men. One said "Excuse me. Are you Mr. T?" I looked at them and replied, "Yes, I am." He introduced himself as Special Agent Blank Blank of the IRS and his partner, Blank Blank. "We want to ask you some questions. Can we go up to your apartment and talk? It will only take a couple of minutes." I said, "No, we can't." Then the first special agent said, "We don't want everybody to know your business, talking here in the street." I said, "You stopped me here on the street, so we talk here on the street." Then he said, "I want to ask you some questions about your tax returns." I said, "I don't answer any questions without my attorney being present." He said, "Okay, but we still have to read you your rights first," which he did. Then he asked again if I still chose not to answer any questions at this time. I told him I understood my rights and I did not choose to talk at this time. He then asked, "What is your attorney's name?" I said, "You will be hearing from him." Then he showed me a tax return and asked, "Is this your signature?" I said, "No comment," and walked away.

I knew somebody in my apartment had probably called in on me because they wondered how I lived the way I did. A black man ain't supposed to be living in an $800-per-month apartment, wearing $400 suits and expensive jewelry and having a limo pick him up every morning. It would be okay if I were white, but not a black man—hell, no!

I hired two tax attorneys, but soon I felt that I couldn't trust them either. They wanted to know an awful lot just to defend me, so I told my two attorneys that since this was nothing more than an audit or investigation, I would supply no more information until I was officially charged with a crime or violation. I was doing nothing illegal. I hadn't cheated on my tax returns. I was not a drug dealer, nor was I a pimp. But these attorneys still wanted to know how I lived. They asked, "How do you pay your rent, have a limo, eat, entertain, et cetera?" I said, "You tell the IRS and anybody else who wants to know that I believe in God and my God is not poor, therefore, I won't be poor. My God didn't put me here to be a failure. So you tell them that, because I have nothing else to say." It really pissed me off when someone would walk up to me and ask, "What do you do?" I look at them and ask, "What do your mama do?" I also told my attorneys the IRS, the police and everybody ought to be glad that I am on the side of the law, because, given what I know and how dangerous I am, I would be a monster of a criminal.

At that time I began to understand the making of some criminals by just observing what happened to me. I can see a man obeying the law, respecting people and their property until he is harassed, violated and mistreated by the powers that be. I began to believe some crimes are understandable because society fails to hear the warnings, or the cries of outrage.

Meanwhile, back in the summer of '79, when I was still having problems with the U.S. Army and the IRS, I had a run-in with the Chicago police, or should I say, they had a run-in with me. The day I got arrested, well, it all happened on a nice humid Sunday afternoon. I had just gotten out of my limo coming from church when I was met by a friend. He told me he was going over to the lakefront to watch the Air and Water Show, an annual summer event in Chicago. He was with his girlfriend, his niece and another child. I told him I would like to join him for the show because we hadn't seen each other for a while. There were a lot of people out that day and traffic was a standstill, but we didn't have far to go, since I lived two blocks from Lake Michigan. When we reached the lakefront, it was a mess. People were everywhere and doing everything. So we started to cross the Outer Drive, but since we didn't see an opening in the crowd, we decided to walk down a little further on the median strip. One policeman said that it was okay to walk on the median strip until we saw an opening to cross at. But as we walked down the median, we were soon confronted by a very nasty, disrespectful Chicago policeman who began shouting at us to get off the median. I stopped and asked the police officer, "Why are you so rude and nasty?" He shouted back, "Are you trying to get smart with me?" I said, "No, I'm not trying to be smart, but I'm a man and there's no reason why you have to shout and disrespect us." Then he cut me off from talking and shouted again, "Do you want to get arrested for disorderly conduct? I told you to get off the median right here." He pointed with his finger. I tried to tell him that the other officer had said it was okay to walk on the median, but again he shouted, "What did I say?" I turned to my friend and said, "I don't believe this," and just at that split second the big, sloppy, unprofessional, ill-trained bully cop grabbed me from behind and started twisting my arm.

Now, I was really shocked because I couldn't believe anybody in their right mind was grabbing me. When he grabbed me, I told him, "If I'm under arrest for disorderly conduct, then arrest me and take me to jail." But he insisted on trying to rough me up, saying to me, "Shut up" and pushing me at the same time. It was very embarrassing because a lot of people were out there and I'm not the type of guy who breaks the law. So I told the policeman again, "Look, arrest me and stop pushing me around." He still continued to assault me, holding my arm behind my back and my suit coat collar in his other hand. He kept on pushing me and twisting my arm. He even pushed me over the hood of a car that was full of people. That's when I told him one more time, and this was his third warning—three strikes and you're out. After he had my back on the car, I told him, "My name is Mr. T, I'm a bodyguard." Then he shouted in my face this time, "I don't give a fuck who you are!"

Well, he shouldn't have said that because I didn't care who he was anymore either. So I pushed him back off me and you should have seen him fly backward. He stumbled back like a clumsy ox. He was embarrassed, shocked and scared to death. He must have thought to himself, Oh Lord, what have I done now. I grabbed the wrong man this time. His eyes were as big as silver dollars and he stood there a few seconds, nervous and shaking, frightened out of his wits. Then he looked around for reinforcement and didn't see any. So this fool, this stupid cop, pulls his weapon out of his holster and aims it at me. After he pulled his weapon out on me, he said, shaking, "Motherfucker, I will blow your brains out." Soon twelve more policemen arrived on the scene and tried to subdue me. They wrestled with me until they finally got the handcuffs on me. A couple of them tried to throw me to the ground and bust my face.

That's when I started to fight. That's right, I was still handcuffed with my hands behind my back, but my legs were free so I told those police, "My legs are just as dangerous as my hands and if any one of you tries to throw or push me to the ground, I'm going to kick the shit out of you." I tell you, it was a free-for-all out there. Police were all over me, trying to wrestle me to the ground, but they couldn't. (I wasn't the city wrestling champion for two years in a row for nothing.) It was three or four police on my neck, two around my waist, three on my legs and the rest were all on the others. After I told them I was gonna start kicking and began to throw them over my shoulder, one of the police said, "Let's get him to the station quick."

I was kept in jail for six hours and my bond was a measly $100. That day I had $968 on me, which made the police more angry. The cop who arrested me was really trying his damnedest to stick it to me. But you see, I didn't have a record, so when they sent my name through the computer, it came back as clean as fresh laundry. The arresting officer was stomping around jail saying, "I want him." Now what he was really saying was that he wanted me to serve some time, because he and his fellow officers wanted no part of me physically. When the police were taking me to the station, they started talking crap. The one who pulled his gun on me said, "You are a sissy wearing those earrings." I said, "If I am a sissy, why did you pull your handgun? Why did it take ten or more cops to put the handcuffs on me? If I'm a sissy, I'll bet I'm the hardest-hitting sissy you ever grabbed." That shut them up. The next day, I went to the Office of Police Professional Standards and filed a complaint against that police officer.

Now just think, I was charged with unlawful use of a weapon and they didn't even find a weapon on me. But the cop who pulled out his weapon, aimed it at me and cocked the trigger, was not charged.

I was charged with five things: (1) unlawful use of a weapon; (2) aggravated assault; (3) theft of lost property; (4) disorderly conduct; (5) failure to register firearms. The court date was set for August 10, 1979. The next day, Monday, July 30, 1979, the news of my arrest was a hot item. It was carried in every newspaper and on most radio stations. It really wasn't news; it was more like a smear campaign or something to discredit me. No, I didn't mind being arrested—I'll do it again if I am pushed and shoved. But because I spend so much of my time working with kids and teenagers, I am trying to set a good example for them to follow. I hated the way the news media handled the incident. Anyway, by the time August 10, 1979, rolled around, I was ready for the trial but the police weren't.

I arrived for my 10:00 A.M. court date at 11th and State Street, the Chicago police headquarters. My limo pulled up at the front door of the police station. I got out and made my way to misdemeanor court on the eleventh floor. I was met by Pastor Henry Hardy of Cosmopolitan Community Church and Pastor T. L. Barrett of Life Center Church. My father was there and so was my mother. The state's attorney wanted me to plead guilty. I said, "Are you mad? You're going to have to find me guilty." Then he offered to make a deal with me about the charges. The police case was very weak, so they wanted to deal with me. They wanted me to plead guilty to unlawful use of a weapon and they would have dropped all the other charges. I said, "Hell, no, because you didn't find a weapon on me; or if that's the charge, you would have to lock me up for life because my hands and feet are deadly weapons." They said, "If you plead guilty to aggravated assault, we will drop everything else." Again I said, "Hell, no!" I would not make any deal; we would go to trial. A new court date was set in a different courtroom, for September 19, 1979.

Now between August 10, 1979, and September 19, 1979, I was being followed by the IRS, my phone was tapped, my bank account and other records were open house for everyone to see. The IRS questioned everybody associated with me. I tell you, it really got to be hot stuff; they followed me around everywhere. I was so excited they thought I made that much money for them to investigate me. I enjoyed them following me; it was better than the movies. It was court time again on September 19, 1979, and we were ready. This time it was a little more of the same but nothing happened. So court was continued until October 19, 1979.

After court I returned home. At about 3:20 P.M., I heard a knock on my door so I grabbed my .357 Magnum and asked, "Who is it?" I was wondering how did they (whoever it was) get past the doorman downstairs. Anyway, I opened the door with my pistol in my hand, standing there with my undershorts and T-shirt on. I asked, "What do you want?" At my door stood a white man and a black man (the latter about six feet one, 180 pounds—I guess his backup). The white guy introduced himself and his partner as MPs. I said, "I can't believe this, I just came from court." Then I asked, "Do you have an arrest warrant?" The white guy said smartly, "We don't need one, we do this all the time." I said, standing in the door, "You're gonna need one for me." Then the white guy said, "If you want us to call the police and make a big scene out of this, we will." I said, "Go ahead, and if they don't have a warrant, you are still in trouble."

They waited outside my apartment door. Meanwhile, I called my attorney and informed him of what was going on. He was bewildered. Soon the police arrived, two whites—one of them I knew, the other one knew of me. They tried to talk me into going peacefully and everything was going okay until that little white MP started running off at the mouth saying, "I don't have all day," and for me to hurry up and get dressed because I was definitely going with them. Well, you know I would get angry behind a statement like that for two reasons: (1) he said that while in my house, and (2) he said that to me, period. I told him, "Let me tell you something and you remember this: If I don't want to go, you guys ain't enough to bring me in, so don't get smart. Don't forget that you are in my house; I don't take no mess in the streets and you know ain't nobody gonna beat me in my own house. Do you understand that?" I called another attorney and informed him. Then I went with the two MPs and two policemen under my condition that I would not be handcuffed coming out of my building. Then the white MP said, "We can't do that, all prisoners must be handcuffed." I asked, "You want me to come peacefully, don't you?" He thought for a second and replied, "Yes."

They took me from my apartment to Fort Sheridan, where they lied to my attorney, saying that they were gonna keep me at Fort Sheridan instead of sending me to Fort Knox detention center. My lawyer really fell for that. Early Thursday morning, at 5:00 A.M., a bus came to take me away to Fort Knox. The ride down there was okay because the driver of the bus was a lady. She was pretty and very kind. Then again, who wouldn't be if they were driving a bus full of army deserters. We finally reached Fort Knox and were introduced to our new home where we would be staying until they found our charges and let us out of their army.

Now down there, I wasn't an easy guy to get along with. I resented the Army coming after me like I killed somebody. They had the nerve to ask me if I wanted to stay in the Army. I said, "HELL NO!" A sergeant who was doing the processing said, "You will be given a dishonorable discharge." I said, "I don't care what kind of discharge you give me; I just want to be out of the Army, like right now." One thing's for sure, they will never forget me at Fort Knox.

While I was there, I gave them hell every single day and night. The first sergeant had threatened to send me to the Fort Leavenworth prison to wait for my orders because I was too mean at the detention center for them. Sure I was mad, because I didn't deserve to be there in the first place. And furthermore, the army people tried to run me through the mill when they found out that I was Leon Spinks' bodyguard. The thing that really pissed them off was when other deserters started asking me for my autograph and pictures. They tried to keep me there as long as possible, until I started to go berserk. I told them I wanted out of the army. Then a sergeant told me I had to wait until they found my charges.

I told him, "Who in the hell do you think you are fooling, you don't arrest no one without knowing what you are arresting them for. You might fool these young kids with that shit, but it won't work on me. If you don't have my charges here pretty soon, somebody is gonna get hurt—that's not a threat, it's a warning. You are treating me like a criminal. Well, I am gonna show you how criminals act. You march us to eat, you watch us like hawks, you have roll call every hour and you keep us behind these barbed wire fences twelve feet high. You got us sleeping in nasty barracks where the shower works sometimes and other times the water is cold."

One night there I will never forget. I was in my bunk when a sergeant tried to bring a guy into our barracks who had the crabs (body lice). I didn't want that guy around me so I hollered, "Don't bring that man in here with crabs." Then that sergeant said, "At ease, Private Tero." I said, "At ease, my foot. I don't want to be around that mess. Why should we take him in, when the third platoon kicked him out. If you want him to sleep somewhere, take him home and let him sleep with your wife and kids." The whole place got quiet then. Then that sergeant said, "Private Tero, I'm gonna write you up tomorrow." I shouted back, "Hell, you can write me up tonight, I don't care because I'm already a deserter and what more can you do to me?"

The next morning I was told to report to the company commander. When I met him, I told him what I was pissed off about. I informed him that I was a bodyguard making $200 per day and now I was losing that pay per day and I was angry. I told him the barracks were unclean and I had been treated like I tried to kill the President. He assured me that he would look into my case and find my charge, which he did. Then he told me that somebody had been sitting on their butts and not doing their job, but he would see that I was out of there by Friday.

But Friday morning in the chow lines one of those sergeants pushed me too far. It started when I stepped inside the mess hall with my cap on, and that sergeant didn't even give me a chance to take it off. He ran over to me and said, "Take your cap off in the chow line." Now I hate for anyone to holler at me so I told him, "You didn't have to holler in my ear, besides I have been coming in here for days. I know how to take my cap off when I enter a building." He shouted, "You act like you got a problem." I told him, "You got the problem, because you think I'm one of these young punks that will take all of the crap. But don't be no fool and get hurt. You see, I get paid for kicking tails and one more won't make any difference. I'm not worried with that Fort Leavenworth talk because if I go there, it will be because I put three or four sergeants in the hospital, not because I talked back to one. Now if you feel froggish, go ahead and jump." It was so quiet in the mess hall that it could have been mistaken for a church that morning. I had no problem from anybody after that, but I was told to report to the C.O. again.

He said, "I can't believe everybody wants me to send you to Fort Leavenworth. I heard about the fight you almost had in the mess hall with one of my sergeants this morning. It's true, everyone is out to get you." That's when I said, "I must get out of here before I go to prison and before I hurt someone, because if I go to prison, I'm gonna hurt a lot of people real bad and that's not a bluff or threat, sir, but it is a prophecy." The company commander said, "I am trying to get you out as fast as I can but you must promise me that you will stay out of trouble. Now, can you promise me that, Private Tero?" I said, "Yes, sir. If they don't bother me!"

That following Monday I was on my way back home; they had kept me for eleven days. Now, I think the real reason they kept me so long was so that the IRS could get a chance to do some snooping around while I was gone. They did contact a lot of people, but what they found out must have blown their minds.

Well anyway, I was now out of the Army National Guard for good. The police incident was thrown out of court. Now that only leaves the IRS. Well, I guess they will be following me all my life, trying to build a big case against me. That's okay because I have no problem with paying my taxes. I know I must "Render unto Caesar that which is Caesar's, but render unto God that which is God's."

9 AMERICA'S TOUGHEST BOUNCER

ORKING AT CHICAGO'S DINGBATS Disco you surely couldn't retire on that salary, but the fringe benefits were just unbelievable. I mean, working at the door of the disco, I got to choose the ladies first, and there were some pretty foxy ladies down there. It was fun because if I wanted to, I could have taken a different woman home with me every night. I became the envy of all the guys. I was the men's fret, the women's pet and sissies' regret (smile). A lot of guys wanted to fight me because of this, but they thought twice about it.

It's really hard for me to describe Dingbats; the place, the people who came there, and the people who worked there. As a disco it was, no doubt, the cream of the crop. There were other discos that were new and more modern in architectural design but the people were phony, fake and plastic. They didn't know how to relax, be cool and have a good time, or just plain ol' get down. At Dingbats the people were known for that kind of activity—nightly. If you came down to Dingbats and didn't know how to dance, I'll bet you learned before you left. Dingbats was a rough and rowdy place simply because it was predominantly black. I didn't allow rudeness. I enforced a dress code, I checked IDs (must be twenty-one years old), I made sure everyone was having a good time, and I checked the men's and women's washrooms periodically to make sure no one was smoking pot. I also mingled with the guests, danced with the ladies, and every now and then I would buy the customers drinks. When there was a problem, I handled it quickly, professionally and quietly. One thing that would get you thrown out by me quickly was disrespecting the women who came down there. If a lady didn't want to be bothered, then leave her alone and don't put your hands on her. Now when a person had too much to drink, I escorted him or her out. I threw a lot of people out of Dingbats—white, black, Mexican, Puerto Rican, whatever. If you were disorderly, I didn't hesitate to show you the door, most of the time with force.

Another thing I didn't take at Dingbats was threats. I didn't let a guy walk out saying he would be back to do this or that to me when he returned. I believe if a person says something he might do it, so I didn't take any chances. At Dingbats I have had over two hundred fights and got cursed out every other day. Why? Because some people wanted me to play favorites and some women wanted me to cut them slack or they wanted to owe me. I would say, "No such thing down here," and then the trouble would start. Especially if the customer was black and didn't have enough money to get in. He would say, "Why are you doing this for the white man, brother? You can let me and my lady in without paying, ain't nobody looking and won't nobody know." I would say, "No," and he would get mad and start cursing me and calling me a "black-ass Uncle Tom" or a "two-bit flunky."

I also threw people out I caught trying to sneak in without paying. When I caught them they would say, "Hey man, I got a pocketful of money, what am I gonna sneak in for?" I didn't let people pay to get in after they tried to sneak in, and that also started fights. I really hated people coming up to me with that "brother" talk saying, "Let me in, brother," or "Can I walk, brother?" Then there's the BS line, "Hey, Mr. T, I saw you on television, man, you sho' is bad." I would say firmly, "Hey, brother, it cost five dollars to get in." Then he would say, "Oh, Mr. T," and I would reply, "Mr. T my foot, if you're coming in, it will be five dollars, get out of the doorway."

Now the thing I was really strong on was IDs. Some days I made everybody show IDs, even people I knew were twenty-one or over. I'd be checking IDs at the door and someone would come up to me and say, "I forgot mine at home" and I'd say, "Then you'd better go home and get it because you can't get in here without it." The next line would be, "Mr. T, I come in here all the time, you don't remember me." I'd look at him and say, "I can't remember people because my memory is about as long as the hair on my head and that's short." A lot of women came up to me and whispered in my ear—they thought they were so fine—but I said, "No deal, sweetheart, you won't be able to get in today." See, the reason I was so hard on them was because they thought a man was supposed to let them in because they were half-naked with an all-right body. I would tell them my favorite line, but first I told them, "I am not like the guys at the other clubs who rap to you and let you in, thinking that they would screw you later. I don't do that and you don't interest me. So either pay the five dollars and come or unblock the doorway." Then the woman would start cursing me out, saying, "You old baldheaded bastard, you ain't shit." I would reply with "Thank you" and a smile. After she would leave, more of that continued in the form of "Mr. T, why are you so mean, you are too cute to be so mean, ain't he, girls?" Now, I'm supposed to be a sucker and fall for that. When she finishes with her talk I say, "I need to see some IDs, ladies." Then one replies with "We don't have any but you can let us in, can't you?" I then tell them, "You are fine and that is true, but I got a lady who would make an asshole out of you. Besides I turn down more women than the average guy gets, so I dont worry about women." They leave all pissed off because they couldn't work their little charm on me.

Some women got mad when I didn't talk to them; but why should I? They come down every night and take a different guy home with them, then they have the nerve to try to talk to me—you've got to be kidding! I remember one woman who was talking to me and I told her I was busy. She kept hanging around telling me what all she could do for me, but I still told her I wasn't interested. I don't want a girl that everybody has had. Some women are like buses—everybody rides on them. She got mad and gave me the finger, then walked up to me and tried to kiss me. I turned my head, she stopped and put her hand on her hip, and said, "I see why you are running away, you can't handle me anyway, I'm too much for you!" I said, smiling, "You're right."

But since no job can be all fun and games, I had my share of work. The work I am referring to are the fights I got into in the men's washroom. One time I caught some guys in there selling marijuana and cocaine. I went into the washroom but had trouble getting past the door because it was so crowded—and no wonder . . . about six guys were smoking reefers and two more were snorting cocaine. I knocked down the door with my shoulder and then I roughed up those guys and the drug dealer. After that I had them arrested. I had a couple of incidents in the women's washroom also. A lot of women thought it was safe for them to smoke or snort in their washroom, but they didn't know that I went into the women's washrooms too. Once I even had to snatch a woman out of the stall who was sitting on the toilet smoking a joint. She was puffing away and when she saw me she said, "What are you doing in here?" I had her arrested too. Like I said, I didn't cut any slack. I was hard but fair.

Like I said, you'll find some of everything happening down at Dingbats. I caught two guys passing out phony money—counterfeit twenty-dollar bills. First I asked the guy to pay for his drinks in real money and then to leave. He said he wouldn't, and attacked me with a wild charge. Then, the guy's buddy tried to jump in also, but I put an end to him with a karate chop to the back of his neck that sent him to the floor in great pain. After I subdued these guys, I had them arrested. There was always something jumping at Dingbats. I had problems with people coming and waiting for women to dance and leave their purses at their table, giving them the opportunity to steal the purses. Some thugs did the same thing with coats. They would say they've lost their ticket to their coat and claim a leather coat or a mink coat as theirs. Once a guy snatched three coats from the coatroom and ran out of the door and down the street. I caught him and taught him a lesson. I also had problems with guys feeling on the waitresses' butts as they went by. I had to collar a couple of guys about that. Of all the things that have happened at Dingbats, I *can* say Dingbats was never robbed. I'm not bragging, but only saying that I don't take no mess.

Being at Dingbats and being a bodyguard, I was sued a number of times, but I won every time. You see, being the top bodyguard around and working at a disco, I was challenged a lot. It's like being the fastest gun in the West—some people would stay out of your way, while some people want to have a showdown with you to see if they can beat you. Now, from all of that, I have been in and out of court fighting lawsuits as a result of my beating up somebody. I have been sued by customers whom I threw out of Dingbats, who claimed that I viciously attacked them without just cause and/or I caused them great bodily harm as a result of the beating I supposedly gave them. One suit claimed that I beat this man and his girlfriend, then threw them out, tore their clothes and caused them much embarrassment. One guy sued me after I refused to let him in because he had a minor (a teenage girl) with him. He got mad at me, cursed me, and then walked away. A few minutes later, he came back, but this time without his girl, and spit on me. Some of his spit landed on my head and the rest on my face. Man, he should have never done that! I mean, you can kick my behind up and down the street, but don't spit on me! After this guy spit on me, he ran. Well, he tried to run. He ran up the stairs and onto the street where his car was parked and his girlfriend was at the wheel. Just before he could get to the street, I tackled him and commenced to beat the stuffing out of him. Then his girlfriend got out of the car with a hammer and tried to bust my head. I picked this guy up and used him as a shield, then I grabbed her, took the hammer and slapped her face so hard her wig flew off. She fell to the ground holding her face. I let them both go, but about two weeks later I heard from their lawyer. I have been called every name under the sun but a child of God. Every time I went to court the other people's attorneys have tried to stress the points of my size, my martial arts skills, my bodyguard duties, and then they say how sweet and innocent their clients are—they are weak, mild and law-abiding people.

You see, some people had this thing in their minds that they would sue me and win their cases real easy. So they would come down to Dingbats hoping someone would hit them so they could file a suit. I even had a woman say to me, "I oughta slap you on your bald head and if you hit me back, I'll sue you." Well, I know you know what I told her. I said, "If you do, I will slap that cheap wig off your head." Then she said, "I was just playing, Mr. T." I said, "Well, I wasn't." One month it seemed like open season on me as far as lawsuits were concerned—in one month alone, I had five lawsuits against me.

Another duty I had to perform was stop ex-employees of Dingbats from beating up the owner and the managers after having been fired. Times could really get rough at Dingbats. I remember when people would be lined up outside in the snow waiting to come into Dingbats (we were really hot then). Parties, girls, celebrities and fun were the thing of the day. But how fast do things change. . . .

. . . I say the place changed so much in such a short time. I saw eighteen different managers in one year and over 140 employees come and go. As far as the employees go at Dingbats, it was like a Peyton Place, sex was the topic for the day. I mean the bartenders were screwing the waitresses, the cooks, the managers, the deejays—at Dingbats you could find exactly what you were looking for. We even had some waitresses turning tricks. One time a guy who was hired to check coats was caught selling shots of whiskey from the coatroom for fifty cents each.

Of all the things I have done at Dingbats, I have never gone to bed with another employee. Remember my old saying, "I never make my honey where I make my money." But really, the best part about the disco was the women who came there.

□ ■ □

One Saturday night (February 2, 1980) about 10:30 P.M. two white men approached me with a proposition I couldn't refuse. These two white men were from NBC-TV, Los Angeles, and their offer was to invite me to partake in a contest they had set up called "America's Toughest Bouncer." I said, "But I'm not a bouncer, I'm a doorman. I hate to be referred to as such." So we talked for about two hours before I agreed to be a contestant, then they left the disco saying that I would hear from them very soon. Well, it surely didn't take long for them to contact me. I received a letter the following week about the contest and its rules. This contest meant the world to me because I was the only black man in the contest. I started training the moment I received the letter.

When I started training, I weighed 245 pounds, and by the time of the contest, I was down to 238 pounds. I stopped at 238 pounds because I thought I needed the extra weight to be able to deal with all the other guys. I thought they would be huge (which some of them were).

The bouncer contest was held on March 25, 1980, at BBC Disco. The contest consisted of three events: the Bounce, where each bouncer would throw a 115-pound stunt man as far as he could; the Blast, where each bouncer would jump from behind a bar, run around a group of tables filled with people, jump over a rail and then run through a four-inch wooden door, after which he must ring a bell to stop the clock; and the Box, where the two bouncers with the highest scores from the Bounce and the Blast would square off in a sixteen-foot ring with boxing gloves and fight. Whoever wins the bout would be the Toughest Bouncer in America. The bouncer contest was sponsored by NBC-TV for a pilot TV program called "Sunday Games."

My training schedule consisted of one and a half miles of running, fifty push-ups, fifty sit-ups, throwing one-hundred-pound sacks, jumping over cars and punching the heavy bag for ten minutes a day. No alcohol, no sex, no parties, no visitors, and no fun! Man, was I mad at the world. I would work out every day. I didn't want to but I had to, because I wanted to win; I was serious about my training. I would wake up in the middle of the night thinking about the bouncer contest. I couldn't sleep. As a matter of fact, for the last week of my training, I slept on the floor so I could be real "mean" on the day of the contest. I know that sounds strange, but I believe in torturing my body because then I will take my pain and hurt out on my opponents. For two days before the contest, I didn't eat. That's right, I was starving. I was hungry. I didn't eat on purpose. That's another one of the tricks I use to make myself mad and angry. But I did eat two things: one whole raw onion and a piece of garlic. Now, that would make anybody mean; it worked on me all right! I told everybody when I was in training that "I don't know or care who these guys are and where they come from, but I do know where they will be going." Man, was I ready! I was so psyched up that I could have killed a brick and stabbed a rock.

I told everybody that I was gonna win that contest because "I trained too hard to lose. Plus, if I wanted to lose, I didn't have to train, right?"

Finally the day arrived, Wednesday, March 26, 1980. On this day, we will find out who really is the Toughest Bouncer in America. I met the other bouncers from across the country. The rules were explained and the contest began promptly at 3:00 P.M. The first event was the Bounce. Well, I didn't do too good it that event, I came in third. The scoring went as follows: first place, 100 points; second place, 70 points; third place, 40 points; fourth place, 20 points, and fifth place, 10 points. There were no points given for sixth place even though there were six contestants. I trained for the Bounce but my concentration was blown at the last minute. Just as I was about to grab the stuntman, here comes Dick Butkus with the microphone asking me some dumb questions. That really blew my mind. Man, I was mad. I wasn't prepared for him to do that. You see, I don't like to talk while I am in the heat of competition. I didn't come here to talk; I came to win! And that's the bottom line.

There was an hour-and-a-half break between events, and you should have heard the things that they were saying about me. Now I was born in Chicago, but I was still an outsider as far as welcome was concerned. I never believed in the home-town advantage jive. The Bouncer contest was held in Chicago but I was still a stranger because I had no support. I was still a "nigger" to the whites. But when those white folks booed and made racial slurs about me, that only made me want to win even more. I *had* to win; I had to win for all the black people. I had to win for all the black people who would be watching the contest, because winning would be an inspiration to other blacks who are in the ghettos all across the nation. So anyway, I didn't let what they said bother me because I came to win.

Now going into the next event, which was the Blast, I knew

I had to come in first in order to move into the finals. Three bouncers had already gone through the door and the time to beat was 10.6 seconds. I knew I could do it and I wasn't even worried about the two guys who went behind me, because they were both very fat and slow. Now the moment of truth; it was my turn.

I surprised everyone when they saw me wearing a towel around my head like I was an Arab or something. I wore the towel just to be different and controversial. Anyway, not only did I finish in first place but I set a new course record with a time of 9.3 seconds. Man, the place went up for grabs. I was jumping with joy and my friends were looking on in disbelief. They just couldn't believe how I got myself around the course, over the rail, and through the door with such speed and force. See, when everybody else got to the bar rail they straddled it. I jumped clean over the whole rail without touching anything and the whole place got quiet. I had collected the points that I needed and I moved into the finals, which happened to be the Box.

My opponent for the Box was a huge, monstrous man from Honolulu, Tutefano Tufi. Wow! He was *big*! He was so big that the headgear could hardly fit on his head. You know they listed him as 280 pounds. Well, I know that was a lie because I was about 238 myself and he surely had more than forty pounds on me. He looked every ounce of 320 pounds to me and everybody else. If you want me to be truthful, since I had to go in the ring with him, he looked like a towering apartment building with no windows, because he stood six feet five inches. I'm only five feet eleven—but, remember, I came to win. The boxing match was scheduled to go only one two-minute round, and if you don't think two minutes is a long time, then you go to Honolulu and fight Tufi! It was about 8:30 P.M. and the ring was all set up. The place was jam-packed. People were betting money on the other guy, of course. Cigar and cigarette smoke was in the air and the bartenders were pouring drinks like never before. The time had come, my big moment.

My huge opponent entered the ring first, then I made him wait for five minutes before I showed up. I had a towel over my head, a robe, and grease all over my body, especially on my face. When I got to the ring, I climbed in and started to loosen up, throwing jabs, hooks, and bobbing and weaving. People were amazed to see me bounce around with so much ease and grace at 238 pounds. I must admit, I was a little bulky but I was still ready.

The ring announcer introduced Tulefano Tufi and the crowd cheered. Then he introduced me and I heard half cheers and half boos. While in my corner, I said my prayers (I always pray). The referee waited until I was finished and signaled the timekeeper that he was ready. With that, the fight began.

I knew I had to strike first, fast and hard, because I couldn't let the fight be close. I knew what would happen if it were close—Tufi would win. So I immediately went on the attack. I took the fight to him. I wasn't afraid of his size because "The bigger they are the harder they fall." It was my strategy to hit and move. I wanted to build up a lot of points and stay out of Tufi's way—what else could you do with a man that big? In less than twenty seconds into the fight, I had Tufi bleeding from the nose. I hit him with a very hard looping left that sent blood pouring from his nose. When I saw the blood, I stayed on the attack, trying for the kill. I went all out because it's just like hunting—the worst thing in the world is a wounded animal.

Then the referee stopped the fight so a doctor could look at the cut to make a decision on whether or not to stop, but he was overruled by some other people.

So the fight resumed and I went at him, pressing the attack again and aiming my punches at his nose. One of my punches caught him in the mouth. Now blood was coming from his nose and mouth. I had to change my style from offense to defense and move away from him. I relied on my quickness and speed. I was tiring him out by moving around so fast and he couldn't keep up. I noticed his eyes, his hands, and his feet. I saw him getting frustrated and exhausted. That's when I knew I had him. So I just stayed out of his distance, because I didn't want him to hit me with one of his wild, lucky punches. Even though he was dead tired, a blow from him could still have knocked me out. I'll tell you the truth, I was also tired. When the bell sounded for the fight to end, I let out a sigh of relief.

When the referee raised my hand as the champ, then awarded me the trophy "The Toughest Bouncer in America," all those earlier boos changed to cheers. I strutted around the ring with my trophy raised over my head saying to the crowd, "Boo now! Boo now!" I knew they didn't like me winning so I wanted to rub it in a little, because if I had lost, they would have done it to me.

After winning the title, I left the BBC Disco. I shouted and I just got down. Women were running up kissing me and the men were slapping me five and shaking my hand. It was just wonderful and I was very happy. I eased away from the crowd for a moment to pray, to thank God for the victory.

The contest was shown on NBC-TV Sunday, April 27, 1980, on the show "Sunday Games." The response was so favorable for the pilot program that the producer was allowed to begin filming for a new show, "Games People Play." That's right, you guessed it, the people in charge decided to have another bouncer contest. People really liked the part of the show about the bouncers.

I wasn't informed until around June 10, 1980, that another bouncer contest would take place on July 16, 1980. Now, I was the champ, so I figured I should have been informed a little earlier, if not first, you know what I mean? Well, maybe that was the whole idea, to contact me at the last minute and try to catch me out of shape and unprepared. A couple of days later I received a call from the program director and he explained to me that on July 16 the regionals would take place, then on August 7 the finals would take place. He also stated he would like for me to go into the regionals because it would really help the show. I quickly replied, "Do I get more money for entering the regionals?" He said, "Let me see, we are trying to work something out." Do you know they never worked anything out? Anyway, I decided to defend my crown. I told him I would enter the regionals and work my way to the finals like everyone else, because I wanted the world to know why I am the best!

After all the talking and arguing, it was June 17 and I only had three and a half weeks to train for the second contest. For this contest, my training was a little more intense. Each day I ran two miles, did one hundred push-ups, one hundred sit-ups, one hundred squats, fifteen chin-ups, four thirty-yard sprints, and I jumped over park benches ten times each. I would also run in place, then dive to the ground as hard as I could. I punched the heavy bag for forty minutes a day.

Now the way I got ready for the Blast was I would go back to the ghetto to condemned old buildings. Even though the signs on the property read "No Trespassing—Condemned, Keep Out," that didn't stop me. I would run through some of the walls. Man, the neighbors in the area thought I was crazy for sure. I wouldn't let them know who I really was, so I would wear a ski cap over my head. One time the neighbors called the police on me and when they arrived, I was sort of trapped in the building. If I had run out, they would have caught me, so I just hid inside. I heard the neighbors telling the police that some crazy man comes in here every afternoon and finds a different building, then once inside starts running through the doors and walls. The two white police looked at each other and then came to the front door of the building. I hid until the police finally drove away, then I waited for about ten minutes to make sure they were gone and jumped out the second-floor window to the ground. When the neighbors spotted me walking down the street, they ran out and got their children off the sidewalks. I trained like that for two weeks, one week on the South Side and one week on the West Side, tearing down buildings. Now, that was dangerous, dirty, nasty, filthy and outright stinky. I mean, nothing smells like an old condemned building, believe me! After training there I knew I was ready to defend my title and the bouncers who wanted my title were in serious trouble. As far as the Blast part of the contest, I was ready.

Now for the Bounce. I would go to a meat packing company and sling, toss and throw huge frozen slabs of meat. I didn't do that for long because I caught a cold there, so I had to find something else. So I started picking up big boulders and heavy cement blocks, some weighing at least 200 pounds. Some I couldn't even lift or budge but I came back every day. Just think, twenty minutes a day throwing boulders, it's rough, baby! My back, shoulders, arms, legs and hands hurt. I trained until my hands turned red and raw. Every time I threw, I would holler, "Got to win! Got to win!" I kept hollering "Got to win" so much and lifting that heavy stuff that I almost lost my health trying to get in shape. But I was ready; at least I had the Blast and the Bounce worked out to perfection.

All I needed was my boxing skills sharpened. So I called up one of my brothers. Boy! Did he work me over. Every day it was truly a workout with him. I would tell him I was tired and he would reply, "Your mind is tired, not your body, beat that bag some more and pretend it's the guy who's trying to take your crown, your title, something you worked hard for." He put emphasis on my "crown" and my "title" until I was thinking like a true champ . . . I trained very hard and very seriously. Some days I worked out twice. I was pumped up so high, I had to stop training four days before the contest because I didn't want to overtrain or reach peak to soon. The days I didn't train I went on boat rides, went to the movies and took long walks to cool myself down.

I was ready for every event now, the Bounce, the Blast, and the Box. I was lean and mean at 218 pounds and I hadn't had sex for four weeks. I wanted to stay mean, stay hostile and keep that angry attitude.

The second bouncer contest started on Wednesday, July 16, 1980. This time there were fourteen other bouncers trying to take my title. There were five from the East Coast, five from the West Coast and four from Mid-America regions. You've heard people talking about a stacked deck before . . . well, that's exactly what they had for me. The biggest, the tallest, and the strongest bouncers were in my region, but it was okay because I had trained for that. I trained for surprises so I was ready, and I had no doubt in my mind that I would win again. As usual I gave no interviews and I didn't talk. I came to do one thing and that was to win! When the competitions started I went into a corner to be alone, to think, to concentrate, to meditate and to psych myself up.

In the Mid-American region for the Bounce I came in first place for 100 points because I threw the stuntman the farthest, twelve feet three inches. In the Blast three bouncers had already broken my old record of 9.3 and a fourth one had set a new house record of 8.4. That was the time for me to beat, and the pressure was on me. I play or perform better under pressure. As I always say, "Pressure makes champions."

It was my turn now; I didn't have a towel this time because I brought a turban to tie around my head. I checked over the course and returned to the back bar. There I was warming up; I squatted a couple of times and nodded my head to the starter to let him know I was ready. He blew the whistle and I was on my way, dashing around tables and chairs. As I began to approach the rail, which stands about four and a half feet tall, I began to prepare my legs for the jump. I jumped right over that rail with the greatest of ease and didn't even break stride but kept on running toward the door. When I hit that door I was going so fast that I hit it so hard I was semi-unconscious, but I rolled over in time to snatch the bell off the wall and stop the clock at 8.3 seconds. That's right! I broke the other guy's record and set a new one myself. I told you I was ready.

I won first place in my region (Mid-American) and moved into the finals. I was going into the finals with the longest throw, twelve feet three inches, and the fastest time, 8.3 seconds. People there were trying to get me to relax and take it easy. I said, "No," because I still hadn't won yet, even though I had a big lead on Wednesday. But today was Thursday and it was do or die. All the bouncers who were in the finals had to be at BBC no later than 1:30 A.M. I arrived even earlier. Once there, I found a nice quiet corner and sat on the floor, not speaking to anyone during the competition. First there was about an hour of interviews with the finalists. Then the TV people wanted more interviews with me, since I was the defending champ. I refused and said again, "I came to win, not to talk."

So the finals got underway, but first Don Ohlmeyer had a suggestion. He said, "We should draw numbers to see who will go first and who will go last." I immediately objected because as the defending champ that privilege should automatically be mine, to choose what order I wanted to go in, and naturally I picked last.

In the first event of the finals all the contestants were good. Every time one bouncer threw, another would top his distance. The bouncer just before me had a real good throw, so good that he thought he had won the Bounce. He didn't think I could beat his distance. Well, he was very wrong.

They called my name and I waited in the background a while to let the cheers and the boos settle down a little, then I stepped into view and onto the platform. I saw the crowds but then again, I didn't see them, just like I heard the noise but again I didn't, if you know what I mean. I paced the platform looking down at the distance marker, flexing my fingers in and out and at the same time waiting for silence from the crowd. Then all at once the entire place got quiet, so quiet you could hear a mosquito urinate on cotton. I shook the stuntman's hand as a little ritual before the throw. Then I picked him up like a barbell, lifting him up three times to my lower chest. Picking the stuntman up a couple of times let the other bouncers know how strong I really was. So you could say I was using a little psychology there also. After lifting the stuntman three times, I started the old heave-ho. I swung him up and back three times, and on the third time, I let out a gigantic yell and let the stuntman fly through the air. When he landed and the dust cleared, he was lying on the fourteen-foot mark, and I was in first place in the Bounce. Now only two more events stood between me and the trophy. The Blast and the Box.

I already had 100 points going into the Blast and everybody knew the Blast was my best event. All I had to do was just halfway do my thing in the Blast. So what if I came in second or third in the Blast, I would still have one of the highest scores. I would still be in the Box, because the rules stated that the two bouncers with the highest scores would enter the Box and decide the champ. Therefore, I wasn't pushed or pressured to do my best in the Blast like I was in the first contest. Both times, I had to come from behind to win, and the pressure was on me. I liked the pressure. I like it when my back is against the wall, then and only then is when I'm at my best. That's when I really put on a show. A performance like you have never seen.

Anyway, I was semi-coasting with my big lead. I was also semi-relaxed, but trying hard not to show it. I hate big leads, it makes you less agressive, less mean, less rough—you don't want to go all out anymore, figuring that you have everything all wrapped up. I kept trying to tell myself that I hadn't won the title yet, but you know that didn't work. Consciously, I was saying one thing, but subconsciously I was thinking something else. Well, I guess you could imagine what happened. My name was called and I did my usual thing. I tied my turban on my head and I inspected the course, so to everyone else I appeared to be ready. I looked mean and wasn't talking, but deep down inside I was putting on an act. I was thinking more about the Box than the Blast. So really I was just going through the motions for the crowd because they go wild when I go sailing over that bar rail without touching anything. I finished second in the Blast, which gave me 70 points. I now had 170 points from the Bounce and the Blast, and was still the highest-scoring contestant.

I advanced to the Box. My opponent in the Box was the bouncer who beat my time in the Blast. Now that was good, because I wanted him to pay for beating my time. After I finished second in the Blast, I was asked by Bryant Gumbel about my performance. I replied, "I wasn't pushed, I had no pressure on me," and I continued on to say, "I just feel sorry for the guy I have to box; I just feel real sorry for him." Going into the boxing ring which would decide just who is America's Toughest Bouncer, I made a prediction; I said, "The fight will not go to the second round." As soon as I said that, it reached my opponent, Mike Donas, who was from Denver, Colorado. I said that I would KO him in the first round. I knew talk like that would make him mad or afraid, and either way, it didn't make no difference. The fight was scheduled for three one-minute rounds, which was a big job to me. I said, "Nobody is going to beat me tonight, nobody!" I was the defending champ and I was planning on retaining my title. I trained too hard to lose.

Besides, I had made a promise to a group of handicapped children that I would win again for them. And you know I couldn't let them down. I remembered that promise. It was back in June 1980 when I was at their school. I told them I was in training for another bouncer contest and because they were so special to me, I would win for them, and they applauded in their own special way. It was a truly touching moment for me. Every time I got ready to leave, another child would grab my hand and say, "Just touch me, Mr. T." Some of the children couldn't talk, so they just reached out their hands to me. Then I would hold them. It was so hard for me to hold back the tears because I didn't want to leave and the children hated to see me go. I didn't want the children to see me crying; they might not have understood. Once outside the school, I couldn't hold it any longer, so I broke down and cried. God knows those children are so special to me and I love them all so very much. But that's another story, a special one at that!

Anyway, getting back to the bouncer contest, the boxing part. Going on into the Box, I thought about them and I would say, "For the kids, Mr. T, for the kids." You see no way was I gonna lose to anybody. I had the force with me, the drive, the push, but most important, those children believed in me.

It was 8:20 P.M., and the referee had just called out, "Five minutes to go." The TV people wanted us in the ring warming up for five minutes to air time, so I was ready, but since I was the defending champ I waited for my opponent to enter the ring first. Then I entered about three minutes later. You know, it's sort of strange. When I fought that big Hawaiian all the other bouncers were in his corner. Now here I am defending my title and I see the same thing, except this time one bouncer is somewhat on my side, the other black guy, from Atlanta. Now you don't think for one minute that it bothered me, because it didn't. I didn't care if he had Angelo Dundee in his corner.

The referee called us to the center of the ring for our final instructions. Once there I gave my opponent the eyeball-to-eyeball stare. I looked him right in the eyes until he couldn't stand it any longer. From that point on, he knew he was in trouble and couldn't nobody help him. He was all alone in the ring with me. I heard people laughing, making other sounds, because of the way I was looking at my opponent. Yes, you could say I was intimidating and psyching him out. That's all part of the fight. Matter of fact, that's a big part of the fight. You try to upset your opponent's train of thought, throw his game plan off and make him scared or mad—either one. You got him beat before the fight starts. After the instruction from the referee, I returned to my corner and said a prayer, then I was ready to go.

The bell sounded to start the fight and I was on the move, straight at my opponent. Wherever he went in the ring, I also went. I was on him like ugly on an ape. I was all over him from beginning to end, pounding away on his head. I tell you, it wasn't a good fifteen seconds before the referee had to pull me off him and give him a standing eight count. As I stood in the neutral corner looking on, I saw I had him in trouble, so as soon as the referee said, "Continue," I was back punching with jabs from my right hand and followups with my left. It was the lefts that were doing all the damage. The referee stepped in again, but this time asking him if he was all right. Apparently my opponent said he was okay because the referee said fight on. I did, until I saw the guy was just outclassed by me and helpless. I made sure he was not faking, so I hit him with three hard right jabs to the head that buckled his knees a little. Then I looked at the referee, figuring that he would stop the fight, but he said, "Go on." God knows I couldn't hit that guy anymore—he was beaten, he was out on his feet. He was just through. I was about to hit this guy one more time, until I saw him wince with pain. That was it.

I threw my hands up and walked away from the guy. I pointed to the referee and shouted, "Stop the fight, I don't want to kill anybody." As I was shouting at the referee, I was walking to my neutral corner and then the referee finally stepped in and stopped the fight. He also had to assist the other guy to his corner. I was a winner by a TKO in the first round, at fifty-three seconds. That's all the time it took me to finish him off. When the crowd saw that I was a clean fighter and a good sport by not going in for the kill against the guy, they stood up and cheered me.

I had successfully defended my title and was crowned America's Toughest Bouncer for the second time. That night I went on record stating I would not defend my title a third time. I didn't want people to think that all Mr. T can do is run through doors and throw people across a room like a monster from the wilds. Besides, the bouncer contest had served its purpose and usefulness to me. It had given me all the exposure I needed. In fact, it was an honor to be chosen to compete both times. I thank God for that.

10 A STAR IS BORN

ELL, WHO WOULD HAVE GUESSED THAT one day I would be in the movies? I certainly didn't dream of it. I have seen many people go to Hollywood and become "has-beens" before they start. I've seen women run away, hitchhike, quit their jobs, or get divorced, just to try to make it in Tinsel Town, U.S.A. Hooray for Hollywood; the bright lights, the glamour and the glitter, the beautiful people, the hookers and everything else. Well now, I've got to say it: I don't go for that jive! . . . I don't like phony people. Most people in L.A. and Hollywood are just like the credit cards they carry—PLASTIC! Everybody wants to be a star, a director, a producer, a writer, a promoter—secretaries want to be starlets, busboys want to be bankers, men want to be women, illegal aliens want to be U.S. citizens. You need a manager, you need an agent, you need a psychiatrist, you need a second home and a third car—that's what they say in Hollywood. Then, if you've got all of that, it's okay to shop on Rodeo Drive.

Hollywood, the place where dreams are made and fantasies are fulfilled. Where else could a movie star become President of the United States? What about the football player who called himself "Hollywood Henderson" while he was playing for the Dallas Cowboys? Hollywood is the land of make-believe, Walt Disney, fairy tales, heartache, pain, and then sometimes death. Yes, there are big mansions there, but they are empty—where is the love? There are a lot of ultra-rich people there, but most of them are miserable, unhappy, sad and lonely. I wonder why?

I remember when I was called to come to Hollywood. It was back in October of 1980. The call was from a lady named Rhonda Young; she was the casting director for *Rocky III*. We talked and she informed me about the movie and the part I was being considered for. I told her that it was an honor itself even to be considered for the part, let alone getting it, but I was interested only if the character was not a pimp role or a dope-dealing role, because I was not the kind of guy who would do anything just to be in a movie or on TV. I have pride and integrity and I am a man of principle. There are some things I won't violate. Doing or being in a movie that exploited blacks just wasn't my thing. Although you may call it acting, I call it insulting. I am not Fred "Nigger Charlie" Williamson, Jim "Slaughter" Brown, Richard "Shaft" Roundtree, Ron "Super Fly" O'Neal, or Ken "Mandingo" Norton, just to name a few. Those blacks who took degrading parts couldn't act and the movies they made were not even entertaining. It was a big black rip-off and the only people who got rich were the white men. Two years later, all of those black so-called stars were in the unemployment lines trying to get a job. That's Hollywood—here today and gone tomorrow.

Well, I was discovered while participating in the "America's Toughest Bouncer" contest on NBC-TV. Over 1,500 black men were auditioned for the part in *Rocky III*—boxers, football players, actors and some bums. But I wanted the part the most.

On January 3, 1981, I received a seven-page script to study in three days. As soon as I got the script, I went to work on my acting ability. I studied in front of the mirror, in the shower; practically everywhere I went. I was in a daze. I kept telling myself that I could do it. I could play the part because this character—Clubber Lang—I had *been* him all my life. You see, the character is mean, bad, rough, hungry and a loner. Now, if you know me, it's easy to tell that Clubber is my make-believe twin and my real-life self. Anyway, I practiced for hours a day; I would wake up in the night hollering, "I am Clubber and I want Rocky Balboa." Plus, all the things that Clubber says are exactly what Mr. T would say—like, "I'll bust you up," or "I will break your arm in six places." You see, that's the way I am all day long. So, I went out to Hollywood with that in mind and I told myself that I would not come back home unless I got the part, even if I had to fight Joe Frazier and Earnie Shavers at the same time—I knew the odds were against me and my back was up against the wall, but that's when I am at my best. I also told myself that Sly needed me just as much as I needed him, he needed a new face in the movie, a different gimmick, and with me he would get both. Sly knew what he had in me, he knew that I already had a name coming in from the bouncer contest, and that I was a world-famous bodyguard.

Well, it was time for me to do my thing in front of the cameras. It was my big day. I'll be honest with you, I was a little nervous, a little tight, but I was ready. I entered the gym where the cameras were set up. Sly was there with Rhonda Young, Linda Horner and some other people there to see my audition. When I stepped into the gym, I was immediately greeted by Sly. He pulled me over to a corner and said, "This is not a one-shot deal. I mean, if you make a mistake, we will do it again, up to ten takes, and keep the best one." He told me to relax and asked if I wanted to read from the script. I said, "No," because I had studied and I was ready. Sly said, "Okay, go for it."

It was so hard for me to believe that I was there getting ready to audition for *Rocky III*. I had seen *Rocky* and *Rocky II*, but I just couldn't believe Sly really wanted me for the part. I felt like one in a million. Anyway, a young lady was there and she read Rocky's part and I would come in with my part. We only did four pages of that, and I think the reason we only did four pages was because everybody there was just amazed at how I was acting and going through the script with ease, like an old pro. One part that really impressed them was the scene where I act mean and then all of a sudden I am sweet. It showed my flexibility as an actor. I glanced over to the side and saw everyone's faces and they were glad and surprised. After doing that, Sly came running over and said, "Cut, good, good."

Then Sly said, "I want to do something, it's what we call improvisation—a lot of actors can't do this. There is no script, we just use our own words. Say what you want to and I will do the same." Sly stood back and said, "Whenever you're ready, T." When I heard the word "Action," I was doing my thing. I was fired up; the words just flowed from my mouth and my body just reached for the words. Sly was so impressed that he could hardly say "Cut," but he did and we went on to the next phase of my screen test.

Sly said to me, "This is the last thing I want you to do. Stand in front of the camera and start talking; first very soft, then build up to anger." So I did and if I might add, I was just super—I amazed myself. Like they say, "When you're hot, you're hot," and I was boiling with energy. Sly said, "That's enough, cut," and everybody started whispering to each other about my performance. I told Sly that I appreciated the opportunity to be given a chance at the part and he said, "I liked what you did and I liked what I saw, but you're up against some pretty tough competition. We'll let you know within a week." I told Sly again as I was leaving, "Thanks for this chance."

So I flew back home to Chicago and waited to hear from them. I had given the performance of my life. And I really couldn't do anything else because *Rocky III* was on my mind. They told me I would be notified within a week, but three days had already passed and I was getting worried. Then, on the fourth day, I received a call from Rhonda Young. She was so excited and glad for me she could barely get the words out. "Mr. T, you got the part and I'm so proud of you." I told Rhonda, "I am thankful to my God, and tell Sly that I will do the best I can to make the movie a success." Then she said, "Go celebrate and we will see you on Sunday when training and rehearsals start." I couldn't wait to tell somebody. I tried to call some people but I just couldn't remember their numbers to save my life, I was so excited and happy.

My mother and father were happy and proud. I had a going-away party and most of the people there thought I was lying about doing the movie *Rocky III*. I mean, these people were walking around at *my* party with cake in one hand and a drink in the other saying, "That nigger ain't going nowhere. Who he think he's fooling?" I learned so much that night. Some people knew I was doing the movie, but they just hated to see me go on to something better.

Anyway, I celebrated for a couple of days, but by Sunday I was ready to leave for Hollywood. When I arrived in L.A., I was met at the airport by Rhonda Young. She was all smiles and she had a big hug for me, and that really made my day, I mean, just to be welcome. Rhonda showed me around town and then took me to get a snack, after which she took me to my apartment. I unpacked and got to bed early so I could be ready to meet the man (Sly) on Monday. The next morning, I was picked up and driven to the gym. I weighed in, changed clothes, wrapped my hands and waited for Sly. Sly came in, we hugged and he said to me, "Welcome aboard." I said I was glad to be there and he said, "You were the right man for the part." I said, "Thanks, I'll give you one hundred and fifty percent every day."

My training schedule for the next three weeks was given to me. The first two weeks I worked out once a day until I got sick. I caught a cold and was laid up for three days. But I started back training on the fourth day. I had to lose about thirty pounds, get my breathing together, develop my muscles and sharpen my boxing skills. Now, I don't know about you, but for me that's a lot of work. Plus I had to study the script every night until I got it perfect. It was a lot of pressure on me and all eyes were watching me constantly. The word was, "Can Mr. T do it? Has he ever acted before? Can he lose the weight? Will he get the big head and try to be a star before it's time?" Well, I knew that a lot of people were worried about me. And I knew there were a few who were in my corner pulling for me and that made me try even harder.

Now, I am not going to lie to you and say it was easy, because it was hard. But it was fair and honest. In my life, I've never trained so hard for anything like I did for *Rocky III*. By the third week, I was working out three times a day. At 6:00 A.M. every morning (including Saturday and Sunday) I would run five miles and do one hundred push-ups and one hundred sit-ups and then go back to sleep until 10:00 A.M., when I would get up and lift weights. After that, I would have lunch, and from 2:00 until 4:00 P.M., I would be in the boxing ring sparring with Sly. And I'll tell you, he really hits hard! We would box every day until my skills got better. He would put me on the heavy bag for thirty minutes and then the speed bag for fifteen minutes. I had to jump rope for fifteen minutes, shadow box for ten minutes, and before each workout was over we would put on some disco music and dance and punch for another ten minutes. I lost eight pounds in one day—I had to change clothes three times that day.

It wasn't easy for me, because at first I didn't even have the energy. Then Sly called in Chris Collins to work with me and help me with my training. I liked working with Chris, he was very understanding and patient with me. He would tell me after each workout if I was improving or not, and he never lied to me. Matter of fact, since Chris spent so much time with me as my trainer, we eventually became good friends. Sometimes Chris would get mad at me because he would find empty cookie bags in my car. Then I would say, smiling, "Somebody

My father's boots

Bigheart

Below:
Doing my best to liven up a kid's hospital stay.

.A-TEAM star Mr. T acts tough but has a
sage to an injured little boy has helpe

Henry Ford Hospital

2799 West Grand Boulevard
Detroit, Michigan 48202

PEDIATRIC INTENSIVE CARE UNIT

TO: Mr. T.
     California U.S.A.

          WARMEST THANKS FROM ALL OF US

            FOR YOUR CARE AND PRAYERS

                  FOR B.J.

          IT DID MAKE A DIFFERENCE!!!

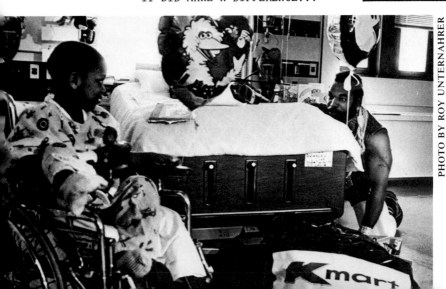

Mr. T fights for little coma boy

I'm really counting on you, little buddy!

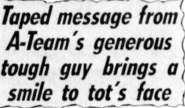

LITTLE Sven Mason raised his arm and smiled when he heard his hero's voice.

Bighearted TV tough guy Mr. T put aside his two-fisted starring role on "The A-Team" to pull off a miracle — his personal message of love has started a dying 4-year-old boy on a fight for his life!

Little Sven Mason had been in a deep coma and on a life support system since the day he was struck down by a car near his home in Rochester, England. There was little doctors could do to revive the boy.

But when Mr. T's heart-tugging message was played at Sven's hospital bedside, the youngster raised his arm — and he smiled!

The growling voice that could stop TV killers cold in their tracks had somehow penetrated the fog that shrouded little Sven's brain and ignited a spark of life.

Sven's anguished parents, Julie and Alan Mason, who keep constant vigil at his bedside, believed their son could be jolted from his stupor by hearing the voice of his hulking hero — Mr. T.

When the garrulous superstar learned that his voice might provide the miracle that could start Sven

Taped message from A-Team's generous tough guy brings a smile to tot's face

back on the road to recovery, he dropped everything, tape-recorded his personal message and had it flown to England. The recording was immediately played at Sven's bedside and the deep, powerfully compelling voice of Mr. T filled the tiny room.

"Little buddy, I'm really counting on you," Mr. T said in his familiar growl. "We're a team, you and me, and we've both got to be tough.

"As soon as you get well, we're both going to be back in the playground, finding the suckers and the fools.

"All the guys in 'The A-Team'

send our well-wishes to you and our blessing for you to get better. So hang in there, Sven. I want you to know that I love you and God loves you. I'll be praying for you every day and every night. God bless you so very much."

A spokesman in Guy's Hospital in London said accident and stroke victims sometimes are roused from deep comas simply by hearing the voice of someone they have a deep affection for.

"It's a miracle for little Sven," the spokesman told The NEWS. "But with someone as dynamic as Mr. T, I guess you can expect a miracle."

© F. WEBB, 1984

Above: Speaking to 16,000 Boy
Scouts outside Chicago, June 1984.
I'm on the right.
Opposite: Meeting and talking with
some disabled children after
addressing the Boy Scouts, 1984

Right: Filming a TV special with Bob Hope in Hawaii, 1984
Below: Showing them how it's done

Left: First Lady
Nancy Reagan had
asked me to play
Santa Claus for the
White House
Christmas party
Below: With New
York's Mayor Ed
Koch after taping a
fair housing televi-
sion commercial,
1984

Chicago, June 1984

else must have put them there." Chris would sometimes jokingly say to me, "If you keep doing wrong, I'm gonna call your mother." I would then say, "Please don't tell my mother; I'll train right." Soon I was training right mainly because I wanted the part so bad.

◻ ■ ◻

Sly started seeing some results and progress in my training and he was glad. I was even happier because I wanted so bad to please him. He would talk to me every day about what it's like in the film business. Sly and I became more than just actors on a set, we became good friends. That made me put out more each day because there was such a relaxed atmosphere between us. I was in the groove now and my boxing skills were much better. My weight was down from 230 pounds to 208 pounds and I wasn't getting sick anymore. I was strong and, more important, I even looked like a fighter.

It was about the middle of March and I had learned the script inside out. I had all the characteristics of a seasoned actor. Sly and I trained from January 8 until the end of March. We started filming in April and completed the entire movie in eight weeks. Imagine that, three months' training but only eight weeks to film! It took so long to train because Sly is a perfectionist and he knew what he wanted, and this was his third Rocky movie.

The whole thing, I mean filming *Rocky III*, was just like a dream come true. It didn't seem real. I felt like Alice in Wonderland, or Dorothy in the Land of Oz, because it was just a couple of years ago that I had been in a local Chicago theater watching *Rocky II* and now, all of a sudden, here I was fighting Rocky Balboa in *Rocky III*. It was just hard to believe. But it was for real and it did happen. I am glad that it happened the way it did because it helped me to keep my head level and also helped me to stay humble.

Meanwhile, back in Hollywood with the rest of the cast of

Rocky III, we were working hard. The fight scenes in the movie were just fantastic. I mean, Sly and I worked so hard in the gym and it seemed like we would never get it right. But by the time we were ready to film the fight scene, everything was moving like clockwork. Even coming down the aisle to enter the ring, I really felt as if I were in a real championship fight—the roar of the crowd, the cheers and the boos!

It was great working with all those stars—Sly Stallone, Burgess Meredith, Talia Shire, Burt Young and Carl Weathers. Everybody there was very supportive of me. Burt Young told me when he saw me act in my first scene, "As one actor to another, you are great!" I responded by saying, "Thank you, I'm just trying to do the best I can." Then Burt, who plays Rocky Balboa's brother-in-law, Paulie, in the movie, said, "I know you are going to be good." I got a lot of help from Carl Weathers too. Carl plays Apollo Creed again, but in *Rocky III* Apollo is Rocky's coach/trainer. Since Carl was in the other two Rocky movies, he knew the ropes. He gave me some good pointers during the fight scene. He also gave me encouraging words many times during the filming, which I desperately needed. Next on my side was Burgess Meredith, who plays Mickey, Rocky's trainer. Now everybody who knows TV and the movies knows how long Burgess has been around. I was really thrilled and excited to work with him, I have so much respect for Burgess as a person and as an actor. After one scene where I holler at Mickey, we later sat together and laughed about it. That's when he told me, "You're a damn good actor." Now for the little lady of the house—I'm talking about Talia Shire, who plays Adrian, Rocky's wife in the movie. Talia and I had many conversations on the set; she is beautiful through and through; she's just as sweet and charming as she looks in the movie.

Last, of course, but not least, there was old Rocky himself, Sly Stallone. Not only did he write the movie, but he directed and starred in it also. When I first got there, Sly told me if I

·ever needed or wanted something I didn't have, to let him know and he would see that I got it. Just before we started filming, Sly took me out on his sailboat, and there he told me, "T, when we start filming, don't worry about making mistakes, that's the last thing we have to worry about. If you make a mistake, we'll do it over until we get it right because we have miles of film. So remember, we are going to make lots of money and have lots of fun." The following week, after filming had started, we had a press conference and everybody was asking about me. One reporter asked Sly, "Can Mr. T act?" Sly replied, "Mr. T was born for the part . . . you don't rehearse Mr. T, you just turn him loose." There was nothing for me to say. Sly later told me that I brought another dimension to the movie that made it more real. He also told me, "T, you are the movie. There wouldn't be any movie without you." That's when he presented me with the pure silver Rocky belt buckle from the first Rocky movie.

Before filming and during the filming I had a lot of fun and I made a lot of money. I met a lot of people and I hope I made some new friends. I was moved by the standing ovation I received from the film crew and cast when Sly announced to everyone that I had just completed my last scene in the movie. I want the world to know that it was truly an honor to co-star in *Rocky III* with Sly Stallone. And to him I want to say, "Thank you for letting me be myself." I want to leave a message to all you critics everywhere, all you nonbelievers, all you negative-minded individuals, and all of you people who were rooting against me: "I'll see you at the movies."

□ ■ □

This opportunity was definitely a chance of a lifetime, and I truly thank God for it. After I finished filming *Rocky III* in June 1981, I returned home to Chicago for some relaxation. I needed the rest because I had worked really hard. The filming of *Rocky III* made me decide to pursue a career in the movies and to give up bodyguarding. I was a little impatient though, and wanted more work, but none was available because I was not a big name yet. Everybody kept saying, "Wait until *Rocky III* comes out, you will be so hot." Now you know that my patience is very short, so I tried to make things happen. It wasn't easy trying to get acting jobs being an unknown. But in August 1981, I got a small part in *Penitentiary II*. I finished filming in September. I came back home and waited for more parts and one came, or should I say, passed me by. I auditioned for a movie called *The Beast Master*. I gave a very strong performance but the producer said he wanted an older actor. So I returned to Chicago and continued to wait. In late December of 1981, I was called to play an undercover cop in one episode of NBC-TV's series called "Chicago Story." I am sure you know what happened after that—more waiting.

Now it was January 1982 and I received a call that the promotional campaign was about to start. Man, I really needed to hear that news, it made the long wait seem worthwhile. In April 1982 I was chosen by the UMPA (United Motion Pictures Association) as Newcomer of the Year, in Kansas City. From Kansas City I went to L.A. for a minipress conference and there I was interviewed by radio, magazines, newspapers and television. I returned home just in time for my twenty-three-city promo tour of *Rocky III*. The tour was fun and exciting but exhausting. I averaged at least six interviews a day and most of the time didn't know where I was. But when I arrived in Philadelphia on May 22, 1982, two days before the world premier of *Rocky III*, you better believe I knew where I was then. Now, I've heard of premieres before, but there was nothing like the world premiere of *Rocky III* in Philly on May 24, 1982. There I was, standing alongside Sly Stallone and Talia Shire—what a night! I really can't describe it to you. All I can say is I wish you could have been there to see, to share and to feel what I felt. The mayor of Philly presented a Liberty Bell to me.

After the premiere, I was back on the road again. This time I headed for the "Good Morning America" show at 7:30 A.M., followed by at least six more interviews that same day. I stayed in New York for two days, then it was off to Detroit for a benefit premiere of *Rocky III* for Operation Push and the Reverend Jesse Jackson. There I received the key to the city from Mayor Coleman Young. The next morning, I was off to Chicago for two guest appearances at different theaters, the Woods and Water Tower. Saturday afternoon, May 29, I was driven to Milwaukee, Wisconsin, for another appearance. I am telling you, things were picking up then. I returned home for three days and then I was off again, to Los Angeles, Phoenix, and then to Las Vegas to be a presenter in the Victor Awards. The next day I was back in Phoenix, Arizona, for a Go-Cart Race for charity. Well, I didn't win, but I did donate $1,500 to the March of Dimes.

The next morning I was flying back to Los Angeles for a press conference and from there I went to New Orleans. Then back to Las Vegas at Caesar's Palace as a guest of the hotel's for the Larry Holmes/Gerry Cooney championship fight. I returned home on June 13, 1982, and was surprised to find out that I was to appear on "AM Chicago" that next morning, June 15, 1982. I had to fly back to Los Angeles for an interview with Bill Harris on Showtime called "Celebrity Lifestyles." I returned home Friday, June 18, 1982, to appear on ABC-TV's Channel 7 news as the guest sportscaster. That following week I was back in Los Angeles to appear on the "Comedy Show Bizarre" on Showtime. I returned home and was interviewed by "PM Magazine," Channel 32 Chicago, Hotline Radio 1390 AM, "The Afternoon Show," cable TV, Radio WGCI FM, and *People* magazine. Then I was flown to New York to tape "The David Letterman Show" for NBC-TV. Upon my arrival back home, I was informed that I was to be the Grand Marshall of the 1982 Bud Billikens Parade. What an honor! All my life, I had watched this parade as a spectator and now I was the main event! I tell you, by August '82, I felt like I had been around the world and was floating in outer space. That was a tremendous high for me.

Now it was September and I was getting ready to move west (Hollywood) to begin filming an NBC-TV series called "The A-Team." Everybody had their doubts about the "The A-Team," which stars George Peppard, Dirk Benedict, Dwight Schultz and yours truly. We put a lot of work and hours into that show and NBC hit the air with a major promotional blitz for "The A-Team." We were special guests at the Superbowl Game (1983: Washington Redskins versus Miami Dolphins), and we appeared on *TV Guide*'s cover. Well, needless to say, "The A-Team" was a hit with very high ratings and was renewed for another season. Everybody had "A-Team" fever from the little babies all the way up to their grandmothers. Even people who at first didn't like the show were hooked on it now. We took our lumps though. The press tried to cut us up by saying it was the most violent show on TV. We knocked "Happy Days" and "Laverne and Shirley" off the air and we were killing our competition. People told lies on us. They tried to get George, Dirk, Dwight and myself to fight each other but it didn't work, because we really love each other and that's most uncommon and unusual in Hollywood. The more bad things they said about us the more fans we got. I told the press, "I don't care what you say about me as long as you mention my name and spell it right." Anyway, we became one of the hottest shows on TV. But the icing on the cake was my own cartoon show on Saturday mornings on NBC-TV, called the "Mr. T Show," what else? From the beginning it was a big hit with all the children, whom I call "Mr. T's Tots," because Charlie's got his angels and Jerry's got his kids, so why not Mr. T's Tots? It seems as though I am a modern-day Pied Piper because everywhere I go, thousands and thousands of children appear.

Suddenly I was on my way with stars in my eyes and big

bucks in my pockets. No more small-time stuff for Mr. T. No more bit parts, no more local talent jive. I have finally taken control of the situation and I am in command of my destiny. I call the shots. No longer do I have to wait in line, run around seeing people and calling them, because the tables have turned. Now they call me and I make them wait. I am in a position to pick and choose. More movies, TV commercials, talk shows, speaking engagements, banquets, receptions in my honor, autograph sessions, the red carpet treatment everywhere I go. Everybody wants to see me. My phone never stops ringing. I am invited to private parties, lunch with millionaires, dinners with politicians, and late-night snacks with beautiful rich women. My career has taken on the snowball effect—the more I roll the bigger I get and the richer I become. Like they say, "There's no business like show business."

Just think, all of this happened to a little nappy-headed, snotty-nosed black boy who was a product of the slums, the ghetto, a broken home and the welfare system. And you thought it only happens in the movies and in fairy tales. I tell you, dreams do come true and a star was born. Now I may not be the brightest star in the galaxy but I do shine and sparkle. In the words of my pastor, Henry Hardy, "Mr. T, you are a shining star. The heavens are warmed by your presence. You are a flower unfolding its petals. The universe is alive with your fragrance. You are a voice caressing the dawn. The silent spaces are filled with your joyous hope. This is your day! Live it in love because you are an expression of the life of God." All in all, I am honored, excited and deeply moved by all my fame and fortune, but the success is not mine alone. I give the credit and the glory to my God whom I serve, because he brought me a mighty long way and he promised to never leave me alone, never alone! And "if God be for me, who in the world can stand against me?" Don't you know, there's no failure in my God!

WILL SUCCESS SPOIL MR. T?

IRST OF ALL LET ME TELL YOU WHAT REAL success is to me, what I believe and what I feel about success. Success! Success! I know it's every man's dream, but I say to really enjoy true success you must have happiness and laughter. If a man is working toward a predetermined goal and knows where he is going, I say that man is a success. My goal is to feed five thousand people like Jesus did, to build a community center for all races of people, and then to become a minister to preach the gospel.

☐ ■ ☐

Now let's examine this word "success" for a moment.

What is success? What does it consist of and how is it developed? I ask you if you can tell me what is success. I bet you have never given it much thought. You know there are probably as many different definitions for success as there are people in this world. Let me give you some examples.

If you ask a businessman his definition of success, he might tell you that being successful means "earning a lot of money." A pro athlete might tell you, "It's making the all-pro team." An architect might say, "It's having beautiful creations on the city skyline." A student might say, "When I receive my Master's or Doctor's degree from college." A young lawyer might say, "To one day become president of my own law firm." A minister might say, "Success is helping someone who is in need and saving souls from sin." I told you that success means many things to many people.

Everyone may have a personal definition for success, but few have really thought the subject through. You see, true success is much more than all the above. We must consider it in great depth and with a broader spectrum to reveal the true definition of success.

Now, one of the most painful aspects of our human life is that few if any of us live to see our fondest hopes fulfilled. The hopes of our childhood and the promise of our mature years are unfinished symphonies. Is there any one of us who has not faced the agony of blasted hopes? Always our reach exceeds our grasp. Shattered dreams are a hallmark of our mortal life. What does one do when a lifelong dream has come to failure?

Some people become bitter and resentful. These people may be extremely cruel to their mates and inhuman to their children. Meanness becomes their dominating characteristic. They love no one and require love from no one. They trust no one and do not expect others to trust them. They find fault in everything and everybody and complain a lot.

Another common reaction of people whose hopes have been blighted is to withdraw completely into themselves. No one is permitted to enter into their lives and they refuse to enter into the lives of others. Such persons give up the struggle of life, lose their zest for living and attempt to escape by lifting their minds to a realm of cold indifference and detachment. They are too unconcerned to love and too passionless to hate, too detached to be selfish and too lifeless to be unselfish, too indifferent to experience joy and too cold to express sorrow. They are neither dead nor alive, they merely exist. Their eyes do not see the beauty of nature, their ears are insensitive to the majestic sound of great music, and their hands are unresponsive even to the touch of a charming little baby. Nothing of the aliveness of life is left in them, only the dull motion of bare existence.

But you must be able to turn a liability into an asset by saying, if there is grief, then I must bear it, but there will be another day and dawn will come. Disappointment, sorrow and despair are born at midnight, but morning follows. Weeping may endure for a night but joy cometh in the morning.

Sometimes days of unutterable joy are followed by nights of overwhelming sorrow. Life brings periods of flooding and periods of drought—when our highest hopes are blasted and our noblest dreams are shattered, we ask the same question Paul Lawrence Dunbar asked, "What is Life?" . . . but,

> A crust of bread and a corner to sleep in
> A minute to smile and an hour to weep in,
> A pint of joy to a peck of trouble,
> And never a laugh though the moans come double:
> And that is life? Well, I guess.

It's not how long you live but how well you live. When I have to meet my maker, when I come face to face with my God and lay my soul bare before him, I will be judged by my deeds, not my degrees, not by where I lived and surely not by the money that I had accumulated, but by my kindness toward others. What I am saying is this: It doesn't matter how long I live, if I die tomorrow or tonight, I would know I lived a good life and I lived a well-spent life because I tried to help others. I did feed the hungry, I did clothe the naked, I did visit the sick and the lonely.

Success is not merely "money grabbing" and success is not the result of making money. Money alone is not enough. That is a shortsighted view, because having money does not make a person successful. I know a man who is a millionaire and he's only twenty-seven years old, but he's a drug dealer and a pimp (tax-free money). Is that man a success? No way! The person who retires at age thirty-two by cheating, conning and chiseling his way to the top is not a successful person. You cannot achieve true success by deluding others. For instance, if you've earned a million dollars, but you lost your family and your home and you develop an ulcer in the process . . . would you call that a success? Or would you be a success if you earned two millions dollars by age thirty but died of a heart attack simply because you tried to burn the candle at both ends?

This is a commonplace enough situation. And, of course, it is obvious to anyone that money itself is not what the man wants: It is the "game," the "thrill," the gratification of "winning" that makes a man keep running long after he has any need to. But I feel that real success is not winning, it's being healthy enough to compete in the contest. What I think is less understood, however, is that a chase of this sort is a substitute experience. And a substitute is always something that we can never have enough of. Man is really always looking for self-esteem, and he seeks to find it by winning the esteem of others. In our society, the fastest and surest way to do this is by amassing a great deal of money. So the money becomes a substitute, a symbol, for the esteem of others.

But in the deep chemistry of the psyche, things do not work out this way. Getting the superficial esteem of others does not give us self-esteem; worthiness comes from the inside, never from the outside. This is why a substitute experience always leaves us hungry for more.

Money is only one example. So are drugs. Sex, of course, is another. The man who chases women (like the one who chases money) can never have enough, can never be satisfied, can never settle down to one possession. The compulsive Lothario is perpetually as insatiable as the compulsive accumulator of money. The same motives operate in this area. When sex becomes a substitute for love, it can never be gratified, but must go on from dizzying triumph to dizzying triumph (and each triumph ends in a kind of internal exhaustion and defeat, convalescence and continuation). The libertine can never find what he thinks he is looking for, any more than the acquisitive man can ever have "enough" money.

Our genuine needs are self-confidence, self-esteem, self-sacrifice. These can be achieved only by *giving*, not by getting. When something in the psyche blocks us from expressing and gratifying these genuine needs, we turn to substitute ones. But no liquid can quench our thirst except water itself.

Not only can the substitute not satisfy us; it also contains its own law of diminishing returns—like the dope addict who needs more and more of a fix in order to maintain the same level of euphoria. Finally, he needs massive doses simply to keep alive, to keep reality at arm's length. Man runs because if he ever stopped, he might drop dead at the mere confrontation of his real needs.

The main reason I think more people do not find true success is because they look for it in the wrong place; they look for it in comparison to others. A man may be more successful than his neighbor, his brother or his father and still be a dismal failure because he has not become anywhere near the person he is capable of being. Even though he is more successful than anyone else he knows, he may be a failure. If he evaluates success by comparison, then the more people he knows the less likely he is to be successful. The years of his life will yield one disappointment after another. But the only valid comparison we can ever make is with ourselves. We must compare what we are with what we have the potential to become.

Another reason so many people fail to succeed is because they equate success with material wealth. They think of money as the end result instead of seeing it as the means to an end. They are sometimes victims of the old myth that there is some "sin" in being rich. They may have misunderstood the Bible's teaching that *love* of money is the root of all evil! Wealth, rightfully gained, is a symbol of success. It is a medium of exchange whereby people trade value. The greatest tribute paid to a person's wealth lies in the fact that they have traded work or a service for it. "The only people who *make* money . . . work in the *Mint,* so the rest of us must *earn* money." Nobody can get rich himself unless he enriches other selves. Every man must have a concern for self and feel a responsibility to discover his mission in life. God has given each normal person a capacity to achieve some end. True, some are endowed with more talent than others, but God has left none of us talentless. After you have discovered what you are made for, you should surrender all of the power in your being to the achievement of that. You should seek to do it so well that nobody could do it better. You should do it as though God Almighty called you at this particular moment in history for this reason. Remember life at its best is a coherent triangle. At one angle is the individual person (me, I). At another angle are other persons (you, they). At the tiptop is the Infinite Person, God. Without the development of each part of the triangle no life can be complete. "I" cannot reach fulfillment without "thou." We cannot truly be persons unless we interact with other persons. All life is interrelated and all men are interdependent. In the final analysis we are inevitably our brothers' keeper. No individual or nation can live alone in isolation. John Donne put it best when he affirmed: "No man is an Island entire of its selfe, every man is a piece of the continent, a part of the maine; if a clod bee washed away by the sea, Europe is the lesse as well as if a Promotorie were, as well as if a Mannor of thy friends or of thine owne were; any mans death diminishes me because I am involved in mankinde; and therefore never send to know for whom the bell tolls; it tolls for thee." This recognition of the oneness of humanity and the need of an active brotherly concern for the welfare of others is the bread of man's life. Keep the bread fresh. Life is a precious thing that we don't know the full value of.

The real greatness of a man is what he has done for others. Did he feed the hungry? Did he visit the sick, the prisoners?

Year after year the U.S. government asks, "What shall I do because I have no room where to bestow my fruits and cheese." I look at the farmers who couldn't get their price for grain and meat so they decided to shoot and kill all of their cattle and burn their grain instead of feeding the poor. "The poor are your brothers and sisters in Christ. You must never be content to leave them just the crumbs from the Feast." If every man were to feed his neighbor, no man would go to bed hungry. I know the man with the fat belly cannot believe that such a thing as hunger exists. So who are the least of these? They are the invisible people, the poor. They are God's children who wake up every day not knowing what to expect next. You know almost two-thirds of the people are hungry? We have people starving to death in Cambodia, Asia, Africa, Mississippi, Georgia, Alabama, et cetera. It's a pity, a shame, a crime against humanity and sin before God. I don't care how many people we have in this world—millions, billions or even trillions—there shouldn't be a single person going to bed hungry at night or waking up and not having anything to eat. It just ain't supposed to be. If I can share, you can share. As long as man holds out, hides, pushes back and keeps away his fellowman, there will always be acts of violence—as long as there is racial hatred, segregation, high unemployment, illness with improper health care, poverty and broken hearts.

"Now, what do you mean by broken hearts, Mr. T?" Broken hearts is when a father doesn't have a job to feed and clothe his family of eight so he leaves home and never comes back. A broken heart is when that mother is left with the children, no job, without enough money to support her family so she goes out and sells her body trying to make ends meet. What a tragic ending to the American Family!

I think most crimes are economics-related. I say 90 percent, and that remaining 10 percent is mental. Some crimes, of course, will always be with us; but most of it could be eliminated by a society that practiced what it preached, and spent on prevention even a fraction of the money it spends on punishment. It now costs $90,000 to build a single high-security cell in New York State; what child of the slums has had $90,000 spent on him before?

□ ■ □

There is a story about a rich man named Dives, and a poor man named Lazarus. The rich man, Dives, went to hell because he passed by Lazarus every day and never saw him. Dives went to hell because he allowed the means by which he lived to outdistance the ends for which he lived. Dives went to hell because he maximized the minimum and minimized the maximum. Dives went to hell because he failed to use his wealth to bridge the gulf that separated him from Lazarus.

Who are the least of these among us? They are the boys and girls who get up day after day and have nothing to look forward to because they can't find a job. Who are the least of these? They are people who see life as nothing but a long and desolate corridor with no exit sign. Who are the least of these? They are the people who have been deprived of educational opportunities; they are the people at the bottom of the economic ladder. Who are the least of these? They are the sick, the old, the unemployed and the ones who don't even have the basic necessities of life. Who are the least of these? They are the ones who sleep on park benches, in train stations, bus terminals, sidewalks and alleys, while the rich sit and sip on champagne saying, "I didn't know people had it that bad." Who are the least of these? They are God's children who live on an island of poverty surrounded by a vast ocean of material prosperity. The Bible says, "Blessed be the hungry for they shall be fed" and "Blessed be the meek for they shall inherit the earth."

□ ■ □

But this does not mean that success is living your life on skid row or in the midst of poverty and disease, as some antisocial, anti-establishment cults and groups might suggest. But if you *choose* to be like Mother Theresa of India and help those on skid row, then that's success to me. Mother Theresa gives her life to Christ's poor in India. Who can doubt the heroism of one who lives as she does—flying tourist class to pick up the Nobel Peace Prize award and turning down the banquet as an insult to her poor? At a public talk, she turned down mere money that came from people's surplus. "If you give what you do not need, it isn't giving." Tough doctrine. Not "Give till it hurts," but, "You have not even begun giving till it hurts." Who can meet the test? Few, very few, like Mother Theresa. That's why she is a saint and I acknowledge her. How many of you know her Nobel acceptance speech? Here is a woman who knows overpopulation and starvation like no one else. She abhors violence of all sorts and she's away from hyperbole. I was so moved when I learned that Mother Theresa won the Nobel Peace Prize and received over $191,000 tax free, while working in the starving areas. She said, "I am not worthy," then she went on to say that she would use the money to feed and shelter life's destitute.

When I see things like that it really makes my heart hurt to know that all the rich and super-rich don't give a damn about anybody but themselves. Because of their feelings, I see a war in the making, and it will be a war between the haves and the have-nots, the rich and the poor. I foresee a bloody, vicious war, too. It's really a shame that so many people in this world are living from day to day, just trying to survive. Now the rich ain't concerned because they don't feel the pain of having sickness, poverty or depression . . . to them, living is self-preservation and survival of the fittest. It's true that the rich get richer and the poor get poorer. It's a dog-eat-dog world out here where only the strong survive because they live off the weak. The Bible says we are supposed to be our brother's keeper, but then again, the reason why we treat our brother so bad is because we feel about him the same way Cain felt about Abel, and you know that Cain killed Abel. I don't know about you but I *hear* the poor people when they sing, "Oh, Lord, Why Am I Treated So Bad?" I will say this, and I said it before, "What shall it profit a man if he gains the world and loses his soul?" Well, that's what is happening in our society today. All around us you will find men trying to get all they can for as little as they can, while sitting on their can. We live in a materialistic world where a man is judged by the things he possesses, like how big a house he lives in or how many luxury cars he owns or how much money he has in so many banks. You know, there is only one difference between a rich man and a poor man: the poor man thinks only of his next meal and the rich man thinks only of the meal that will be his last. So I say to you, do not, I repeat, *do not* aspire to wealth, and labor not only to be rich, but strive instead for happiness. Try to be loved and give love in return and then the most important thing is to acquire peace of mind and serenity.

Oh, I hear that welfare mother saying, "These things are impossible without gold or money." I hear the unemployed father saying, "Who can live in poverty with peace of mind?" I then hear the beggar saying, "How can one demonstrate love for one's family if he is unable to feed, clothe and house them?" What is my answer to that? Well, it is this: I say to you, "Sorrow, weeping, despair, poverty, hunger and hate may endure for a night, but joy will come in the morning." I say every day there is a new hope. "But try telling that to the people in Cambodia, Mr. T, or India or Africa or even the people in the United States who are starving to death. Try telling them to wait on tomorrow and listen to what they will tell you. They will tell you tomorrow only brings more pain, more agony, more death and more heartache." So I say, "Just like death comes to the poor, it comes to the rich." Death sits at the rich man's door like a hungry dog guarding a kitchen; he knows that eventually the kitchen will be left unattended. Death waited for Nelson A. Rockefeller, the once governor of New York and once Vice President of the United States and always millionaire. His money couldn't buy the bone or feed the hungry dog of death. Death waited for J. Paul Getty, the billionaire, who had so much but didn't have enough. Death waited for Aristotle Onassis, the "Man with the Money." Death waited for Howard Hughes, who had enough money to wrap himself up in it, who became a recluse and withdrew from society. They all had money and they all had access to all that money could buy, but they didn't have the joy of living, for money cannot buy what it takes to have a good time in this life. Some of the most miserable people in the world are rich people.

Yes, I hear that poor man when he says, "Give me a million dollars, and let me suffer for a while." Well, I got news for him: the grass always looks greener on the other side. Think about all of those rich people and then take them one by one and analyze, study and evaluate them. Then you see the loneliness, the depression, the pain, the frustration and all those tranquilizer pills. Oh yeah, if you thought it was all pleasure and no pain, you are mistaken. Ask the man who became a millionaire and lost his wife and children in the process. Ask the rich widow who drinks her life away. Ask the wealthy executive who threatens to shoot himself three times.

But why do the rich suffer? Well, they suffer because they do not share, they do not give to those who are less fortunate than they are. The Bible says, "Blessed be the cheerful giver" and "It is better to give than to receive." You know something I just don't understand? When we say, "Peace on Earth and good will to all men," then right across town people are homeless, no food, no clothes and nobody cares. The only thing society is concerned with is keeping the poor in their place and away from the rich.

The only answer to the problems of the world is "God." Man is not God, Money is not God, Gold is not God and Guns are not God. Jesus said, "I am the way, the truth and the life."

We must worship God, praise him and be thankful. That's the reason why I never touch my food until I have blessed it first, and given thanks. I will always remember that there is an unfed mouth somewhere.

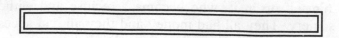

Will success spoil me? . . . I doubt it seriously. Let me tell you why it won't spoil me. It won't spoil me because it's been too long of a wait and too hard to come by. I know many, many people will say, "Yes, it will spoil him," out of jealousy and envy. You see they hate to see anyone get ahead, especially if it is someone who was very poor and someone they were once higher than. They don't want to see me make it—don't you know that misery loves company?

The first thing I want everyone to know is that I never had it made; I was not spoiled. I made up my mind a long time ago that one day I would have the things I want. Being the youngest son, I picked up a little bit of character from each one of my brothers. I also learned a lot from my father. I can't begin to explain the joy and pain I have experienced in being a member of a family of twelve. I know how it feels not to have something. I know all too well about hand-me-downs, second-hand this and secondhand that. Sure, now I can afford the best life has to offer. But let me tell you something, I have paid my dues to get where I am today, and I will continue to pay my dues to stay here.

I didn't get where I am because someone felt sorry for me! I have had many setbacks. Many doors were slammed in my face, many people laughed at me. I was told, by a lot of people, that I was stupid and uneducated. I was disappointed so many times, I have been rejected, turned down and pushed to the side. I have been told to wait on many occasions. Everywhere I looked and turned people were injecting my arm with negative doses of nothingness. So I prayed to my God and asked him for strength and good health. I kept this song on my mind: "Lord Don't Move the Mountain, but Give Me the Strength to Climb." In spite of all the obstacles, all my failures, all my hardships, and despite all of my sorrows, I decided I will and I can. I've always had a positive attitude. I got to be so confident that I didn't believe that there was anything in the world I couldn't do or have. From that point on, I was on my way.

But if you think for one minute that it was easy, you have another thought coming. I went a lot of days without food to eat, I went a lot of days and even weeks wearing the same clothing and the only thing that kept me going was my dream. My dream was that one day, things would be better, and that one day, all of my hard work would pay off. When I got in a down mood, I would think about great men and women who made it in spite of obstacles. I think about Alexander Graham Bell, he didn't make it on his first try; I think about Wilma Rudolph, a black girl born with polio and who doctors feared would never walk, but not only did she walk, she ran, she ran so fast that she won gold medals in the Olympics. I think about Jackie Robinson, the first black major league baseball player, who was the best player on an all-white team but had to sleep outside with the animals, and was cursed at, spit on and booed, but through all of that became a member of the Hall of Fame. I think about George Washington Carver, a black man who made many discoveries from just one peanut. You see, I know it was not easy for them, they never had it made.

So I say to you, if you are down and out like I was, don't quit. Because it's important that you understand it is not where you come from, but where you are going that counts. If you get tired—rest, but don't quit. Life is full of challenges and tests and they will make you or break you. I had to keep telling myself, "I'm going to make it."

Sometimes I look back and I wonder, "Oh, boy! How I got

over." Now if you ask some people they will tell you that I got over like "a fat rat in a cheese factory." Some will say that I was really lucky. Some will say that I knew the right people. But none will say that I had the *right stuff*. Regardless of what anybody said, I knew I had what it takes. I had the love of God, and that's power. Seek ye first the kingdom of God and his righteousness, and all these other things will be added unto you. Do I need to go any further? My success is so simple because God made it all possible. Didn't Jesus say, "Ask anything in my name"? But in order to serve God you must have faith. Didn't Jesus say to the man with the withered hand, "Your faith has made you whole"? And what is faith? The Bible says, "Faith is the substance of things hoped for, the evidence of things not seen."

You know we all want to go to heaven but nobody wants to die. We all want to be rich but we all don't want to work for it. We don't want to sacrifice, we don't want to pay our dues, but we still want to get over. You know some black people figure they are supposed to get something just because they are here. Some blacks think just because they wear an Afro hairdo, clench their fist real tight and shout, "Black Power," they can get any job they want, whether they are qualified or not. Well, they got another think coming. Those blacks are born on welfare, raised on welfare, and will die on welfare. They have a welfare mentality and poverty sensibility. They say, "Why work when I can get a check once a month for doing nothing?" I pity them because they live in a small world. Don't you know that plans and dreams alone would swallow them up alive? They can't stand it! They are afraid of real success, it frightens them even to think about it.

When I did start to make it, a lot of people were trying to hold me back and wanted me to stay down in the bottom of the barrel with them, but I couldn't stay in the mud. I was born to be a star up there with the rest of the heavenly bodies. I soon became the person that everyone hated or disliked—

why? Because I wanted to *be somebody*. I didn't want to be a dropout, I didn't want to be a jailbird, and I knew that there just had to be a better way. I had it hard and my family was very poor. I would go and steal food to feed my family. I would ask to be forgiven because I didn't want to steal, but I had to. I remember when I would beg people for money, I would say, "Mister, could you give me some money, I'm poor and I don't have anything to eat at home and I haven't had anything to eat all day," and if you looked at me you could tell I was not lying. I had holes in my pants and you could see my dirty drawers. My gym shoes were ragged with holes in them and my feet were touching the sidewalk when I walked. My shirt had only one button.

I just did what I had to do in order to survive. I never robbed anyone, I never broke into anyone's house, I never snatched a purse. I was like Robin Hood, I only took from the rich and gave to the poor, which was my family. I would steal from the bakery every day, and the milk company. I used to break into the trucks as they waited to unload at the super-market and bring big boxes of food home. I didn't like to steal, but I stole because my family was hungry and I wasn't going to let them starve.

☐ ■ ☐

We call America the land of opportunity. Well, if the white man can make it, so can I. You know I really get tired of all that white man jive. I mean all I hear from black brothers is, "The white man got all the jobs, and the money." Well, I say, "Cut the crap." If you black, low-lifed, good-for-nothing, uneducated, and funky so-called men would get up off your dirty tails and stand up, you can be rich, too. But all you want to do is criticize and wait on your welfare checks every month. I see why the white man calls us blacks shiftless and lazy. We get a good job that pays good money but we won't come to work or if we do come we are late and then we want to leave early. Then when the white man says, "You're fired!" we holler racial hatred, and if another black gets promoted we call him an Uncle Tom just because he comes to work on time every day and does his job. You are the people who holler, Will success spoil Mr. T? You are the ones who say, "Mr. T sure has changed since he got a little money!" Or the most famous line: "I remember when he didn't have anything." Or, "I remember when he couldn't buy a sandwich."

I still remember how my mother kept the family together with a prayer and hope. I remember how unconcerned and selfish a lot of people were toward me, and those were the people I thought were my friends. They turned their backs on me, they talked about me, they laughed at me and yes, they even tried to hurt me. I remember who helped me and I also remember who tried to hold me back. I know about smiling faces; they tell lies and I got proof. What I am saying is this: "People (white or black), don't tell me about how I should act or be, when I paid my dues to get where I am. You didn't help me or you didn't want to help me get where I am. You wouldn't even give me an encouraging word, but soon as I get money you want a part of it." To you I say this, "If you didn't help me when I was at the bottom, well, I don't need you now that I am at the top." Don't you know you only get out of something what you put into it? In other words nothing from nothing leaves nothing. So don't come trying to tell me how to spend my hard-earned money that you didn't give or loan me, okay!

Now let me clear the air for a moment about this word success and what it means to me. First of all the dictionary defines success as: "The favorable or prosperous termination of attempts or endeavors; the attainment of wealth, position, or the like; a thing or a person that is successful." Well, that's what the dictionary says, but my religious teachings tell me that, "Prosperity without God is unwise and God without Prosperity is unnatural." Jesus said, if you want to be successful there are three things that you must do: *Ask,* and it shall be given; *Seek,* and you shall find; *Knock,* and the door shall be opened unto you. Success to me is not money per se, the most important part of success to me is my health. My mother always told me, "Son, when you got your health you got your wealth." Well, that is so true because I know a lot of people who are millionaires but they arc sick unto death and all their money can't save them either. That's kind of sad, isn't it? You see now there are some things that money just can't buy.

Please don't get me wrong—I am not saying it's wrong to have a lot of money or to try to get it. But what I am saying is this: If I didn't have God in my life, yes, I would get the big head and success would spoil me. Because I am very success-ful, I am a millionaire and the money keeps coming in and adding up. Everything I touch turns to gold. My Mr. T dolls have been breaking sales records everywhere. When the dolls first came out three million were sold in three months. My dolls outsold the Cabbage Patch dolls by ten million. I was invited to the White House, where I met the President of the United States, Ronald Reagan, and his wife, Nancy—what an honor. I went to Hawaii and did the hula dance with Bob Hope. I was interviewed by Barbara Walters on a special. I was roasted by Dean Martin and his friends in Las Vegas. I was voted male star of the year by the fans at the People's Choice Awards. I was given the key to the city of New York by its major, Ed Koch. I was given the key to my own city of Chicago by Mayor Harold Washington. I was invited to Amsterdam, Holland, where the members of the A-Team were met at the airport by 15,000 screaming fans—what a feeling!

You see what I mean. It would be so easy for me to trip out on my success and think I am so great. I am not great, but the God I serve is great. All I want to do is keep my feet on the ground and my head toward Heaven. Success to me is helping someone, feeding the hungry, clothing the naked and visiting the sick. It's being a good loving father, unselfish and upright. It's being a good role model for the young children to emulate, and most important, it's living the life of God.

I'm not interested in being a "movie star," some kind of media celebrity. I don't take that seriously. I know I'm just a piece of meat here in Tinsel Town. I know soon they'll be tired of Mr. T and be looking for someone else. That's the way it is. You only go for so long, but you got to know and understand what's happening. I know I can be replaced. They been making movies before I got here, they're going to be making movies after I leave.

When they get tired of Mr. T, I won't be mad, I won't say, "Oh, they're getting rid of me because I'm black." No! I'll say my usefulness has ended here. I'll take my money and invest it well and go on to bigger and better things. Like I said, I'm called by God to do what I'm doing. This is an avenue for me to reach people. This is my platform and I'm taking advantage of it.

I plan to go into the ministry in four or five years, so when people come up to me and say, "Mr. T, how long you think this is going to last?" I say, "You forget that I'm doing God's work, so I'll be occupied for a long time." I'm not just about making a lot of money. If that were the case, I'd be short-changing myself and God. Money can't bring total happiness. I see that every day on Sunset and Wilshire and everywhere else. This is a platform for me to reach people, to reach kids, these rich folks' kids, strung out on drugs. Mr. T is reaching them. These poor kids who don't have any hope. Mr. T is reaching them. These middle-class kids all confused about everything. I'm reaching them.

☐ ■ ☐

Now you want to know the real reason why I am so success-ful? There is only one reason why I am so successful: I believe in God and I serve him faithfully. I try to live life fully. I enjoy being alive. I am glad to get out of bed every morning. I think every man should be doing a job he likes because if he is doing a job he likes then he will do it well. I have this relentless pursuit for life and I go about it as though it is impossible for me to fail. Man should be taught to expect success from life . . . as the acorn is destined to become the oak. I am successful because I give and when I give I get it back ten times. Press down, shaken together and running over. The Bible says, "Blessed be the cheerful giver." Well, that says it all. I get so much because I give so much. Don't you know that you can't beat God giving? But I think I should point out to everyone that I have been blessed; I am not lucky but blessed. I am successful mainly because I *think* success, I *believe* I can be successful if I apply all my God-given talents. My Bible tells me that "Whatsoever a man thinketh in his heart, so is he." I think success, therefore I am successful. Do you understand what I am saying?

Well if you truly understand what I am saying about my Bible and my God, then don't get mad at me just because I believe and in return I am blessed for it. In other words I am saying, "The Lord is my Shepherd and I shall *not want*." Because I live right I don't want for anything and if I desire it, then it's mine. What I am saying is this, "My God is not poor therefore I will never be poor because my God is more than able and nothing is impossible for God." Now I must say this so I won't be misunderstood: The belief that God will do everything for you is as untenable as the belief that you can do everything for yourself. That is based on a lack of faith. And you must learn that to expect God to do everything while you do nothing is not faith, but superstition. For if God does everything, you will then ask for anything and God becomes little more than a "cosmic bellhop" who is summoned for every trivial need. What I am saying is, "God helps those who help themselves."

So the answer to your question, "Will Success Spoil Mr.

T?" is a big fat NO! But I am not here to try and convince you because I know how the human brain works, and you are going to believe what you want to believe. Now I will say this: If you stop worrying about Mr. T and concentrate on your own life you will be a much better person, and success just might come your way if you live right and treat other people right.